C000213357

SHENTON OF SINGAPORE

ALSO BY BRIAN MONTGOMERY

Biographical:

A Field-Marshal in the Family
Monty's Grandfather

SHENTON
OF SINGAPORE

Governor and
Prisoner of War

BRIAN MONTGOMERY

LEO COOPER
in association with
SECKER & WARBURG

© Brian Montgomery 1984
First published by Leo Cooper in association with
Secker & Warburg Ltd,
54 Poland St, London WIV 3DF

ISBN 0–436–28440–5

Photoset in Great Britain by
Rowland Phototypesetting Ltd
and printed by St Edmundsbury Press,
Bury St Edmunds, Suffolk
Bound by Mackays

CONTENTS

TO
BRIDGET

Daughter of Sir Shenton and Lady Thomas

ACKNOWLEDGEMENTS

The author and publisher offer their sincere thanks to the publishers and copyright holders of the books which are listed in the Bibliography for their kind permission to reprint extracts from their works.

I shall always be grateful beyond words to the Countess of St Germans and Lord and Lady Thomas of Swynnerton for inviting me to write this biography as my own work, not subject to their approval, and for giving me the privilege of full and unrestricted access to their family papers; particularly those in the Rhodes House Archives of the Bodleian Library. My warmest thanks are also due to Mrs Hugh Thomas and Mr Stephens Thomas, for information from their family records and to Lady Laidlaw and Colonel Robin Prichard for important details of Sir Shenton's career in East Africa. Without such wealth of basic information, supplemented by my late wife's stimulating comment during our research, I could not have attempted the task.

Apart from these family sources my story would still be in the making, without the benefit of wide research in the United Kingdom and elsewhere in order to confirm its historical accuracy, particularly where personal memories have been responsible for so much detail and description. I therefore owe a great deal to other sources on which I have drawn extensively and which I gratefully acknowledge below. I have received the encouragement and help of a great many individuals as well as institutions.

In chronicling the early years and education of Shenton Thomas I relied much on information supplied by E. J. Hartwell (Headmaster of St John's School, Leatherhead), Simon Reynold (Headmaster of Aysgarth School, Bedale) and Dr D. W. Boweet (President of Queen's College, Cambridge).

My wife and I made a research journey to Singapore and Malaysia our first essential, and the advantages we derived were incalculable, due to the massive help we received from so many people before and during the visit.

The High Commissioner for the Republic of Singapore in the U.K., His Excellency Jek Yeun Thong, assisted me greatly over my visit to his country, particularly in obtaining permission to enter the Istana (the Presidential Palace) and the restricted area of Changi Gaol, while Mr I. T. Tan, Chairman of the Singapore Tourist Promotion Board smoothed our path throughout our journey. In Singapore I owe much to the British High Commissioner Mr J. H. Hemmings, who arranged for me to visit the site of the Naval Base and much else I would not otherwise have seen. In Malaysia and also in London I owe a deep debt of gratitude to Tan Sri Dato Mubin Mervyn Sheppard Al-Haj, who gave me much helpful advice about Shenton Thomas's governorship, combined with extensive hospitality. Without Sheppard I should not have met Mr

W. Bentley, British High Commissioner at Kuala Lumpur, in his beautiful and historic residence at Carcosa.

In my Foreword readers will see the tribute I have paid to Professor Wong Lin Ken and his staff at Singapore National University. I am particularly grateful for the access I was given to Shenton Thomas references in their University records. Later, in London, I had the good fortune to meet Mr Chit Chung Ong who is writing a thesis on Shenton. I find it hard to express sufficient thanks for the generous hospitality, assistance and timely advice that I received in Singapore and Malaysia from Mrs Gerald Beale, Captain Bogaars, Michael Gorrie, who literally guided my footsteps in Singapore, Sir Anthony and Lady Hayward, Eric Jennings, who was a mine of information on everybody and everything before, during and after the Second World War, "Curly" Lee with his long and expert knowledge of Malaya, and Roderick MacLean. I shall never forget the high standard of comfort, service and general well-being that prevails in the Goodwood Park Hotel, which we made our base for the research task overseas.

A number of sources have made this book possible by the quality of the information and support which they gave me, in consultation, correspondence or comment, especially new evidence of which they had special knowledge or which had not so far been published. In this context I owe a deep debt of gratitude to: Freddy Bloom, Dr T. C. Carter, Sir John Fletcher-Cooke, Professor E. J. Corner, Leslie Davis, Andrew Gilmour, Vyvyan Frampton, Harry Grumbar, Hugh Humphrey, Cecil Lee, Captain H. W. McClelland R.N., Nigel Morris, the late Mrs Savage Bailey, J. C. Sharp, Mamoru Shinozaki, and Dr Cecily Williams.

Friends and acquaintances of the Shenton Thomases, his colleagues during his thirty-seven years' service overseas and thereafter, as well as many people who never met him but were interested in his life and career, have all been unstinting in the help which they have offered me. A great number have sent memoranda, some with completely new evidence of men and events, including private diaries, quotations from their own or other works, and personal reminiscences – not a few with photographs, sketches or pictures. Only the limitations of space have precluded the publication of all that has been offered. For these invaluable contributions I owe particular thanks to Sir Adetokumbo Ademolo, Charles Allen (of the B.B.C.), George Allen, T. L. Avon, Mrs J. G. Barry, Group Captain H. T. Bennett (Japanese interpreter), Sir Robert Black, M. J. Bowen, B. T. Bramwell, J. S. H. Cunyngham-Brown, Major Donald Callander, Mrs Kathleen Clark, Sir John Colville, Miss Sawrey-Cookson, Commander R. H. Vaughan-Cox R.N., Dr Charles Cruickshank, J. L. H. Davis, John Drew (Shenton's orderly in the P.O.W. camp), G. Evans, Lady Galleghan, Dr Martin Gilbert, Sir Andrew Gilchrist, Commander Clifford Gill R.N., Major-General Sir Peter Gillett, Sir William Goode, Major-General J. R. Graeme, Mrs William Handcock, W. K. M. Haxworth, Lieutenant-Colonel H. T. Heard, Professor F. H. Hinsley, A. J. W. Hockenhull, H. Schweitzer-Sten (International Red Cross), Mrs Eric Keegan, Major-General B. W. Key, the late Ronald Lewin, E. S. Lomax,

Colonel and Mrs McGladdery, Commander C. W. McMullen R.N., R. F. M. Millard, Lieutenant-Colonel J. Montressor, Colonel B. J. Murphy, Sir Rex Niven, C. O. Oates, Sir John Peel, Mrs Molly Puckeridge, Captain R. Sarrell R.N., the late Sir Robert Scott, T. D. Shepherd, Wing Commander A. Staveley, Brigadier Ian Stewart, William Swaffield, Lieutenant-Colonel Ivor Thomas, Miss Mary Thomas, Lady Templer, Sir Harry Trusted, Mrs Molly Vlasto, Dr C. B. Wilson, Mrs Mary Wilson (widow of Bishop Wilson).

I am very conscious of the varied advice I received during my research and writing of this volume and my sincere thanks are due to: Dennis Ambler, Christopher Blake, Colonel J. B. Coats, Philip Crawshaw, Air Vice-Marshal J. Elton, Mrs E. E. Emms, L. E. C. Evans, Mrs R. Grumbar, Brigadier Rolo Gwyn, Donald Headley, the late Lady Huggins, Harry Miller, Lieutenant-Colonel J. B. Palmer, the late Lady Brooke-Popham, Air Vice-Marshal Ramsey-Rae, the Rev. Robert Robinson, Dr J. S. N. Sewell, Frank Steele, Miss Marion Stewart, Ian Urquhart, and the late Sir Dennis White.

I am grateful to the staff of the following departments of H.M.G. for valuable assistance: Miss E. Blayney and F. Sedgewick-Jell of the Foreign and Commonwealth Office Library and Records, Colonel Peter May and John Smith of the Ministry of Defence, H. L. Theobald, E. E. Thomas, and D. A. Morris of the Historical Section at the Cabinet Office.

I am very grateful to the members of the following institutions for their unfailing help, particularly for their ever-prompt assistance in locating and producing the books and material to which I requested access:

Dr Noble Frankland, formerly Director and Dr Alan Borg, Director, Robert Crawford, Dr Dowling, Roderick Suddaby and the staff of the Imperial War Museum; Dr Bingle, Anthony Farrington and all the staff at the India Office Library and Records; the British Newspaper division of the British Library; Miss Patricia Methven, Archivist, and the staff at the Liddell Hart Centre for Military Archives, King's College, London; F. E. Leese, the Librarian and Alan Lodge, the Archivist, of the Rhodes House Library of Oxford University; all the staff at the London Library; Group Captain D. Bolton, the Director, and staff of the Royal United Services Institute; the Library of the Army and Navy Club; the staff at the Public Record Office; the Librarian and staff at the royal Commonwealth Society; Captain J. Rumble R.N., Director General of the Royal Overseas League; the (former) British Empire Leprosy Relief Association.

I have received editorial assistance from Tom Hartman, aided by Auriol Stanton. My thanks are also due to my agents Graham Watson and Andrew Best. I must pay high tribute to my two secretaries Sheena Barber and Susan Cowley, for much hard work, accuracy and patience in coping with my terrible handwriting and requests for re-typing at short notice – including invaluable correction of my spelling and other manuscript errors. I was fortunate in having Ann Hoffmann as a very skilful and experienced indexer.

Finally, none of the sources which I have listed are responsible for any errors of fact or omission which may remain, and for which I am responsible, including the views expressed in this book, which are my own.

LIST OF ILLUSTRATIONS

AUTHOR'S NOTE

How this story came to be written

When the British Army in Malaya surrendered to General Yamashita at Singapore on 15 February, 1942, I was in Rangoon in South Burma, and the Japanese 15th Army was closing in on the city. When we heard about Singapore we said, "It's our turn next"! Fortunately we were wrong, but it was only by a miracle that we escaped being surrounded and broke out in time. Otherwise I might not have been given the opportunity to write this story.

In the nineteen-sixties and seventies at least ten writers published accounts of the Malayan campaign, but, with one exception*, all the books were written without access to the written records of the Governor. In this respect all previous accounts of the Malayan catastrophe must to some extent resemble *unfinished stories*, as they lack the personal record of the most senior officer on the spot.

In 1981 I was invited by the members of Sir Shenton Thomas's family to write the authorized biography of his life. His personal papers are lodged, under embargo until 1990, in the Bodleian (Rhodes House) Library, Oxford, with authority for access controlled jointly by Shenton's nephew, Lord Thomas, and his daughter, the Countess of St Germans, who kindly gave me right of access.

B.M.

---

*In 1967 Lady Thomas gave Noel Barber limited access to the Shenton Thomas material when the latter was writing his *Sinister Twilight*.

FOREWORD

"Eric Jennings here, I hope you had a good flight. I'd like you to lunch with me, if you will, at 12.45 p.m. today at the Singapore Club. It's on the 11th floor of the Straits Trading Association. You should have no difficulty in finding it; it's close to Shenton Way. But it's 'Men Only', so I'm afraid I can't ask your wife."

This was the telephone call that woke us at 8 a.m. on Thursday, 2 March, 1982, at the Goodwood Park Hotel, where we had arrived from London late the previous night. It was our first visit to Singapore and Malaysia, and we had been warned about the need for rest to offset jet-lag, but evidently it was not to be! Indeed it was the start of two of the most energetic and eventful weeks we had ever experienced: non-stop research with expert help and advice, and very generous hospitality, provided by many kind people. Without this latter I am sure my task would never have been accomplished.

Before I went off to lunch that morning I kept wondering what sort of life Shenton Thomas had led in Singapore, in particular during those months of the Second World War, over forty years ago, before hostilities came to the Far East, when he and his wife were in residence at Government House. Shenton had kept two daily diaries, both written in pencil in his small but neat handwriting. One was a leather-bound, pocket-sized volume, with five brief outline entries on every page for the five consecutive years, 1941–1945. The other, written on lined foolscap, gave his own personal day-to-day view of the events and the people he met, from the first day of the Japanese invasion of the Malay Peninsula on 8 December, 1941, until the day preceding the surrender at Singapore on 15 February 1942.

Experts say a biographer should try, as it were, to live with his subject, even *invade* his thoughts. So I had with me some copy from his five-year diary, and took a random look at it before I met Jennings. The contrast between his life at Government House and as prisoner is striking:

1941 Sept. 26.   Sir Earle Page arrived from Australia. Golf with Daisy. Then dinner for forty incl: the Brooke-Pophams, Duff Coopers, G.O.C., the Laytons, A.O.C., Gen. Gordon Bennet. A.I.F. Band.

1942 Mar. 2.   I scrubbed our floor this morning. Davis came with a sack of ground nuts, some pork and beans.

For strangers the first sight of Singapore, the new, dynamic city-state with its huge, multi-storey buildings, the capital of a nation of 2¼ million people on an island the size of the Isle of Wight, is breathtaking; especially when seen against its foreground of shipping ceaselessly entering and leaving what is now the second busiest port in the world. Yet I had to see under all that and recapture the atmosphere of the old colonial capital as it was in the late 1930's when the Second World War began.

To have the privilege of entry to the Istana, now the home of the President of the Republic of Singapore, is to view again the Residence where Shenton Thomas and his family lived for over seven years. The same dignity and ceremony are there, perhaps even strengthened, but for those who are familiar with the ambience of the residences in which British Colonial Governors lived, there is a subtle difference – of degree, not of substance. For the old Government House is now the Palace of a Head of State, with a new dimension which is right and proper for its status. Yet, if you shut your eyes, you can still visualize H.E. The Governor and his Lady coming down the grand staircase on some formal occasion. It must have been difficult in a long frock!

The day we spent at the Singapore National University at Kent Ridge was perhaps the high note of our tour. The Head of the History Faculty had very kindly offered his help and it soon became clear that his department's knowledge of my subject was exhaustive. The University, with its 10,000 undergraduates, virtually all Singapore Chinese, its spectacular new highrise buildings, built on the summit of the Ridge and dominating the countryside, creates its own atmosphere – a climate of learning and scholarship urged on by desire for expansion. New faculties are being created, teaching hospitals and more science laboratories are being built. Everything on Kent Ridge is bright, new and shining, spotlessly clean and neat; it could not be otherwise in this island state.

We lunched in the staff restaurant with Professor Wong Lin Ken and some of his dons, including one British and one American; both the latter were visiting Professors from Oxford University. That meal, and the discussion that followed, were highly rewarding, ending with the gift to myself of two Academic Exercises on the Administration of Sir Shenton Thomas by two Chinese graduates (Ho Peng An and Teoh Chai Lean). Meanwhile Professor Wong Lin Ken had given me an introduction to Mr Chit Chung Ong, currently in London studying at the School of Economics for a Ph.D thesis on Sir Shenton Thomas.

Of course we saw Raffles Hotel and the many old houses remaining from the British Colonial era. In sum they still create "the feel and the smell" so often depicted in historical novels with a Singapore/Malaya setting. The famous Y.M.C.A. building, where the infamous Japanese Kempetai tortured their prisoners, was being demolished when we saw it. It is said that the screams of the tortured victims can still be heard after night falls.

For me the British Empire in Singapore and Malaya, its former power and influence, became indelibly etched on my mind after visiting these places where for so long British men and women had led their lives: St Andrew's Cathedral and the other Christian churches of various denominations, the Fullerton Building which housed the Singapore Club, the Cricket Club, where my wife lunched with kind friends that first morning, the Municipal Building and the Parliament House, with the old suspension bridge over the Singapore River, and of course the Botanic Gardens with the old houses remaining in the Tanglin Road area.

I could not have written this book without seeing Changi Gaol, where so many thousands of British prisoners of war and civilian internees were incarcerated. The Gaol is now a maximum Security Prison to which access, other than to visit a prisoner, is prohibited. However, Mr I. T. Tan, Chairman of the Tourist Board, arranged entry for my wife and myself. The pathos of the place is unforgettable, nowhere more so than in the silence, the stillness and the stark beauty of the little prison Chapel, perched high up near the roof. I was taken to the oldest block, built in 1936, to a cell where individual prisoners of importance were held. It was a grim sight, only reached after passing through nine massive steel gates, or doorways, and tramping down long, echoing, concrete passageways. The cell was a concrete box, ten feet by seven, with no bed or furniture, no facility of any kind, save a lavatory, and one electric light bulb controlled from outside.

During the Japanese occupation one of the British prisoners in Changi, an artilleryman, was taken ill, like many hundreds of others, and was transferred to the prison hospital, housed in a barrack block where a British infantry regiment had formerly been quartered. This prisoner, Bombadier Stanley Warren, was an artist, and clearly one of merit. The murals, all scenes from the life of Christ, that he painted on the walls are remarkable for their sensitivity, their colour and their scope. Evidently his fellow prisoners were models for the paintings, which seem to appeal to the viewer for compassion, forgiveness and understanding. The scenes of the Crucifixion are particularly moving.

If you drive across the island to the northern shore to see the site of the great British Naval Base, the vast dock big enough to take the *Queen Elizabeth I* and the Causeway to Malaysia, you will also see the Kranji War Memorial. No traveller should pass it by. It is wonderfully sited on high ground; its columns bear the names of every man and woman, of all ranks and races, of all the armed and civil forces who died on active service in Singapore and Malaya in 1941–45. The effect is touching, and, though beautiful, not sad, and impossible to forget.

The following week we crossed to Malaysia, another new State, but so different in racial composition and topography. Somehow I felt it would be easier to write about Sir Shenton in the different atmosphere of Malaysia. The physical nature of the land – high mountain ranges rising to 7,000 feet, with forests and dense, tropical jungle, important mineral resources, particularly tin and wolfram, enormous rice cultivation and rubber plantations, with relatively sparse rail and road communications – all seemed familiar. It brought back memories of Burma, which had also seen retreat and disaster, with two and a quarter million refugees, disease, privation and terrible hardship.

I

THE LOSS OF FORCE Z

On 8 December 1941, Sir Shenton Thomas, Governor and Commander-in-Chief of the Straits Settlements and High Commissioner for the Malay States, received the following letter at Government House, Singapore:

> Japanese Consulate-General
> Singapore
>
> 7th December, 1941
>
> Dear Excellency
> I thank you very much for your gracious letter which I have just received. It is exceedingly kind of Your Excellency to ask me to have lunch with you tomorrow, 8th December, at 1.00 p.m. I feel I am highly honoured and I shall be delighted to accept your kind invitation.
> Believe me, I am
> Very sincerely yours,
> Suermasa Okamoto
> (The Consul General for Japan)

The Governor endorsed this in pencil:
"The Japanese attacked us at 2.15 a.m. on December 8th"! This was the last letter Sir Shenton Thomas received through the normal post and telegraph system before active war conditions came to the Far East.

The Japanese attack on Malaya was one of four carefully planned invasions of sovereign independent countries, synchronized to within a few hours of each other in the early morning of the same day. The International Date Line causes considerable local variations, but, using Tokyo time as standard chronology, Malaya was attacked first at 2.15 a.m. on 8 December; then came Pearl Harbor at 3.25 a.m. (it was actually Sunday there and the Japanese knew most of the United States fleet would be in harbour); the landings at Singora, in Thailand, took place at 4 a.m., and the Hong Kong invasion began at 8.30 a.m.

Speed was the essence of each operation: Hong Kong surrendered after eighteen days' resistance, on Christmas Day, 1941; at Pearl Harbor the American Pacific fleet was virtually destroyed within a few hours; the invasion of Thailand met with no resistance; in Malaya it took General Yamashita only seventy days to roll back a British Imperial Army over 400 miles and force its surrender at Singapore on 15 February, 1942.

In all Malaya, including its dependencies, no issue of substance, political, civil or military, could be resolved without reference to the Governor, who was responsible to the Crown and the British Government in London. This constitutional fact became even more important in war, because the Governor, by title, was also Commander-in-Chief of Malaya, though he had no executive control of the armed forces operating in or from the country by land, sea, or air. All military operations therefore affected him, but he had no control over them. The effect of this anomalous position will be referred to frequently, particularly in extracts from Sir Shenton's private diaries. We shall see how he became involved in certain military problems which had a decisive effect on Singapore and certainly contributed to the disaster there.

First, there is an entry in the Governor's diary for the day preceding the outbreak of war in the Far East.

> Sunday December 7 1941
> Up at 4 am for an urgent cypher cable from Colonial Office. Early church at St Andrew's Cathedral. Work all morning. Impey, Daily Mail War correspondent, came to lunch. The Japanese ship convoy moving West across the Gulf of Siam has disappeared, but more single ships seen. Perceival[1] told me that one Japanese ship had fired on a reconnaissance aircraft of ours. D and I went to tea with the Laytons[2] at the Naval Base.

It is now matter of history how the Prime Minister, Winston Churchill, and the Cabinet in London decided, before the war with Japan started, to send a reputedly strong naval task force (Force Z) to Singapore. This contingent consisted of six ships. The flagship, H.M.S. *Prince of Wales*, was our latest and most powerful battleship, of some 36,000 tons, 29 knots speed and armed with 15-inch guns; her armour and overall protection was heavier than that of any battleship yet built and she had the reputation of being "unsinkable". She was accompanied by H.M.S. *Repulse* and four destroyers. The former was an old battlecruiser, built in 1915, still capable of 28 knots and armed with 15-inch guns, but lacking in modern anti-aircraft weapons; her

---

1 Lieutenant-General Arthur Percival, G.O.C. Malayan Command.
2 Admiral Sir Geoffrey Layton, C-in-C China Station.

horizontal armour-plating, for protection against air attack, was out of date. This force arrived at Keppel Harbour on 2 December and later in the day concentrated at the Naval Base in the Johore Strait.

The whole saga of Force Z, with its tragic misconception, has recently been retold by the distinguished naval historian the late Professor Arthur Marder in his book *Old Friends, New Enemies**. Marder wrote thus of the arrival of Force Z at Singapore on 2 December:

> The *Prince of Wales* and *Repulse* were greeted on their entry into Keppel Harbour, the City's port, 'as though they were the main attraction of a seaside carnival'. . . . The press played up the arrival of the capital ships as though, with the fleet there, the Royal Navy had command of the Eastern seas. . . . It spoke of these ships making 'a magnificent and imposing sight as they were silhouetted against a background of blue sky and green islands. . . . Enthusiasm everywhere was very noticeable'. . . . A peacetime atmosphere pervaded the city, which was gay, brightly lit, and, on the surface at any rate, confident that the advent of the Eastern Fleet would counteract and lull the insistent sabre-rattling of the Japanese war lords. . . . The old sleepy colonial way of life persisted . . . with a general feeling that "They [the Japanese] might do it to the Americans, but not to us. They wouldn't dare; it's bluff – they won't come". . . . The evening of 3 December, Rear-Admiral E. J. Spooner, commanding the Naval Base, gave a party in honour of the *Prince of Wales*. "Everybody felt cheerful and confident. 'There was a sound of revelry by night.'" Friends were made, and future plans discussed of meetings, of tennis and golf.

Then comes Marder's dramatic final sentence to the paragraph:

> Early the following day [4 December] all leave was stopped.

The Governor wrote of these events in his diary:

> *December 1*   7 a.m. Telegram from Colonial Office saying position getting worse. Meeting with Brooke-Popham, Percival, and Jones [Colonial Secretary]. Orders to the Volunteer Forces. Admiral Sir Tom Phillips, Admiral Palliser, Commander Goodenough, lunched at G. H. Duff Cooper and Sir Harry Trusted [Chief Justice] dined with us.
> *December 2*   Peaceful. Hot and showery. H.M.S. *Prince of Wales*, *Repulse* and 4 destroyers arrived at Naval Base at 5.30 p.m. We are invited to party there tomorrow.

* Oxford University Press, 1981.

The Governor and his wife did not go to that party on 3 December.
Perhaps discretion had its way, though we do know that they "went to
tea" in the Naval Base on 7 December.

Of course the Governor was actively involved in the events in
Singapore on the first day of the Japanese invasion, but his own part in a
decisive conference in the War Room at the Dockyard Offices of the
Singapore Naval Base, and the vital decisions then taken, have so far
been published only in Professor Marder's book.

It is easy to criticize the thoughts, decisions and consequent actions
of those who held the reins of power in those troubled and dangerous
days. We tend to forget that their thinking was limited by their lack of
reliable information, while subsequent criticism is too often based on
being "wise after the event". As Professor Marder wisely cautions, "to
look at yesterday with the eyes of yesterday, that is the historian's real
task".

In London it was certainly hoped that the arrival of Force Z might
induce second thoughts in the Japanese. The Head of the British
Admiralty Delegation in Washington thought it quite possible that the
Japanese would "hesitate for a moment, as the presence of the *Prince of
Wales* would necessitate their dispatch of a capital ship escort with any
expedition southward, and they may not feel inclined to do this." On 1
December Admiral Sir Dudley Pound, the First Sea Lord, had sent a
personal message to Admiral Sir Tom Phillips, Commander of Force
Z, suggesting the desirability of sending either the *Prince of Wales* or the
Repulse, or both, "*away from Singapore*" in order that the uncertainty of
their whereabouts would disconcert the Japanese, while remaining
there himself. Later, when intelligence reached London of the sighting
of three Japanese submarines off Saigon proceeding southward, probably to watch Singapore, Pound repeated his suggestion to Phillips:
"that one or both British battleships get away" to the eastward. But
Phillips did not respond.

By 6 December the Admiralty knew that Japanese ship convoys were
moving west across the Gulf of Siam. Was an invasion of Thailand
imminent? If so, it was very important *not* to intervene from Singapore,
unless Britain was certain of the armed support of the United States.
Britain must not be seen to make the first move to breach Thai
neutrality. So nothing was done about it in London that day and the
Japanese had no difficulty positioning their ships in readiness for their
invasions of Thailand and Malaya.

Finally, one last chance to pre-empt a Japanese attack was narrowly
missed. On 7 December, when the Governor and his wife were invited
to tea at the Naval Base in Singapore, Lord Halifax, then British

Ambassador at Washington, telegraphed to London that the United States would regard any Japanese invasion of Thailand, Malaya, Burma or the Dutch East Indies as a hostile act, and that Britain was requested to attack Japanese ships sighted steering *west* or *south-west* across the Gulf of Siam, "since they must be going for either Thailand or Malaya". The Admiralty repeated this information to Phillips but it was too late; their signal reached him at 2.18 a.m. Singapore-time 8 December; the Japanese had attacked at Kota Bharu at 2.15 a.m.

It is easy to see the dilemma in which Admiral Phillips was now placed. What should be done, and could he do it? Briefly he had to decide whether (a) to stay at Singapore and risk being bombed to destruction, or (b) to sail to some remote area, far from the danger of air attack, or (c) to sail "at once" to attack Japanese transports and warships probably about to land on the east coast of Malaya. He did not then know of the Kota Bharu landings. In this situation Admiral Phillips called a conference, held in the early morning (around 2.30 a.m.) on 8 December in the War Room at the Naval Base. Present were:

Admiral Sir Tom Phillips, with two staff officers,
    Commander Goodenough, R.N.
    Commander Beardsworth, R.N.
Commander Greening, R.N., staff officer to Admiral Layton
Sir Shenton Thomas, accompanied by two senior civil officers*
Air Chief Marshal Sir R. Brooke-Popham (B.P.) C-in-C Far East
Captain Back, R.N., Naval liaison officer of B.P.
Air Vice-Marshal C. Pulford, Air C-in-C
A Brigadier and a Colonel from the Headquarters of General Percival,
    G.O.C. Malaya

Apparently no official minutes of this important conference were kept and there would now be no written record of it whatsoever but for the prescience of a young naval officer, Lieutenant-Commander J. W. McClelland**, who was then Naval Base Signals Officer. McClelland's account of what transpired at the meeting and how he came to record it are best told in his own words:

---

* Almost certainly these must have been the Colonial Secretary and the Defence Secretary, but both are now dead.

** Now Captain J. W. McClelland, D.S.O., O.B.E., R.N., who very kindly showed the author his record of this meeting, and what followed thereafter, in July, 1982.

I do not know when C-in-C China, Admiral Sir Geoffrey Layton, became aware of Phillips's intention to hold this conference, but most evidence suggests that he (Phillips) had decided to call it long before the event. Layton told me after the war, when he was C-in-C Portsmouth, that he had spent long hours trying to think of some way of avoiding it and its inevitable conclusion, even to the extent of sticking his neck out and sending a signal to the Admiralty saying that he thought that Phillips should be ordered to withdraw westwards, as the two capital ships were at serious risk and their Admiral had been placed in an impossible position . . . . Greening told me that in these circumstances Layton was particularly anxious that I, as an unbiased witness, should the disaster he foresaw occur, should hear what was said, and, being aware of my (signal officer's) cubbyhole at the far end of the War Room from the conference table, he considered that, with the lights left off at my end, I might easily escape detection. Greening, Layton thought, might be asked to leave, although in fact this did not happen, because the China Station Command had already lapsed at midnight.

It was decided deliberately that no minutes of the conference should be recorded, but that those attending it should agree to stick to the conclusions reached, to save time at a future joint conference held to co-ordinate the employment of Force Z. It would also give the participants time to mull over their commitments. Layton had hoped to exclude the C-in-C Far East, Air Chief Marshal Sir Robert Brooke-Popham, as that would give the Air C-in-C, Air Vice-Marshal C. W. Pulford, who was two grades junior in rank to B.P., a chance to speak his mind, which Layton thought would be more valuable than hearing the Air Chief Marshal, who should have been left on the retired list he was so little use!!

Phillips opened the meeting by saying that he did not think the Japanese would deploy capital ships or aircraft carriers in Malayan waters as long as the United States fleet remained undefeated. (The news of Pearl Harbor had not yet reached Singapore.) His main danger, he thought, was from Japanese submarines, and, after that, attacks by aircraft. He dismissed high-level bombing as unlikely to achieve any significant results, in the face of his anti-aircraft armaments, unless he was extremely unlucky. Dive-bombing was likely to cause damaging hits, but should not cripple either of his two capital ships; in any case he understood that the Japanese naval dive-bombers only operated from carriers, and he had already said that he did not expect to encounter one. As the torpedo was the weapon to which heavy ships were especially vulnerable, the principal danger from aircraft came from the torpedo bomber, as had been amply demonstrated in the case of the *Bismark*. But, in the thick north-east monsoon weather then prevalent, the execution of simultaneous attacks was very difficult and the torpedo bomber itself was very vulnerable to attack by fighters during its approach to the dropping position. Against this form of attack his protection by shore-based fighters thus became essential, as his arrival without carrier escort meant that he was completely devoid of any fighter protection whatsoever.*

He wound up by saying that, if the factor governing the situation was the preservation of his ships so that they could be used to greater advantage later in the campaign, there was no doubt at all that he should retire to the westward and await reinforcements. He then sat down. (According to McClelland, all this was merely Phillips' way of handling the conference. He had already *decided*, before the conference, to take the offensive and what to do, but he wanted to test his hearers' reaction as to when and how he should do it.)

A dead silence followed which nobody seemed inclined to break. Finally the Governor gave his views. The heavily built, but fit, Sir Shenton Thomas, a Cambridge man, quiet, scholarly, dignified and even-tempered, always said that he knew nothing about warfare, except of the tribal kind. But he certainly had a clear mind when the occasion arose to talk about it, as now. It had, he said, come as a complete surprise to him to learn that the arrival of the battleships was only a bluff, and, further, that the Japanese might be about to call it. If they did, would not this change the circumstances completely? Ought they not immediately to ask the Government (in London) what they wished the Admiral to do now? After all was said and done, the Japanese must be as aware of the shortcomings of the British Force as the Admiral himself, and would make every effort to exploit them.

Brooke-Popham then spoke. He disagreed with Thomas, said it was useless to ask for fresh orders, and made disparaging remarks about Japanese efficiency. He did not expect a Japanese sea-borne attack during the north-east monsoon, and still hoped the occupation of Thailand was the Japanese objective. He finished with his usual cliché, that "Once he is in a fight, the only way to get a Jap out of it is to kill him"! Pulford (Air C-in-C) spoke next and very briefly. He emphasized the limitations of his aircraft, the lack of training of his fighter pilots in a fighter-protection role, stressing particularly the difficulties they would run into out of sight of land. However, within these limitations he would support the Admiral's plan, whatever it may be. Pulford thereupon left the meeting.

Shenton Thomas then said he would like to add a few words in the

---

* The original composition of Force Z included the aircraft carrier H.M.S. *Indomitable*, but she ran aground at Jamaica before she could join the Force.

assumed capacity of an "umpire". As he saw it, given another week the
Admiral would have sufficient destroyers* to permit offensive operations as far as Japanese submarines were concerned; but, on the other
hand, the provision of fighter protection during any operation was
obviously a vital factor in the safety of the battleships. In his opinion,
therefore, the ships should not be employed on any offensive task
unless fighter protection could be guaranteed and he wished that the
AOC-in-C had not left and could hear him say so. But probably
C-in-C Far East would agree and could give the necessary assurances?
Brooke-Popham did not reply to this – perhaps he realized his aircraft
were still on the ground when they should have been attacking any
transports approaching Kota Bharu? Instead B.P. said to Phillips: "Do
you know, Admiral, that I am beginning to believe that *if* the Japanese
intend to attack, your intervention is the only thing that can prevent the
invasion suceeding.

According to McClelland this last remark by Brooke-Popham was
exactly what Admiral Phillips wanted to hear. He (Phillips) was not the
man to risk, in any avoidable way, a couple of valuable ships, only
to discover that the C-in-C Far East was quite confident that he
(B.P.) could repel any invasion without any naval help *in the early
stages*.

Admiral Phillips made no reply to this sudden declaration by B.P., but
Sir Shenton Thomas, after rubbing his chin for a little while, said gently,
yet very clearly, that "he sincerely hoped that Brooke-Popham's original
conception (about the inferiority of the Japanese and his conviction that
war in the Far East would not happen) was correct, because, if it was not,
"it looked as if they would be in a regular pot-mess and no mistake".
Talk on these lines was going on but was suddenly interrupted when
"Air Raid Warning Red" (an attack is imminent) was announced. As it
was too late to get to the Base shelters, those in the War Room lay down
on the floor under the conference table. When the "All Clear" was
sounded the meeting broke up in a hurry.

A detailed search, including the Public Records at Kew, appears to
prove that no official minutes of this highly important conference were
kept, and there is no mention of it in the *Official History* or any other
published material except Marder's book. Fortunately McClelland
recorded what happened immediately following the meeting. That
Thomas's judgement was right (and events certainly proved him so)

* The Americans had already promised Phillips they would send him a division of U.S.
destroyers.

underlines the fact that, *as a civil Governor, he challenged the opinion of a professional service commander.*

Admiral Phillips, when he left the War Room, sent an immediate signal to the Admiralty. He had in fact drafted it and had it encyphered in *Prince of Wales* ready for urgent dispatch before he went to the meeting. We know beyond doubt, from McClelland's signal office data, that this signal was dispatched from Singapore to London about 6 a.m. on 8 December, and that London sent its "Answer back" (proof of receipt) by 9.30 a.m. Singapore-time that same morning. Marder said, "I have been unable to find this signal," which is extraordinary in view of its importance. Furthermore, Admiral Phillips gave the gist of his cypher telegram orally to McClelland, whom he knew well, in the War Room at the Base immediately following the meeting:

> It's at present "most secret", but I'm taking Force Z out this evening to try to scotch the Japanese round Kota Bharu. I rate the chances of getting there no higher than fifty-fifty, but I'm sure it's the only way in which to halt the invasion and if it can be halted, they should find it impossible to start it again. Surprise is absolutely essential, but it is just possible in this thick monsoon weather, given even an average amount of luck. But, if we are spotted, which is bound to happen sooner or later, we shall be attacked. . . . I've drafted a fairly long urgent signal to send to the Admiralty, to tell them what I intend to do.

This strange sequence of events – an unrecorded meeting of high importance attended by the King's representative and a missing telegram from Admiral Phillips to the Admiralty – will crop up again later.

Meanwhile, it is a matter of history that Force Z was destroyed because both battleships were launched on an offensive task without any guaranteed fighter protection against enemy torpedo bomber aircraft. Furthermore Phillips grossly underestimated the range of Japanese naval bombers and the efficiency both of their crews and the torpedoes they carried. Meanwhile, McClelland noted the implication of that missing signal:

> Phillips must have been aware that he was taking a risk, which was impossible to calculate, with two valuable ships. He may have hoped to receive the comments of the Admiralty on his intentions, as expressed in the signal which I sent for him. But he would most certainly have wished to give the First Sea Lord time to instruct him (Phillips) NOT to take the risk, if, for reasons not known to him, Admiral Pound did not wish him to take it. But Phillips *received no reaction to his signal.*

To this Marder adds a terrible indictment:

> High Authority in London stood transfixed, unable to decide on a
> course of action in time to influence the unfolding tragedy.

He therefore acted on the brief he had received from the Admiralty
dated the 7th, to attack Japanese shipping sighted steering west in the
Gulf of Siam, having the concurrence of the C-in-C Far East with his
plan. He sailed from Singapore on the evening of 8 December,
notwithstanding the information he received from the Air Commander-in-Chief as H.M.S. *Prince of Wales* was passing through the boom
defence at the entrance to the Johore Strait. It was a visual signal,
flashed from the Changi fortress signal station, which read: "Regret
fighter protection impossible". Phillips's reaction is said to have been a
shrug of the shoulders and "Well, we must just get on without it". The
irony of it was that he knew that Japanese land-based aircraft were now
operating from Saigon in Indo-China, including torpedo bombers. But
he thought that their radius of action, based on comparable British
aircraft performance, was about 200 miles; the truth, *which he did not
know*, was that the Japanese Zero fighter (torpedo bomber), which
destroyed him two days later, could operate up to a radius of 1,000
miles.

This question of fighter protection for Force Z, its feasibility or
otherwise, and the unwisdom of sailing without it, will continue to be
argued about. Thirty-five years after the event, in 1976, it was claimed
that no less an authority than the A.O.C. Malaya himself (Air Vice-
Marshal Pulford), supported by the Admiral commanding the Naval
Base (Rear-Admiral Spooner), had blamed Sir Shenton Thomas for
the absence of aircraft protection provided for Force Z.

> Pulford and Spooner were adamant that the Governor of the Straits
> Settlement, Thomas, had exercised a malign influence on the conduct
> of the whole Malayan campaign. They charged that as soon as he knew
> of the possibility that fighter aircraft might be diverted from the air
> defence of Singapore to provide air cover for Force Z, he had protested
> most vehemently against their use for this purpose.*

According to Marder this grave charge was made orally by Pulford
and Spooner before they both died, after the surrender at Singapore, of
exhaustion and malaria. These two distinguished officers had managed
to escape the Japanese; with some fifty-three others they embarked in a

* Marder pp. 428–429.

patrol boat to reach an island off the coast of Sumatra where, after two months, all but twelve had died. During this period they had bitterly aired their grievances, and their views on the loss of the two battleships and of Malaya, to a survivor of the party, who recorded what they said. It is strange that no mention of this alleged, improper protest appears in either the *Official History* of the campaign, the official dispatches of the C-in-C Far East and Air Vice-Marshal Maltby, or in the Brooke-Popham papers in the Liddell Hart Archives. Sir Shenton himself flatly denied any such accusation by Pulford, and the matter had evidently reached high level, for in a letter* of 20 April, 1954, to Sir Folliott Sandford, Parliamentary Under-Secretary at the Air Ministry, Sir Shenton wrote: "I repeat I had no knowledge of the matter at all, and in my opinion this was right. It did not fall within my province."

Be all that as it may, this unresolved problem quickly lost its topical importance when it became known that British aircraft in Malaya were in any case outdated and inferior in performance to Japanese aircraft. Unfortunately British pilots, early in 1941, had been told that "the best of the Japanese fighters were old fabric-covered biplanes which wouldn't stand a chance against the [British] Buffalo Fighters".

One more facet remains about the naval battle of Malaya which is important, for it reveals a condition which might have changed the whole course of events on the night of 9 December and therefore what happened the following day. Briefly, the radar installation in H.M.S. *Prince of Wales* was defective when she sailed from Singapore about 5.30 p.m. on 8 December; her surface-scanning set was not working.

For what follows I am indebted to a distinguished scientist, Dr T. C. Carter, O.B.E., D.Sc., F.R.S.E., who at the time was a squadron leader in the R.A.F., and in February, 1941, had been sent to Singapore to form and command a Radar Installation and Maintenance Unit (R.I.M.U.) for Far East Command. He recalls the following incident, which is published here for the first time:

> I believe the *Prince of Wales* had two radar sets, operating on different frequencies, one used to search for aircraft and the other, a higher-frequency set, for surface-scanning; and that the surface-scanning set was unserviceable. About midday on December 8th 1941 I was at the R.I.M.U. (dispersed under rubber trees two miles east of Seletar) when I was told that the Navy needed technical assistance, and that I should ensure my best radio mechanics were sent to help them. I went myself, taking a couple of Radar Mechanic Sergeants. In the Naval Base I went upstairs to find details of what was required of me. . . . The news I

* Imperial War Museum.

received was that a radar set on *Prince of Wales* was unserviceable, the
Navy had been unable to repair it, and would we please do so by that
evening. I took my sergeants aboard and found that the set was of a type
that none of us had seen before. I was somewhat irritated when I found
that the set had been unserviceable throughout the week that *Prince of
Wales* had been in Singapore, and it was only now, when she was
obviously being prepared for sailing, that we were called in and asked to
do the job "at once"! In the event we could not. It was the usual trouble:
radar apparatus designed for U.K. conditions failing to stand up to the
humidity and temperature (in that order) of the tropics. Had we been
called in a couple of days earlier we might have been able to do the job,
which probably included rewinding transformers. So *Prince of Wales*
sailed with that radar set unserviceable.

In 1977 Martin Middlebrook and Patrick Mahoney published their
thrilling and well-documented book* in which they recorded the fact
that at one time during the night of 9/10 December there had only been
five miles between Force Z and the Japanese cruiser *Chokai*. They
added the following:

> Indeed, it is surprising that *Chokai* had not been picked up on *Prince of
> Wales's* radar, which had a theoretical range of up to twenty-five
> miles. . . . If the two sides had met the result of the battle can only be
> conjective. The British had the heavy 14-in. and 15-in. guns; the best
> the Japanese cruisers had were 8-in. Moreover the British gunnery
> could be radar-controlled in darkness, and although this type of fighting
> was still in its infancy, the use of radar generally would have been an
> immense advantage to the British in night action. . . . If the British guns
> could have got to work at close range, they might have blown the
> Japanese ships out of the water. If Japanese torpedoes had found their
> marks, the British ships might well have been crippled, or at least slowed
> down for the morning.

In view of Dr Carter's report, it is indeed tempting to wonder what
might have happened if *Prince of Wales's* surface-scanning radar had
not been unserviceable, and she had spotted *Chokai!*
Marder (page 447) gives in detail the radar capability, of both
surface-warning and air-warning sets, in *Prince of Wales* and *Repulse*
and in the escorting destroyers; and it may well appear inconceivable
that neither of these great battleships was able to detect large surface
targets only five miles away. It is also well known that Admiral Phillips
had issued strict orders for complete radio silence. Did this mean that

---

* *Battleship, The loss of* **Prince of Wales** *and* **Repulse**, Allen Lane, p. 142.

no set capable of transmitting radio waves was to be used, whether it was W/T, R/T or radar set? There seems to be some doubt about it. Captain C. W. McMullen, D.S.C., R.N., a survivor of *Prince of Wales*, writes as follows:

> The late Professor Marder contacted me twice but did not comment on the radar queries. What seems more likely is that the opposing ships were very much further apart – may be twenty miles not five; three Japanese float 'planes were sighted at dusk on the 9th, so from then our radar would have been free to operate, even if some restricted radar silence had been ordered previously.

When all is said and done, it may be that the *Chokai* incident will join other unresolved and controversial issues which continue to span the history of wars.

Of course we should know more if Tom Phillips had decided to transfer his flag to one of his escorting destroyers; he was the Fleet Commander, not the officer commanding *Prince of Wales*. But what should be well known by all, and is utterly beyond doubt, is the incredible courage and superb performance of all the officers and their crews in both *Prince of Wales* and *Repulse*. They were rightly proud of their fine ships and fought the battle magnificently to its inevitable ending.

II

THE BEGINNING

When Hong Kong fell to the Japanese on Christmas Day, 1941, and six weeks later the British Army in Malaya surrendered to General Yamashita at Singapore, I was in Rangoon in South Burma. I doubt if many of us there appreciated the full significance of these events; we were too preoccupied fighting the Japanese 15th Army, which had invaded Burma and was closing in on Rangoon. When we heard about Singapore most of us said wryly, "Of course it's our turn next!" Fortunately we were not right, but it was only by good luck that we avoided being surrounded and managed to break out in time.

We heard no news during our long retreat to India, and months passed before I knew that Sir Shenton Thomas and his wife were prisoners of the Japanese. I had only met Sir Shenton once but I had long known his wife, for she was my cousin, née Daisy Montgomery, and her parents had lived close to our family home in Co. Donegal.

When the Thomases were released from their three-and-a-half-year captivity they settled in London, where, after the war, my wife and I often met them. They talked quite freely about their experiences during Sir Shenton's long career in the British Colonial Service, including their years in Malaya. Old friends and ex-colleagues of Shenton and Daisy, including men, like Sir Robert Scott*, who held or had held high office under the Crown, at home or overseas, often called on Shenton Thomas when I was there. I recall how I listened avidly as they discussed controversial events and the leading personalities involved, particularly during those momentous war years.

I used to ask Shenton why he did not publish his own account of what happened during his time in Malaya and Singapore and during his captivity. In addition to the *Official History*, published in 1957, General Percival, the British Army commander in Malaya, Ian Morrison, a distinguished journalist, and many others had published their views, some of which were very critical of the British civil administration, for which Shenton was responsible. But he replied that he had directed

---

* Sir Robert Scott, G.C.M.G., C.B.E., formerly Permanent Secretary Ministry of Defence, Commissioner-General S.E. Asia, etc.

that his private and personal papers and diaries should not be revealed during his lifetime. If he published his own story about Singapore, he said, "many heads would roll", and he would not like that to happen. He wrote letters and articles in national newspapers and magazines, about such matters as economic, social and industrial development in British colonies, including Malaya; and he sent his personal comments on the *Official History of the Malaya Campaign* to the Cabinet Office, including his own assessment of Malaya's war effort, but none of his reports were published by H.M.G.

After his death more authors, both historians and servicemen, and including Japanese writers, published their versions of the Malayan campaign; but all these books were written without access to the personal records and opinions of the Governor.

In 1981 I was invited by members of Sir Shenton Thomas's family to write his authorised biography. His private papers are lodged, under embargo until 1990, in the Bodleian (Rhodes House) Library at Oxford, with authority for access controlled jointly by Shenton's nephew, Lord Thomas of Swynnerton, and his daughter, the Countess of St Germans, who kindly gave me right of access until my task was completed.

I first met Shenton Thomas in rather unusual circumstances. It was in 1930 and I was a passenger on the old *Llangibby Castle*, en route from Mombasa to London via Cape Town, when the ship called at the port of Dar-es-Salaam. A battalion of the King's African Rifles (K.A.R.) was stationed there, and in those days the regimental stores included a four-oared boat, a gig, manned by askaris in special nautical order of dress with a shawesh (sergeant) as coxswain. The crew were very smart in khaki drill shorts and blue puttees, khaki tunics with sailors' collars, and a scarlet tarboosh (headdress) with long black tassel; they were barefoot because, before the Second World War, K.A.R. askaris were not issued with footwear of any kind, no matter what the occasion or weather; yet no one could outmarch them. They never tired and were certainly never footsore. These soldiers handled their boat in true Royal Navy fashion. It was their duty to meet V.I.P.s from incoming vessels anchored in the harbour – the port had no deepwater quays for big steamers – and convey them to the landing pier on shore. V.I.P.s were given a similar escort when departing by sea.

Sir Shenton Thomas, then Governor of Nyasaland (Malawi), was in Dar-es-Salaam, where he had been attending an East African Governors' Conference, and was returning via Beira to his post. I remember watching him arrive in the gig to board *Llangibby Castle* and be received on deck by the Captain. I was then a junior officer in the

K.A.R., going home on leave, and I had no idea who this V.I.P. was or where he was going; by his dress and bearing, and the deference shown to him, he was clearly a person of great influence. Had his wife, my cousin Daisy, been with him, I would of course have recognized her. Anyway, at that particular moment I was feeling extremely ill and I went back to my cabin.

At lunchtime I asked for the ship's doctor, who arrived, took my temperature and told me it was 105°, though, he added, "That's of no importance"! This rather alarmed me and I certainly got no better. However, two days later Shenton came to my cabin (he had seen my name on the passenger list), with his A.D.C. and another passenger, the Principal Medical Officer in Uganda. This P.M.O. gave me strong quinine injections (in my behind and most painful!) and I very soon recovered. I have good cause to recall with gratitude my first meeting with the subject of this book.

Colonial Governors are now a thing of the past, evoking memories of potentates who lived in tropical climates, in considerable style and with much ceremony, were called "His Excellency" and were provided with a large and splendid mansion named Government House. From there they presided over the destinies of many thousands of subject peoples.

Although this brief memory picture covers only the trappings of high office, it is true that by the early years of this century the British Colonial Service had begun to evolve a type of professional career officer who, by his training and experience, could be categorized as "an average British Governor". This officer was invariably what was commonly called a "gentleman" (from the upper-middle classes, seldom the nobility), was always white, and drawn mainly from the rural counties of the United Kingdom. He was well educated, at a British public school or grammar school, and was always a Church of England, or other denomination, Protestant* and certainly a practising Christian; by and large he was hard working and incorruptible. From school he went to University. Unlike the Home, Foreign and Indian Civil Service, he could normally join the Colonial (Overseas) Service by nomination and selection, without a qualifying examination; the only exception to this practice was the Malay Civil Service which still insisted on its cadets passing the I.C.S. entrance examination.

Daisy's husband served sixteen years as a Colonial Governor, and we should therefore look first at his background, upbringing and edu-

---

* The Sovereign, by style and title, is Defender of the Faith. The Governor, as the Sovereign's representative, was seldom therefore a Roman Catholic.

cation, to see if these pointed the way to the eventual outcome of his career.

Shenton Thomas Whitelegge Thomas was the eldest son of the Reverend Thomas William Thomas, Rector of Newton-in-the-Isle, Cambridgeshire, and his wife Charlotte Susanna Whitelegge. Born on 10 October, 1879, Shenton had four brothers and one sister; his youngest brother, the late Hugh Thomas, C.M.G., also had a distinguished career in the Colonial Service and was the father of the well known historian Lord (Hugh) Thomas of Swynnerton.*

Shenton was brought up as a child in the atmosphere and environment of a large country parsonage in rural England. His father, as Rector of the Parish, lived with his wife and family in a lovely old Georgian house, with a large garden, and they usually had two or three domestic servants. There was no electric light or power, no water supply other than from a well from which water had to be pumped daily, and of course there were no motor cars, so the family depended for transport on horses. Altogether it was a happy childhood for the Rector's family, and in due course the eldest son went to his preparatory school, Syderstone, near Wicken Fen in Norfolk.

St John's, Leatherhead, has always been primarily a public school for sons of the clergy, so young Shenton was sent there in 1890 when he was ten years old. One or two letters that he sent to his parents from school have survived; they show the attitude typical of a young boy of his generation in his first term at public school:

> Dear Mother,
>   I hope you are quite well? I am quite happy now, so do not fret about me. Thank Will for his letter. We, that is Hamilton and I went out for a walk this afternoon. I think it is a very pretty place. We have the Ancient and Modern Hymn Book in Chapel. I have not got one yet, but please do not send one. I got in my Eton suit alright this morning. I was afraid I should not. Please will you ask Herring to write as soon as he can. We have very nice lessons here. Do not write more than twice a week it upsets me so. Mr. Skeen's son has only spoken once to me. I am not in the Choir. Love and Kisses to everyone and a lot for yourself.
>
>   Your loving
>   Shenton

He did very well at both work and games, particularly cricket, becoming a member of the 1st XI for his last three years. He had a bent for the classics, and in 1898 gained a scholarship to Queen's College

---

* Currently Chairman of the Centre for Policy Studies.

Cambridge, where he was an undergraduate that year. He graduated B.A. with 2nd class Honours in 1901, and always kept his links with Queen's College of which he was made M.A. and an Honorary Fellow in 1936.

Shenton was not academic, though he was certainly a scholar, and this may explain why, on leaving Cambridge, he elected to join the teaching profession. For the next seven years he was a master at Aysgarth Preparatory School, in the Yorkshire Dales and probably the best known school of its kind in the north of England. While he was there he took a year's leave, in 1904, and journeyed round the world by sea, with a member of his family. He was a keen fisherman and also maintained his reputation at cricket, playing regularly for Cambridgeshire and for the M.C.C.

Against this record we can see an image of Shenton Thomas emerging, as he joins the British Colonial Service early in 1909.

He is now twenty-nine, still a bachelor, and in good shape both physically and mentally. He is a short powerful type of man, vigorous and active, and gives an impression of robust health. He has little or no private means as his parents' finances were overstrained in caring for and educating their six children. He is very popular and gets on well with people, having absorbed all the practice and traditions of the British public school system in the late Victorian and Edwardian eras. Like many of his contemporaries from similar backgrounds he is influenced by the ethos of the educational establishments that he had attended, which bred admiration for skill at games and sport. He is a firm believer in *team* spirit, and therefore in a code of discipline at all levels, be it family, school or chosen occupation. He has travelled widely; it was possibly his voyage round the world that gave him a sight of the scale and prestige of the British Empire, then at its peak, and led him towards a career overseas. He was a parson's son and always a strong churchman.

At this time one strong influence on his approach to life generally may have been the fact that, after leaving university and going to Aysgarth, the ambience of his working conditions did not change; altogether he had lived, and was employed, in a school-university-school community for over twenty years. Was this good or bad for a future officer in the Colonial Service? We may see the answer to this later. Meanwhile it is perhaps worth quoting the "Ten Command-ments of a Public School Boy", cited in *Rulers of British Africa**, as a

---

* By L. H. Gann and Peter Duigan, Croom Helm, 1978.

semi-facetious comment on the background to British Colonial Rule:

I   There is only one God, and the Captain of Football is his Prophet.

II   My school is the best in the world.

III   Without big muscles, strong will, and proper collars, there is no salvation.

IV   I must wash much, and in accordance with tradition.

V   I must speak the truth, even to a master, if he believes everything I tell him.

VI   I must play games with all my heart, with all my soul, and with all my strength.

VII   To work outside class hours is indecent.

VIII   Enthusiasm, except for games, is in bad taste.

IX   I must look up to the older fellows, and pour contempt on newcomers.

X   I must show no emotion and not kiss my mother in public.

III

AFRICAN EXPERIENCE (1909–1934)

> We all broke from our ambushes with a yell. I rushed to the entrance, and there we had entrapped forty-nine fully armed Kikuyu raiders from Tetu. My Masai spearmen were out like lightning and began to kill at once. The whole affair was quick and quiet, and, as it all occurred in the open and within a few yards of me, I had an excellent view when I was not myself kept busy. I held the entrance with my bayonet, being shielded by two Masai with their massive shields of buffalo hide. A good number of the enemy bolted for the door, but none got past me. I was surprised at the ease with which a bayonet goes into a man's body. One scarcely feels it unless it goes in to the hilt. But one frequently has to make a desperate tug to get it out. In the end not a single one of the enemy escaped, all being killed.

This horrific account of human slaughter is the personal testimony of an officer of the King's African Rifles, Lieutenant Richard Meinertzhagen, who served in the British East Africa Protectorate not long before Shenton Thomas arrived there at the end of the first decade of this century.[*]

British rule and government in Kenya, as in virtually all other colonial territories of the European empire-builders in Africa, had begun as a result of private commercial enterprise. The industrial revolution of the mid-nineteenth century, particularly the advent of steam, and later electric power, fostered an urgent need to develop legitimate commerce and create new wealth by supplying European industries with fresh sources of raw materials, cotton for example, and thereby find new markets. This was the mainspring of the so-called scramble for Africa in the late Victorian and Edwardian era.

In East Africa the chief promoter of the enterprise was a Scotsman, Sir William Mackinnon, who in the late 1880s founded a chartered company, The Imperial British East African Company, which actually governed the whole of Kenya until the turn of the century. But white men like Mackinnon who produced this "New Imperialism" brought

---

[*] Quoted by Nicholas Best in *Happy Valley, The Story of the British in Kenya*, Secker & Warburg, 1979.

with them other influences, notably abolition of slavery and the lucrative slave trade, together with the arrival of missionaries, whose teaching of the Christian faith and its true meaning, especially in those early days, was looked on by indigenous Africans as anti-pagan, or anti-muslim, and disruptive of firmly rooted tribal disciplines, laws and practices. Mackinnon himself was almost fanatically religious. He became very rich with vast shipping and trade interests, yet he firmly believed that all he did was in accordance with God's will and judgement, and that he had earned the Almighty's favour by his Christian conduct and example!

In this setting the time soon came when political power in the new colonies could not be exercised without the use of physical force. Traders, local officials, administrators and missionaries all had to accept that pacification of tribal lands, and their native populations, often could not succeed without military action; wars of conquest could not be avoided and were certainly not infrequent. When this happened the British in Africa relied almost entirely on locally raised native troops, commanded by British officers*. The massacre described by Meinertzhagen, beyond words to deplore in the values of today, should therefore be viewed in the context of his time and judged accordingly. The truth of the matter is that violence, either inter-tribal or black African versus white man's rule, always existed in East Africa; terror was never far below the surface, though generations of African, Arab, Indian and European families lived very happy and prosperous lives, in Kenya in particular, notwithstanding terrible atrocities during the Mau Mau (Kikuyu) uprising as recently as the mid-nineteenfifties.

I have emphasized past history in this way because the K.A.R. are symptomatic of the locally raised military forces with which Shenton Thomas was inevitably associated during his long service overseas, particularly when Governor and Commander-in-Chief of British territories in East and West Africa, where the local forces were under his direct control. Furthermore, as later pages will show, Shenton's daughter married his A.D.C., who was a British regular army officer serving with the Royal West African Frontier Force.

In Kenya Sir William Mackinnon's Chartered Company collapsed financially just after 1895. Mackinnon had founded the famous "B.I. Line" (British India Steam Navigation Company Ltd) and could bring

---

* The situation was identical with that of the British East India Company (a trading corporation) some two hundred and fifty years earlier; the Company, when attacked by Indian Forces near Bombay, raised and trained its own army of Sepoys which became the forerunner of the Indian Army.

his goods to Mombasa by sea, but he did not have the finance and resources to build a railway inland, without which his company could no longer trade at a profit. The British Government had therefore to step in, and early in 1896 construction began of the 600-mile single-track, metre-gauge line planned to link Mombasa with Lake Victoria Nyanza. No story about East Africa could be complete without mention of this railway which became the life-line, the jugular vein, for all communities in Kenya and Uganda.

When Shenton Thomas left Aysgarth School to join the Colonial Service he found there was in fact no such profession, like the Home Civil Service, the Diplomatic Service or the Indian Civil Service. People talked glibly about a "Colonial Service" but it was not formed, as such, until 1933. Until then the Colonial Office in London dealt with nearly forty separate governments, large and small, each with its own administrative service, as well as medical, agricultural, forestry, public works, police and military departments. Duration of tours, leave and scales of pay and pensions differed considerably, and every candidate, like Shenton, signed a separate contract of employment with an overseas colonial government before he was finally accepted. It seems strange how long this seemingly archaic system was allowed to continue; one reason may have been the fact that the staff of the Colonial Office were all Home Civil Servants who themselves did not serve overseas. They had no experience of life in the Colonies, though they were solely responsible for selecting the young men who were sent out to administer all the countries of the British Empire.

This was a huge task, for a colony could vary from a small group of Pacific Islands to a vast territory like Nigeria, with a very mixed and complex racial, social and political structure. The choice of background in this recruitment policy is interesting, particularly at the time when the Colonial Office took over the administration of British East Africa. An analysis* of the two hundred young Englishmen who joined the administration in Kenya between 1895 and 1918 shows that at least one-third had been to a university, and half had attended a public school: one in five had served in the armed forces and one in five were the sons of parsons. Perhaps even more interesting, vis-à-vis Shenton Thomas, is that only one in twenty became a Colonial Governor. Finally *one in nine* died in service.

Thus Shenton, one of the "parson's sons", sailed from London for Mombasa early in 1909 in the "B.I." vessel S.S. *Rohilla*; she was a

---

* T. H. R. Cashmore "Studies in District Administration in East Africa Protectorate", (Unpublished Doctoral Dissertation, Cambridge University, 1965).

7,400 ton, single-screw cargo liner, coal-fired, with Goanese stewards and comfortable accommodation for the 1st class passengers. In those days formality and discipline extended to everyone in passenger line vessels. A bugle call summoned you to meals, and all males at dinner must wear dinner jackets with starched shirt and cuffs, and high winged collar, while ladies must wear evening dress. In tropical waters the ship's band played for dancing on deck.

For most young men this sea voyage, lasting at least three weeks, with calls at Gibraltar, Port Said and Aden, was a delightful time, including the organized, or unorganized, social life. But Shenton was handicapped by shortage of money. His pay was only £250 a year and he had had to buy his colonial outfit, the purchase of which, from a contractor nominated by the Crown Agents for the Colonies, could not be avoided. Some of the equipment he bought, from F. P. Baker in Golden Square, would look very odd today, but in the event he found it invaluable, particularly the "camp kit". Camp kit consisted of a green canvas bath on a folding wooden frame, a similar style canvas wash-basin and bucket, with two folding chairs and a folding table. Then there was the *chilumpchi*; this was a strong tin wash-basin, with a tight-fitting canvas cover strapped down over the top, and deep enough to contain all your essential personal gear, shaving and washing kit, pyjamas, etc., even a bottle of whisky! With his *chilumpchi* and his canvas valise (bedding roll) a district officer had all he needed for a long *safari* if necessary, not forgetting his snake-bite remedy carried always in his pocket. This a short, sharp, narrow-bladed knife, the handle of which was hollowed out to contain a phial of permanganate of potassium. When bitten by a snake the victim must at once incise the bite deeply with the knife and then pour a permanganate solution into the self-inflicted wound!

When Shenton Thomas disembarked at Mombasa vast areas of Kenya's 225,000 square miles were still virtually untouched by British rule; particularly the lands of the great martial races like the Masai whose territories covered high mountain tracts and dense forests as well as dry and arid country. More than half of all Kenya, then as now, was inhabited by nomadic, pastoral tribes (Somals, Galla, Boran and Turkana) whose semi-desert lands stretched from the frontier with Ethiopia southward to the Equator and the Kenya Mountain ranges. Mombasa Island was still very undeveloped and Kihindi Harbour as we know it today did not exist. But the port was always busy with ships arriving with thousands of Indians – Muslims, Hindus, Sikhs, skilled and unskilled, and all with their families – for construction work on the branch lines of the Kenya–Uganda railway; the main line had reached Kisumu on Lake Victoria some eight years earlier.

These factors – vast, remote, underpopulated tribal lands through which ran the white man's railway, accompanied by increasing thousands of immigrants from India – now set the stage for the arrival of a third, and highly dynamic, influence. This was the advent of white settlers – farmers and their families from Great Britain – who came seeking prosperity in new lands, attracted by fine high country, seemingly unused and unexploited. The first of these white settlers, and certainly the most prominent, was Lord Delamere; in 1903 he was granted 100,000 acres at Njoro in the Highlands, mainly from Kikuyu territory and between 5,000 and 7,000 feet above sea level, astride the Equator.

I have attempted this brief description of important factors influencing Kenya some seventy-five years ago because these were conditions that remained virtually unchanged for the nine years that Shenton spent in the Protectorate*. Overall it was a picture of tribal lands gradually slipping into other hands, which eventually became a grievance with far-reaching political, social and racial power changes. Meanwhile the first impact of it all on a newly arrived civil servant was an instruction that he must quickly learn Hindustani (Urdu), as well as Ki-Swahili, the lingua-franca of all East African lands.

Shenton Thomas was only one of a batch of new, young Assistant District Commissioners to report at Mombasa. In the Colonial Office they had been interviewed by Sir Ralph Furse who had impressed on them the importance and variety of their future duties, particularly the advantage of service in an out-station in remote areas, where they would quickly learn responsibility and decision-making. Furthermore, life in an out-station would be far more adventurous, with splendid opportunities for big-game shooting. Imagine then their surprise, even dismay, when the posting-officer at Mombasa told them he had no idea where each young officer was to report; he had therefore decided to put all the vacant appointments at a dozen stations throughout Kenya in a hat, and they would then draw lots to determine their first job!**

Shenton drew Nairobi, on appointment as Assistant to the District Commissioner; he could not have known then how very fortunate he was to have missed one of the coveted out-stations.

In those days Nairobi was a small and unattractive township clustered round the railway station area, still where it is today but made up entirely of functional corrugated-iron huts, sheds, workshops, locomo-

---

* Kenya did not become a Crown Colony until 1920.
** Unpublished memoranda by Lady Thomas.

tive turntables for enormous wood-fired steam engines and marshal-
ling yards. The only road from the station, later called Government
Road, led to the nearby bazaar with a few European-owned shops and a
large Indian quarter. There were a few small hotels, but the only one of
any standing, fit for Europeans, was the Norfolk which had opened a
few years earlier and is now a large and well-known tourist resort. The
British officials and senior railway officers lived on Nairobi Hill, where
the Nairobi Club now stands. Their houses, all bungalows, were built
of mud bricks, raised on concrete piles, with the inevitable corrugated
iron roofs; this was the type of house that was allotted to Shenton as the
new Assistant District Commissioner.

Although white settlement on African tribal lands was already
accepted and established by the early nineteen-hundreds, nevertheless, in all East and West African colonies, British officials generally
followed a political policy first introduced by Lord Lugard. This policy,
defined as *indirect rule*, was based on acceptance that British rule and
government was not a permanency; it was therefore necessary to foster
and educate natives in tribal and local government, as well as to
promote African trade and commerce. This was the philosophy underlying British power in colonial Africa, against the day when *direct* native
rule became fact, which indeed has happened. Later a Conservative
Secretary of State for the Colonies formally announced that: "The
interests of the African natives must be paramount, and if and when
those interests, and the interests of the immigrant races, should
conflict, then the former should prevail." Looking back, it is not
difficult to see how easily trouble began, and burgeoned, when successive governments in London, and the local colonial administration,
endeavoured to operate and maintain two conflicting policies – indirect
rule *simultaneously* with white farmer settlement and white business
management.

It was in this setting that Shenton Thomas met, and in his day-to-day
work had much to do with, Colonel J. A. L. Montgomery, a British
official who was the first officer to hold the new appointment of
Commissioner for Lands and Settlement in British East Africa. James
Alexander Lawrence Montgomery, C.S.I., C.B.E., after a long and
distinguished career in the Indian Civil Service, with great experience
of land settlement work in the Punjab,* had been posted to East Africa
in 1905. At this time India was sending experts throughout the Colonial

---

* After the demise of the East India Company, large-scale, complex and difficult land
settlement problems remained throughout India. A Commissioner was always a very senior and
high-ranking officer.

Empire to assist in every administrative field, particularly in railways and irrigation works. When Shenton arrived, the Colonel had already been nearly four years in Kenya, and had been joined by his wife and three daughters. He was my uncle, and also, therefore, of my brother, Field-Marshal Viscount Montgomery of Alamein, who had then just joined his regiment in India.

Although Nairobi was still very much a "shanty" town, it had already become Kenya's capital city, and every would-be white settler, applying for a grant of farmland in the Highlands, had to visit Nairobi and see the Settlement Commissioner. He also had to report to the local District Commissioner's office, so there were few of the white settlers that Shenton did not meet. Faced with this broad view of Kenya's problems, and through his contacts with Colonel Montgomery, he soon became imbued with the notion of trusteeship inherent in indirect rule. He became intimately aware of the impact on indigenous peoples, and their lands, of the arrival of white men, generally well-born upper-class Englishmen with their families, seeking new homes, new lives and prosperity in tropical Africa. Probably Shenton did not appreciate it at the time but his early experience in Nairobi was to influence, and profoundly affect, his thinking on the conduct of colonial rule in the British Empire.

Colonel Montgomery and his family lived in a large bungalow befitting a senior civil officer on the southern slopes of Nairobi Hill, where the Kenyatta Hospital now stands; there were wonderful views over the grasslands of the Athi plains, which had already been designated a game reserve. Wild life – antelopes of all kinds, zebra, wildebeeste, even leopard and lion – were sometimes found in the outskirts of the township in those days, so it was not really surprising when the Montgomerys' nearest neighbours had a very alarming experience. One fine sunny afternoon (the climate in Nairobi, just south of the equator at an altitude of 5,200 feet, is glorious) the family could not find their black spaniel bitch anywhere. Eventually the teenage daughter of the house looked under the double bed in the spare room and there, to her horror, was a full grown leopard, asleep, with the carcass of their spaniel which he had just eaten! The leopard had trapped the bitch in the garden – to spring on her and kill her would take but a moment – and brought her body into the bungalow, through the open French window, to be consumed under the bed; then, sated with his meal in the hot afternoon, the great cat had fallen asleep*.

---

* The African leopard will rarely attack man unless interfered with; his body, about 4 feet long, would be invisible under a large bed. The panther, 7 feet long with similar markings, is the ferocious and always dangerous spotted cat of Africa.

The young English girl showed great calmness and courage; she crept from the bedroom without making a sound, shut the door and told her father (fortunately it was a Sunday and he was there) who took his rifle and shot the leopard through the window. The animal's skin was proudly kept and displayed by the family.

Shenton Thomas's bungalow stood just behind the Nairobi Club, and there he first met Lucy Marguerite Montgomery, always known as Daisy, youngest daughter of Colonel Montgomery and five years younger than Shenton. She was attractive and petite, with dark hair and eyes widely spaced, a high forehead and very firm mouth and chin; she gave an impression of composure and determination, coupled with a neat and orderly mind, characteristics she would certainly need during the next thirty-seven years of her life in tropical Africa and Asia. She was born in Simla and, except for school years in England and France, had been strictly brought up in all the tradition and atmosphere of the British Raj. Her father had been a member of the Legislative Council, as well as a Commissioner, in the Punjab. Thus the frontiers of Daisy's world had been bounded by the taboos and formalities of life in large cantonments like Delhi and Rawalpindi, with hot weathers spent in hill stations, Simla and Muree, or in Kashmir. She was keen on horses and loved riding, but in those days girls always rode side saddle and, as she herself wrote: "In India we young girls were never allowed to go for rides with any young men alone."

Not surprisingly with this background, Daisy had had two proposals of marriage in India, both of which she accepted. First, in Muree, from a young officer in the British infantry about whom she wrote:

> He was very popular, most amusing, a good actor, and danced beauti-
> fully; but I soon realized I was not in love with him, merely flattered, so I
> broke it off. The following season we were in Simla where Lord
> Ampthill was Viceroy, and Lady Ampthill was wonderful to all young
> people. She used to give dances where she was the only chaperone, and
> parents were *not* invited. In those times young girls never went to dances
> without a chaperon, so we all had great fun.

In Simla she met and became engaged to an officer of the Indian cavalry, who was much older than she was and, perhaps fortunately, it all came to nothing, though Daisy wrote: "I was very unhappy for a long time."

It must have been a great change for the Montgomery sisters when they joined their father in Nairobi late in 1906. Compared with the routine and stability of cantonment life in India, their living conditions in Kenya were distinctly rough. There was no ice supply and no cold storage of any kind, no ceiling fans and of course no electric light or power; there were clouds of fleas and flies and those red *safari* ants, which invade your bungalow and can only be driven out by burning with quick lime. The jiggers which burrow under your toe nails and have to be dug out by your African boy, who is well versed in the procedure, were another painful annoyance. It was essentially an open-air life because all movement, away from the axis of the railway, depended solely on animal transport or manpower – camels (huge camel carts were seen in Nairobi until the 1930s), horses, mules, donkeys, ox carts, bicycles, rickshaws, hammocks, or just Shanks's pony. As Land Commissioner Colonel Montgomery travelled the length and breadth of Kenya, using every form of transport including African porters to convey stores and baggage – invariably carried as headloads. In East Africa porterage had been a long-established profession for generations, and was always the main transport of the slave trade in particular.

Daisy's father, always known in our family as Uncle Jimmie, kept a lengthy diary for every day of the seven years he was in East Africa, many of which were spent on safari, accompanied more often than not by Daisy or one of her sisters. A typical entry from his diary while on safari shortly after Daisy had arrived reads:

> *March 6th, 1907* In the Bamboo Forest of the Aberdare Mountains. Daisy with me, transport 15 donkeys and 30 porters. We ride when possible but mainly on foot in the forest. Increasingly girls here wear breeches and boots and ride astride.

This, then, was the type of life that Daisy Montgomery was leading when she first met Shenton Thomas; it was all very free and unconventional by comparison with her life in India. Gone were the days when "girls were never allowed to go for rides with any young man alone". And there were still comparatively few white women who mixed freely in social life in East Africa. Just before Shenton arrived Daisy wrote of a gymkhana "at which all Nairobi was there, 60 men and 30 women".

Daisy and Shenton very soon became great friends. He was good at all games, especially cricket, and the arrival of a newcomer who was a county cricketer and had played for the MCC and well-known clubs like the Free Foresters made him very welcome at the Nairobi Club. Daisy wrote of those days:

> In Shenton I knew I had found the ideal man; we became engaged in no time, and were blissfully happy. But our trouble was that his pay was still

only £250 a year, and I had no money either, so there was simply not enough to make both ends meet and we had to wait two years to get married.*

However, in one way their problems were solved, for Uncle Jimmie's appointment ended and he retired to his home in Ireland, taking Daisy with him.

For Shenton the next two years were fortunate, even though he was parted from Daisy. Evidently his classical education paid dividends for he passed the Higher Standard examinations in both Ki-Swahili and Urdu which brought him a bonus of £100. Next he was sent on tour to report on the standards of African education in every district of Kenya, and the result, with his recommendations, was obviously a success; for he was promoted to be an officer in the Government Secretariat in Nairobi with a rise in salary to £400 per annum.

Meanwhile Kenya was becoming well known for its social and sporting activities, which Shenton certainly appreciated; he always enjoyed parties and entertaining, which figure prominently in his later professional life. In those years the famous era of the Happy Valley set, as it was called, had scarcely begun; that came later, after the First World War, together with the founding of the Muthaiga Country Club, described as "a pink-walled, rambling structure erected on the site of an old Masai *manyatta*, which has probably seen more fornication than any other club of its kind in the world!"

But Shenton had now made his mark in altogether different fields; he was "in the Secretariat" which counted a lot in both official and social circles and his skill at games was well known. Nairobi was the only town of any size, and the famous characters who dominated the Kenya scene between the two world wars were beginning to gather in the Highlands. Meinertzhagen was still there (he became a Colonel in the K.A.R.), and Ewart Grogan, who had already made his famous march on foot from the Cape to Cairo, and there were many others to be found daily in the bar of the Norfolk Hotel or at the Nairobi Club.

Shenton met them all and, of course, knew all the stories, generally extravagant, that began to circulate beyond Kenya's frontiers. Winston Churchill had already visited the country and so had Theodore Roosevelt, ex-President of the United States of America. Then King Edward VII's brother, the Duke of Connaught, with his wife and their young daughter, the Princess Patricia, arrived to "see East Africa".

* The salaries and allowances of District Officers in East Africa before World War I were deplorable.

This was just before Shenton arrived, but Uncle Jimmie and Daisy were both there when the following unexpected event occurred. Uncle Jimmie often talked about it.*

The Government of Kenya was determined to entertain the royal guests suitably and did everything possible to ensure that they were insulated from the "rough" side of Kenyan life. However, on one occasion everything went completely wrong. The Connaughts were lunching just outside Nairobi with a prominent and wealthy settler, Mr James Elkington, who employed Masai tribesmen as herdsmen for his cattle. All went well until the party moved into the garden for a cup of locally grown coffee after lunch. It was then that Elkington, who had rehearsed his servants endlessly, suddenly became aware of a towering African figure, completely naked, though carrying a long Masai spear and shield, advancing purposefully towards the Duchess across the croquet lawn. Her Grace, with the young Princess in tow, levelled her lorgnette, thinking perhaps this presaged some gift from a loyal subject. She saw instead this enormous man displaying his tremendous specimen of very well-developed manhood – tremendous because the Masai tie a brick on it during childhood to make it longer – bearing a note for the embarrassed host. It was the Duke who smoothly retrieved the situation. Turning to Elkington he said, "Wow! The Elkington livery, I presume!"

In 1912 Shenton completed his first African tour and went home on five months' leave. He and Daisy were married on 11 April at a large family wedding in St Jude's Church, Kensington, attended, inter alia, by Lieutenant (later Field-Marshal) Montgomery. Afterwards Daisy wrote of this period: "I had quite an ordeal meeting my husband's family for the first time as he had four brothers and a sister; but they were wonderful to me and his father (he was a typical country parson with rosy cheeks and white hair) and his mother were darlings." Of course Shenton had to visit Daisy's home at Moville in Ireland where her father, Colonel Montgomery, was High Sheriff that year for County Donegal. Motor vehicles were still comparatively few in that remote and sparsely populated county, and Uncle Jimmie excited considerable attention when he bought a Model "T" Ford, an open two-seater coupé. He employed a driver in chauffeur's uniform and was driven everywhere sitting bolt upright wearing his bowler hat and looking very dignified in the passenger seat. But his appearance only caused derision at nearby New Park, where his brother, my father Bishop Montgomery, lived. The numerous young people there used to

* Also quoted in *Happy Valley*.

say, "Of course, Uncle Jimmie thinks he is back in India riding on his elephant beside the mahout." So much for dignity!

Meanwhile the First World War was soon to start, though, when Shenton and Daisy returned to Nairobi, nobody thought it could ever happen and Daisy wrote in her diary:

> Nairobi was very gay in those days and we had heaps of friends, and used to stay with various settlers, including the Delameres and the Coles, who had lovely farms (some with stone-built houses now). During Nairobi Race Week settlers and people from up-country used to come in, and there were dances and all sorts of things going on. Then suddenly war came in August, 1914, and it all stopped. For me too our daughter, Bridget, was born just then.

The fighting in East Africa, between British Kenya and German Tanganyika (now Tanzania), by comparison with the great European campaigns, was but a side show; though in the end more than 30,000 British Empire troops were deployed against the Germans under General Paul von Lettow-Vorbeck. On both sides disease claimed more casualties than enemy action in this strange campaign which ranged over vast distances. Malaria, heatstroke, blackwater fever, dysentery, rotting feet caused by uncontrollable jiggers, all took their toll. Also, in a way, it was possibly the last of the "gentlemen's wars", for it was fought, almost literally, with great good humour on both sides, as if it was some big boy scout exercise! This was due to two factors: the character and attitude of von Lettow, who captured the imagination of both his German public and his British opponents, and the sporting instincts of British settlers who formed many squadrons of a newly raised regiment, The East Africa Mounted Rifles (E.A.M.R.). Their men, riding horses or mules and accompanied by K.A.R. guides and trackers, were the reconnaissance element of the British.

Von Lettow was a professional officer, very active and efficient, a front-line soldier who believed in always leading his men and seeing the enemy himself. His African askaris – German equivalent of the K.A.R. – adored him and did their best to protect him from E.A.M.R. patrols, who sometimes spotted him and tried to shoot or capture him, but did not succeed. In this fashion a sort of *rapprochement* developed between both sides.

Von Lettow was completely cut off from his own country and could get no news direct from Germany. So, when the Kaiser promoted him to the rank of General, a British officer, bearing a large white flag of truce, went through the German lines to deliver the good news, adding, of course, the British commander's personal congratulations! When it became known that von Lettow was ill the British sent him medicines and enquiries after his health in the same way. One story has it that they sent him a cake on his birthday! Sadly, that is apocryphal, though it is a fact that when a British veterinary officer was captured he was exchanged, *on the spot*, for three bottles of whisky, which the German officers had not seen for months! Von Lettow was a great and fearless leader who never tired. If his horses or mules were not available, or unsuitable in the African bush, he led cyclist patrols along grass trails, until even his bicycle was shot from under him.

But by 1918 the game was up. He was completely out-numbered, without food or ammunition, and had to surrender to a senior officer of the K.A.R. by whom he was treated with honour and courtesy. His name will live in British history as the only German commander during the first World War to have invaded British territory: in 1914 his troops got within twenty miles of Mombasa and flew the German flag on British soil.

Shenton tried hard to join the K.A.R. directly war began but was ordered to remain at his post in the Secretariat, though with compulsory extra duties in the auxiliary armed police, which involved night guard duty. His life was therefore very strenuous, particularly when he was left in personal charge of the Secretariat with only one junior assistant officer. Here again he was lucky in that, as time passed, there was little he did not learn about the administration and central control, in peace and war, of colonial government in tropical Africa, a great help to him in his future career.

Daisy wrote of her own experiences during those war years:

> I joined what was known locally as "The Wild Women", actually the Women's War Work League, where we did every conceivable job that women can do! We met the casualty trains coming back from the front lines, and gave them tea, etc., while they waited to be taken to hospital. We saw the grim side of war, as soldiers, with dreadful wounds or diseases, arrived in the awful cattle trucks into which they had been packed. There were no proper ambulance trains or mobile field ambulances in East Africa, and soldiers, wounded in battle or disease-ridden, generally began their journey to hospital either in an ox cart, or on a stretcher on the back of a camel. I also did typewriting at Army Headquarters though I was not at all good at it, and one day I very nearly precipitated a religious crisis. My office chair was rather low (I am only 5'2") so one of the officers fetched what he said was a cushion "lying about in an adjoining room" and gave it to me. I folded it and found it very helpful until he rushed back in a great state, to say it was actually the

prayer rug of our Muslim clerk, young Ali Khan! It was put back at once and hopefully he never knew.

Then one day in 1916 Uncle Jimmie suddenly returned to Nairobi! He had been called out of retirement and appointed Commissioner of the Red Cross in East Africa, with the rank of full Colonel in the Army. He made his home with his daughter and son-in-law, to their mutual advantage, for he contributed to their household expenditure, while Shenton in the Secretariat gave him official government support. As Red Cross Commissioner Uncle Jimmie was a great asset. He toured the combat areas with a view to improving the ambulance and field hospital facilities and organization; it was by his efforts and recommendations that proper hospital trains and mobile ambulance equipment began to arrive from India and the United Kingdom.

Early in 1918 Shenton was promoted and appointed Assistant Chief Secretary in Uganda (again a Secretariat post) at Entebbe, the capital city. He and Daisy had had nine happy years in Kenya and they hated leaving, though there were compensations as Entebbe is a lovely place on the shore of Africa's largest inland sea, Lake Victoria Nyanza, which is 200 miles long and nearly half the size of England and Wales. After Germany had capitulated they were able to sail right round the lake, where German gunboats had been operating, in the steamship *Sibyl*: she was a 600-ton ship of the Uganda Marine, built in Scotland and sailed to Mombasa, where she was taken to pieces for transport by rail to Kisumu dockyard and reassembled there. It was a novel experience for the Thomases, as the *Sibyl* had standards of comfort almost unknown in East Africa in those days, with electric light and power that provided ceiling fans and piped water, with proper bathroom and lavatories; Uncle Jimmie called them *pukka closets*. It seemed strange also, when the long rains broke and there were violent storms causing huge waves, to find passengers sea-sick on a lake in central Africa.

For Shenton Uganda was valuable experience in a colony that did not have the complications of white settlement, but had a government largely in African hands with a population of 4,000,000 and a stable economy based on cotton, coffee, sugar and timber.

After the First World War when Shenton and Daisy, and their young daughter Bridget, were in England on leave from Uganda, Shenton was told that he would not be returning to Entebbe, but was to go as Principal Assistant Secretary to Lagos, the capital of Nigeria in British West Africa. It was promotion again, and also a significant change. Nigeria, which then included the Cameroons, had a population exceeding 21,000,000. He remained there for the next six years, being promoted again in 1924, to Deputy Chief Secretary. He must have done well in that appointment, for in his recent biography Sir Rex Niven describes him as "possibly the ablest man we ever had".*

Shenton Thomas spent more than ten years in Government Secretariats at Nairobi and Entebbe and was in similar employment in Lagos. The Secretariat was the mainspring of a colonial government, the vital link between the Administration and the Districts, and, equally important, with the Governor himself. No minute or paper ever went to the Governor without a recommendation, or otherwise, from the Colonial Secretary, who was Head of the Secretariat. Shenton had become a "Secretariat man" and would never be a District Officer, which many in his service regarded as an essential field experience (up-country) without which promotion to gubernatorial rank ought not to be allowed. This was similar to the thinking of many army officers who felt strongly that experience as commander of troops in the field was an essential prerequisite for promotion to general officer rank. Argument on these lines, in all British government service, is with us to this day but no one has yet resolved the issue by making it a principle, or a general rule one way or the other; for individual talents, characteristics and tendencies differ so widely and seem to defy solution by rules. In Shenton's case his ability to write in a style that was clear, concise, legible and devoid of ambiguity no doubt counted much in his favour. All important decisions at the Secretariat level of a colonial government were still recorded and kept on file in handwritten office minutes. In East and Central Africa the clerical staff were mainly Goanese, but on the West Coast well-educated Africans were generally employed as clerks.

Shenton's service in West Africa was marred by long periods of separation from his wife, for they had both decided that she must be with their daughter, Bridget, in England. From Lagos Shenton wrote frequently and at length to Daisy and extracts from his letters, which were often twelve pages long, show the deep and lasting bond of love and affection between them, as well as the vagaries and vicissitudes of life for a senior civil officer in West Africa more than sixty years ago:

Lagos Nov. 25, 1923

My own belovedest

Well, what think you of the news of "our David" coming to visit West Africa? It has caused a good deal of excitement here and also some disgust, as he arrives just before Easter and that will ruin some holidays. I expect you will say you must hurry out to be here (and I shall ever be

* *Nigerian Kaleidoscope* by Rex Niven, C. Hurst & Co. Ltd, 1982.

grateful for that) but I believe he is only going to spend one day in Lagos, though apparently as soon as he gets out of touch with Father he alters his programme to suit his own wishes! Makes sense too when I think of the poor youth spending four days in the train (to Kano and back) in the hot weather with a temperature near 120° in the shade! I *wish* you were going to be here, but don't forget Bridget's (Easter) holidays. Maybe they're more important to you than just one dance with – a very dissipated young man!

"Our David" was a reference to the then Prince of Wales, later H.M. King Edward VIII, who toured West Africa in 1924.

Nigeria gave Shenton his first experience of the administration of a vast territory, Britain's largest African colony, with a population almost entirely African, mainly Moslem or pagan. From south to north the topography varied greatly; first a belt of mangrove swamp, sometimes 60 miles wide, along the entire coastline, followed by a huge zone of tropical rain forest and oil-palms; then a complete change of vegetation to attractive open woodland and savannah, until, in the northern tracts, the scene changed to an arid semi-desert plateau, rising to an altitude of 4,000 feet.

The climate, too, changed with the type of country; rainfall varied from as much as 172 inches in the south, where the heat and humidity, particularly in Lagos, were terrible, to under 25 inches in the dry extreme north. Finally there was the River Niger, 2,600 miles long and navigable by large steamers for 1,000 miles. With its tributaries, this great river crossed and dominated the country from the north-western frontier until it spilled out into the many mouths of its delta in the Gulf of Guinea.

In Shenton's time the Nigerian oil fields, now so vital, had not yet been surveyed, but there were important tin and coal mines, as well as the growing palm oil industries, the traditional farming, forestry and fishing and huge exports of timber, hides and skins. In sum it was a land of great extremes, in climate and geography, in race and religion, as well as in its social and political problems. It was barely forty years since Lord Lugard had begun the process of pacifying this enormous territory, previously under the rule of all-powerful tribal kings and chieftains, to bring the population under the protective umbrella of his *indirect* rule.

In this setting Shenton clearly saw far-reaching implications for British administration. Years later he wrote:

In West Africa it was our bounden duty to lay down policies and programmes so that the African could be given his rightful chance to become a good citizen. You cannot force the development of the soul as if it were a hothouse flower; the process must be gentle and gradual. So the true progress of Africa, in our day, did not necessarily fit in with plans for urgent economic development. As trustees we had to keep this in mind; self-government was of course the ultimate aim, but not always actually in sight.

In 1926 Shenton is nearing the end of his service in Nigeria. Daisy is again with Bridget in England and he writes accordingly:

Lagos June 11, 1926

My own beloved,

Old Lord Leverhulme – "Soapy Bill" – is here with yacht complete. H.E. gave a dinner and dance for him last night. The old boy is 75, but he danced away like anything – deaf as a post and drops his "h's" all over the place! Tomorrow I go to dine on the yacht. H.E. was asked, but has refused in a four page letter in which he emphasises all Soapy Bill's complaints about his administration, and says he will not accept anything from him until he apologises!

I enclose H.E.'s confidential report on me – and you! Bring it back with you as it must be an heirloom! It isn't bad, is it? And can do no harm I think, though I don't know how much attention the Colonial Office pay to H.E.'s "ravings". You observe "I am fit for any job that's going"!

Meanwhile you'll soon be packing to join me. What joy . . .

What a bore about Bridget's school fees. Even so I suppose it's cheaper than most schools. Are you very hard up, you poor thing? Soon I shall have paid off the overdraft and I shall then have to begin paying off Way – about £100. I have £45 a month at home after paying your allowance and Mother's. In fact when you leave there will be just enough in the bank to pay your passage!

Always your own loving
Shenton

"Soapy Bill", the first Lord Leverhulme, was the founder of Port Sunlight and chairman of Lever Limited, which had already amassed vast holdings in the palm oil, copra, groundnuts, cocoa and allied industries in West Africa. H.E. the Governor of Nigeria was Sir Hugh Clifford G.C.M.G. He was unusual in the British Colonial Service in that he was a Roman Catholic and an aristocrat, of the family of Baron Clifford of Chudleigh. Evidently his good opinion of Shenton did bring dividends for, not long after this, Shenton was promoted Colonial Secretary of the Gold Coast. Many years were to elapse before his pay fully matched his needs and he now had to assist his mother financially following his father's death. Way was his tailor in London.

When he became Colonial Secretary at Accra he must have realised
that it should lead to a Governorship if he did the job well. This he did,
as indeed he was expected to do, for he already had many years'
experience in the Secretariat. Furthermore, once again the wheel of
fortune turned in his favour. The Governor of the Gold Coast, Sir
Ransford Slater, became ill and had to return to England six months
before the end of Shenton's tour, so he was made acting Governor. In
that capacity he was styled "The Officer Administering the Government" not "His Excellency"; but it meant that he and Daisy had
forthwith to leave their comfortable bungalow (the Gold Coast has a
cool climate compared with the extremes of Nigeria) and move into
Government House. The impact of this sudden change on them both
was well described by Daisy:

> Shenton did not seem to have any worries at becoming acting Governor.
> But our boys (we took our own personal servants to G.H.) were thrilled,
> and our cook certainly rose to the occasion. When I first told him he
> would now have to cook for thirty people or more, instead of six or eight,
> he at once said: "Well, it no my fault"! And he didn't seem to mind in the
> least. Otherwise too the change made domestic life easier for us. In
> those days there were no frigidaires and we always thought we were
> fortunate in having an old government ice chest. But in Lagos our
> garden boy had to walk three miles into the town, to the cold store, and
> came back carrying a large block of ice on his head, wrapped in a cloth.
> Of course it kept his head cool, but there was generally very little ice left
> for the ice box! However in G.H. there was no bother about ice. Just
> before we left Accra in 1929, for leave at home, Shenton told me he had
> been offered the job of Governor of Nyasaland, in place of Sir Charles
> Bowring, an old friend from our Kenya days, who was retiring. Shenton
> must have done well so far, for he was made a C.M.G. that same year.

Thus, at the age of fifty, Shenton Thomas had almost reached the
peak of his profession, the Governorship of a British Colony, though
not yet in the top grade. Nyasaland was one of thirty-odd non-self
governing colonies in the Empire, of which eighteen were in Africa; it
was a small Protectorate tucked away in Eastern Central Africa along
the western shore of Lake Nyasa, 50,000 square miles, producing tea,
coffee, tobacco and cotton. It had been the hunting ground of slave
traders until discovered by Livingstone and Stanley and was still
comparatively primitive, or at any rate Shenton thought so on his
arrival. Zomba, the capital city, was a lovely place in the mountains
4,000 feet above sea level and Government House was rather like a
large English country manor.

In all British colonies the Governor was the most prestigious and influential official. He was the head of the Government and the Sovereign's personal representative, and, in that dual capacity, his word was regarded as law. Not long after Shenton arrived as the new Governor and Commander-in-Chief a London newspaper correspondent wrote the following:

> Shenton Thomas descended on the Nyasaland Government like a meteor. For years nothing had been done for agriculture; a place that had been asleep was suddenly jerked awake. Within a short time he brought out a new Director of Agriculture, Dr Small (then in Ceylon), who had been with him in Uganda, and the sailing list of liners soon included names of civil servants going home on retirement; they were men who the new Governor thought would not help Nyasaland to attain the position he knew it should occupy.

Equally important for the King's representative, Shenton's prowess at games, particularly cricket, delighted the population – Africa, Indian and British. Very few Governors of African colonies can have equalled his score at one cricket match in which he was put in to bat first "and made a century, not out, before breakfast, having hit three sixes". They began early in the tropics.

Shenton and Daisy were to remain as a Governor and "Governor's Lady" for the next sixteen years and, for them both, Nyasaland was the prelude to much they had to learn and practise. They had to become capable of separating official pomp and ceremony from their human "ordinariness"; yet at all times they had to retain dignity, as well as appearing "non-stuffy" to friends and relatives, or in any circumstances where informality was natural and proper. To put it another way, they had to remain relaxed, affable and tolerant, without prejudice to the dignity and obligations of their official position. It was in Nyasaland, in 1930, that Shenton got his "K" (a K.C.M.G).

Daisy found the peaceful atmosphere and conditions of life at Government House in Zomba a very great help, no matter how great the pressures of engagements and functions. The gardens were lovely, full of English roses, with a river running through the grounds and a water garden. In particular the mass of flowering trees and shrubs entranced her. However, Shenton was not so content for, to my surprise, I found a letter from him to Daisy, when the latter was in England, which read:

> I wish to goodness I could give up all this and retire, but I don't see how I can with my mother to look after.

His salary as Governor was then only £2,000 per annum which seems little enough in today's terms. However, a few months later Daisy wrote:

> When Shenton came home on leave from Zomba he was offered the Governorship of the Gold Coast, which he could not refuse as it was promotion; besides the salary there was £4,000 per annum.

Shenton's two years as Governor at Accra (1932–1934) left a lasting impression on him because, for the first time, he found himself strongly opposed to the political aspirations and ambitions of some black African members of the local legislative Council. Again it was the problem of timing that he had met in Nigeria nearly ten years earlier – the need not to force the pace of political development – and he would not give way.

Despite strong opposition, he insisted that the Council should enact his Gold Coast Sedition Ordinance, aimed at suppressing subversive propaganda against the established constitution. African politicians criticized him in the local press; and even went so far as to send a delegation to London to present their protest to the Secretary of State:

> This legislation is a disgrace to any Governor who sanctions it. Sir Shenton Thomas, the reactionary Governor, has imposed the Ordinance on the country against the wishes of the chiefs and other moderate members of the legislative Council. On the strength of his firmness no doubt Sir Shenton's stock went up at the Colonial Office . . . But shame on him.

It is now 1934, twenty-five years since he landed at Mombasa, and he has earned the reputation of being a strong man, in every sphere of life.

While Shenton and Daisy were in London on leave he was offered the appointment of Governor and Commander-in-Chief of the Straits Settlements and High Commissioner of the Malay States, the most important post in the Colonial Service. At first Shenton was not interested, but all his friends told him he would be mad to refuse. Daisy wrote:

> Of course Shenton accepted when he found out more about it and what a wonderful job it was. When he went to Buckingham Palace, to be received by the King on his appointment, George V told him he looked on Malaya as the blue ribbon of the Colonial Service. This was very nice to hear but Shenton was embarrassed when the King, talking about life in Africa, suddenly asked: "And how many elephants are there in

Africa?" Shenton had no idea whatever so made a wild guess, but was later told by an expert that he was several thousands wrong in his reply!

Before they could sail for the Far East Shenton and Daisy had to pay particular attention to the outfits they would need in Singapore. A Colonial Governor had to have two basic uniforms: one white with a white helmet decked with red and white plumes, and one dark blue with a cocked hat and white plumes. Each tunic bore gold and silver gorgettes, with epaulettes, brass buttons, sword belt and court sword. These outfits were very expensive and it is not known when Way, his tailor, was eventually paid off!

IV

SINGAPORE PRE-WAR (1934–1939)

Sir Shenton and Lady Thomas, with their daughter Bridget, travelled by sea from England to Malaya in the P. & O. liner *S.S. Ranpura*. They landed at Penang Island on the north-west coast on 9 November, 1934, being greeted by a seventeen-gun salute from a visiting warship of the Royal Navy, with the full civil and military pomp and ceremony befitting the arrival of a new Governor and Commander-in-Chief. That night they went on by rail in the Governor's train, consisting of two well-appointed *wagon-lit*-type coaches (one for their Excellencies and one for their staff) attached to the night mail express to Singapore. There were advantages in travel by rail; not only was it quicker and more restful than by road, but both coaches were air-conditioned, providing a standard of comfort and convenience seldom found in Malaya in the early 1930s, and certainly not installed in the Governor's residence.

Coming down from Penang Shenton and his family had their first sight of mainland Malaya, beginning in the early morning as they passed through thousands of acres of cultivated rubber. They had seen rubber in West Africa, but not with such density as in these plantations, where up to a hundred trees per acre were planted, making the country's annual rubber production, then approaching half a million tons, the third largest in the world. Around Kuala Lumpur they saw the signs of open-cast tin mining which bared and lacerated the earth, but which nevertheless, together with the enormous development of the rubber industry, provided the country's main source of revenue. Of course they were familiar with tropical jungle and forests in Africa, but not perhaps so thick as here.

In the 1930s Shenton Thomas wrote a brief description of Malaya, which is worth quoting:

> The small island of Singapore is just ninety miles north of the Equator, and separated from mainland Malaya by the narrow Strait of Johore. This mainland is about the size of England without Wales, some 50,000 square miles in area and 400 miles in length, from the Thai frontier in the north to Singapore in the south. The total population in my day was

about 5,500,000. Down the centre of the country there is a wide range of mountains up to 7,000 feet in height. On the eastern side of this range the population is relatively small, save in the extreme north, because for the most part the land (on this eastern side) is not suited for cultivation. The intensive development of resources and communications which the country has witnessed for so many years, has therefore been confined almost entirely to the western strip.

After the war Daisy wrote of their first arrival in Malaya: "I doubt if we realised the full shape and extent of Shenton's new responsibilities until we were in Government House and had talked with the Private Secretary and others."

Shenton Thomas's "Empire", as his friends called it, was quite unlike any of the African colonies where he had served so long. At Singapore he held three posts simultaneously. First, he was the Governor and Commander-in-Chief of the four Straits Settlements which jointly constituted a single Crown Colony, though the four territories were geographically far apart, consisting of:

1. Penang Island, with the larger area of Province Wellesley on the mainland opposite Penang. This was the oldest of the Settlements, ceded to Great Britain in 1786.
2. Singapore Island, with Christmas Island and the Cocos and Keeling Islands in the Indian Ocean under the Governor's administration. Singapore was ceded to Britain by the ruler of Johore in 1819.
3. Malacca Settlement, with a history of Portuguese, Dutch and British occupation – ceded to Britain by Holland in 1824.
4. Labuan Island, off the coast of North-West Borneo 700 miles from Singapore, ceded to Queen Victoria by the Sultan of Brunei in 1846.

Next, as High Commissioner Shenton Thomas had responsibilities stemming from past diplomatic treaties with the rulers of the following ten individual Malay States, all of which were under British protection.

First and foremost were the four Federated Malay States (F.M.S.) of Perak, Selangor, Negri Sembilan and Pahang, with their federal capital at Kuala Lumpur (K.L.). This Federation had its own Parliament consisting of Legislative and Executive Council, a Federal budget controlling the main sources of revenue and expenditure, and a Federal Secretary at the capital, through whom a British Resident in each State was responsible to the High Commissioner. Federal Heads of Departments controlled their technical staffs in the four States. In this setting British civil officers, responsible ultimately to the High Commissioner, exercised considerable administrative control in the F.M.S. by virtue of the 1896 Treaty of Federation. But in the five Unfederated Malay States (U.M.S.) of Johore, Trengganu, Kedah, Kelantan and Perlis, the political and administrative picture was quite different. Each State had a British Adviser (not a British Resident as in the F.M.S.) and there were no official parliamentary Councils. Administration was carried out with the aid and advice, and persuasion when necessary, of British officers of the M.C.S. Only in matters of foreign affairs and defence were there overriding British powers (the *quid pro quo* for protection!).

The tenth State was that of the Sultan of Brunei, on the north-west coast of Borneo, which had been under British protection since 1888. The importance of this territory lay in its production of crude oil, for which the Shell Oil Company had the concession. There was a British Resident in the State, and an Assistant, also British.

Overall, the High Commissioner's powers were limited by certain factors common to all the States. Shenton Thomas could *not* give orders to any Malaya ruler. The States, although "protected", were not part of the possessions of the British Crown, and their inhabitants, though British "protected" persons, were *not* British subjects. Sovereign power belonged to the Malay rulers, not to the British Crown.

Finally, Shenton was the Agent for British North Borneo and Sarawak, two vast areas covering over 80,000 square miles with a total population exceeding half a million. Although the British Agent had no authority over either territory, the Government in London relied on him to keep them informed of political, social, economic, financial and commercial developments. They were among the last of the independent states of the British Empire to be owned and controlled entirely by commercial or family interests.

British North Borneo was administered by a Civil Governor (Mr C. R. Smith when the war with Japan broke out) who was appointed by the Court of Directors of the British North Borneo Chartered Company in London. The Charter empowered the Company to raise revenue, pass legislation, issue currency and postage stamps, and recruit its own administrative service, police, customs, medical, public works and other staff. Sarawak was also an independent State but was ruled by Sir Charles Vyner Brooke, who had succeeded his father in 1917. The latter was a nephew of the famous Sir James Brooke (1803–1868), the so-called "first White Raja", an English adventurer to whom the Sultan of Brunei had ceded the territory in 1842. The Rajas of Sarawak appointed their own administrative and other services under a Chief Secretary, the last of whom (Mr Le Gros) was killed by the Japanese in 1945; both territories were finally ceded to Great Britain in 1946.

In view of the geographical distribution of his responsibilities, the Governor and High Commissioner was provided with four official residences on mainland Malaya, in addition to Government House at Singapore. At his discretion he and his family could leave Singapore and travel through the Malay peninsula to stay at:

The King's House (Istana Tetamu) at Kuala Lumpur. This charming and comfortable residence, situated in the famous Lake Gardens, was Shenton's home in K.L. in his capacity as High Commissioner for the F.M.S. Next door was *Carcosa*, the house of the Federal Secretary, now the residence of the United Kingdom High Commissioner.

The King's Pavilion at Kuala Kangsar, the capital of Perak, one of the four Federated Malay States. The Sultan of Perak was the senior ruler in the F.M.S.

Bel Retiro, the Governor's house on Penang Island at the summit of Penang Hill, approached by a funicular railway. From the top there are magnificent views over Georgetown and Butterworth on the mainland, extending on a clear day to the rice plains of Kedah and Province Wellesley. It must have been delightful to stay at Bel Retiro, always cool and pleasant and an escape from the heat and humidity of the plains.

Finally *The Lodge* at Fraser's Hill in the central mountain range, a few hours drive by car from Kuala Lumpur, and approached by a road with innumerable hairpin bends. The Lodge was the High Commissioner's hill station residence. It was here, in October, 1951, that Sir Henry Gurney, then High Commissioner, was shot dead by communist terrorists.

Government House, Singapore, the principal residence of Sir Shenton and Lady Thomas, had been constructed mainly with convict labour from India and was completed in 1869. It must have been a pleasant place in which to live and work, particularly in those peaceful days before the Second World War; and it was commensurate with the trappings of high office, as befitted the home of the King's representative and supreme authority in what could rightly be described as one of the richest and most important colonial possessions of the British Empire. Evidently Daisy Thomas appreciated her life there for she wrote at length about it:

> Government House was a most beautiful building, of white stone, very large and imposing; it was set on a low hill with wonderful views overlooking the entire city and the shipping in Keppel Harbour, with the islands beyond. All the rooms had high ceilings and broad verandahs,

which kept it delightfully cool and fresh compared with the tropical heat outside. There were beautiful reception rooms and fine chandeliers, and upstairs a huge ballroom opening out of the drawing room; for the latter we found some lovely French chairs and sofas which had been stored away and become very shabby, so we had these re-covered with brocade; one sofa was beyond repair, but a Chinese carpenter copied it exactly making the gilt frame look identical with the original.

The servants were excellent; we had an enormous staff of over seventy (Malay, Chinese and Indian) excluding the garden boys. The Indian bearers waited at table wearing a very smart uniform of long scarlet and gold tunics, with flat red and gold hats dating from the time of the old East India Company; there were Chinese cooks and boys for the rooms, and three wonderful Chinese amahs (maids) – one each for myself and my daughter Bridget, and one for the guests. Malays and Tamils generally looked after the gardens and were clerks and chauffeurs. There was a very good Comptroller who was in charge of the staff and used to consult me about the menu for the day's meals every morning; he was an ex-serviceman, a gunner, who had served several years at G.H. and was invaluable.

I think it was the grounds and gardens at Government House that gave us the most pleasure; their beauty and tranquillity gave us peace and relaxation. It was like living in a Park of some hundred acres, with a nine-hole golf course, six lawn tennis courts besides one hard court, and a small enclosed swimming pool. The grass lawns were wonderful, and so were the many coloured tropical flowering shrubs and trees. The Chinese gardeners grew marvellous orchids in pots, and always arranged attractive ferns and flowers flanking the steps at the main entrance, and also up the lovely staircase that led from the central lobby to the first floor.

Another asset of the Governor's life lay in its financial and material advantages. Unlike similar appointments elsewhere in the Colonial Service, particularly in Africa, the Governor at Singapore could live comfortably with his family and carry out all his duties, including very extensive travelling, with virtually no need to touch his salary. His expense account covered the cost of most of his entertaining, official or private. His salary, excluding all his allowances, was £5,500 per annum.

Sir Shenton Thomas came as a complete stranger to the people of Malaya and there was much speculation, including articles in the *Straits Times*, as to what sort of man he was and why he had been sent at all. It was known he had done less than two years in the Gold Coast and that an African delegation had gone to London to protest to the Secretary of State about his policy. On the other hand his transfer to

Malaya was clearly a promotion and before he arrived the *Straits Times* gave him a fair press. On 16 July, 1934, the paper said:

> We know nothing of the origin of the difficulties which Sir Shenton encountered in West Africa. He has been singled out for very consider-able advancement, and that is not a treatment which is accorded to failures. Moreover it is well known at the Colonial Office that local feelings became very strained on several occasions during Sir Cecil Clementi's* régime as a consequence of the flouting of public opinion. Is it reasonable to suggest that the Colonial Office, knowing the delicate position which had arisen in Malaya, would single out deliberately as the next Governor a man who possessed in an exaggerated degree the shortcomings of his predecessor? What is needed is a man of pro-nounced administrative ability and a large measure of tact, who will order our affairs in the best interests of Malaya and at the same time soothe feelings which have been sadly ruffled during the past three years.

This brought out into the open what to this day many of Shenton's associates and friends have not realised – that he was promoted and sent to Singapore as a replacement for Sir Cecil Clementi, who was removed from his post because he was a failure. After the war Shenton said to me, "The lot of a British Colonial Governor, in spite of the apparent conveniences of life in G.H., was not easy; it was often subject to difficulties and painful embarrassment, with either the government in London or locally, and this sometimes caused great personal stress."

Sir Hugh Clifford, who was Governor of Nigeria when Shenton was Deputy Chief Secretary at Lagos, had been made Governor of Malaya in 1927. Professor Heussler wrote of him:**

> Malaya was the reigning passion of his life, the subject of many books he wrote after long years of service in the M.C.S. However, his mental state on his return to Singapore was not good. In Pahang, the State he knew best, he was welcomed as a hero. . . . There was great excitement in Kuantan where many remembered him. . . . But in the Federal Council he often got things muddled and his behaviour became rather odd at times. . . . Gala receptions were a trial for the Private Secretaries. On one occasion Clifford lined up all the ladies and presented kisses and beads to those with the best ankles.

Finally Sir Hugh had to retire and his place was taken by Sir Cecil Clementi, who had been Governor of Hong Kong for the previous four

---

* Sir Shenton's predecessor at Singapore.
** *British Rule in Malaya, 1867–1942*, Clio Press, 1981.

years. He was a tall, handsome and impressive man, with a severity of manner that did not endear him to his colleagues, and this gave him a reputation for being tactless; certainly he was anything but socially inclined and did not enjoy his obligatory social functions. Furthermore it did not help him that Lady Clementi was an eccentric and very outspoken woman, as definite in her opinions as her husband but much less reticent. What in the end ensured Clementi's premature retirement was his unwise discrimination against the Chinese population of Malaya, who bitterly resented their exclusion from plans for rice cultivation and educational grants.

It must have been somewhat daunting for Shenton Thomas to succeed a man who had considerably strained the relations between the Governor and the governed. However, in the event he did not disappoint local opinion. In his first public speech, to the Penang Legislative Council after disembarking, he said:

> It is my earnest desire that, during my tenure of office, co-operation between all government officials and the public shall be sincere and fruitful. For myself I welcome this early opportunity of stating that I am prepared to listen to anyone who may feel able to offer me useful advice, and I hope he will not wait for me to ask for it. I shall take no decision without first inviting the views of all parties interested, and giving them the fullest consideration.

Shortly afterwards the *Malay Mail* reported:

> Malaya has at last found, in Sir Shenton Thomas, a man who has not only the willingness to consult others, but appears peculiarly well suited by disposition and personality to do so.

Shenton lost no time in touring the country in order to become acquainted with Malaya's problems and population. As Governor, he had a private steam yacht of 800 tons for his sole use, in which he could travel on official visits at his discretion. His wife wrote:

> We had a lovely yacht, the *Sea Belle II*, in which we used to visit the various states on the Malay coast, east and west, and Penang, as well as voyages to Borneo and Sarawak.

Early in January, 1935, he began his first official tour of two Straits Settlements, Penang and Malacca, and four Malay States, Kedah, Perak, Selangor and Negri Sembilan. Two months later he toured the east coast, visiting Kuantan, Kuala Trengganu and Kota Bharu; he made this trip in *Sea Belle II*, entertaining the Malay rulers and other notables on board the yacht and going ashore for functions at the rulers' Istanas (palaces) and at the official residences of the British Advisers. The *Sea Belle* had comfortable accommodation for ten passengers, excluding officers' cabins, and in the saloon the Governor could hold an official dinner party for twenty guests. The yacht carried a wireless operator for communication with Singapore, and the Private Secretary, who always accompanied the Governor, had charge of the diplomatic and other cyphers for H.E.'s secret telegrams to London and elsewhere.

Whenever possible, Daisy went with her husband on his official tours, as she had done in both East and West Africa, but she particularly enjoyed being with him on the yacht. They used to visit offshore islands such as the Perhentians or Tioman where the bathing from beautiful white sandy beaches was marvellous, and they could have picnic meals with their guests, relaxed and undisturbed by the formalities or obligations of governorship. The first years in Singapore were very pleasant for Daisy; the whole ambience of her life there was far wider than during her previous experience in Africa as Governor's lady:

> It was certainly a busy life – we had a great many guests coming and going, most of them very interesting; our first were the Chief Scout, Lord Baden-Powell, with his wife and their two daughters. After much talk – it was not easy! – Lady Baden-Powell agreed that Malay girl guides could wear their national dress as Malay Muslims, to avoid the incongruity of having to wear the English-style guide uniform; and very charming they looked in their bright blue sarongs, with little white cravats.

Of other visitors she added:

> The British fleet stationed in Hong Kong used to visit Singapore frequently and their Admirals and Captains generally stayed with us at G.H. I remember once we had two Admirals as our guests, and I found that a junior midshipman, a cousin of mine, was on board one of the visiting warships, so we asked him to come and stay with us. We only heard afterwards about the send-off he had when he left his ship to go to G.H. A Government House car was always sent to meet our guests, with a large station wagon for their baggage; so all his friends lined the rails to cheer as this junior midshipman stepped into the large car by himself while his only luggage, a small Hong Kong wicker basket, was solemnly put into the station wagon! However, he thoroughly enjoyed his visit, as we were able to let him have a car in which he could go to the swimming club, and see the fascinating Chinese bazaar, play golf and tennis, etc.

During the 1930s the Governor's A.D.C. was sometimes an officer of the Malay Police Service. Nigel Morris*, then a young officer of the Straits Settlements Police, has given an account of certain aspects of social life, as seen by an A.D.C. at Government House during those carefree years:

My main recollections of those early days are the usual pursuits of all young officers anywhere, i.e. games, girls, and parties, in between doing one's job and keeping out of trouble. The A.D.C. (who was of necessity always a single man) lived in Government House where he was provided with a bachelor flat on the top floor, and a very comfortable office-cum-sitting room on the ground floor well away from the Governor's office. In this setting the A.D.C.'s quarters became a favourite haunt after parties at the Tanglin Club or elsewhere, particularly when H.E. was making an official visit up-country and was provided with an extra A.D.C. from the State he was visiting; when that happened, the substantive A.D.C. was often able to remain in Singapore during the absence of the Governor.

Thus it was that very few of the attractive young unattached girls in Singapore would refuse a late night invitation to Government House, and their mothers, mistakenly, were unlikely to object! The alternative was a bachelor mess or parties which no mother would have knowingly permitted. For us impecunious young officers an added attraction lay in the free drinks to which the A.D.C. was entitled and which were charged to Government House funds. Furthermore there was the swimming pool, where young things, late at night, after a strenuous evening of dancing and drinking, could often be persuaded to cool off even though they were unlikely to be carrying their swimsuits. Although these parties were obviously more frequent during the absence of the Governor on official trips in *Sea Belle*, there were also some memorable occasions when both Sir Shenton and Lady Thomas were in residence. Of course the parties held then were more circumspect, though obviously not as quiet as they should have been, and, on hindsight, both Sir Shenton and Lady Thomas must have known what was going on; yet on no occasion did either of them give any inkling that they knew some uninvited guests were being entertained.

I also recall that if the lure of the A.D.C.'s office, the free drinks and the midnight swimming, was insufficient to break down the resistance of a young lady visitor, at least on one occasion, when the Governor was away, the attraction of the gubernatorial bedchamber was conclusive. . . . Official parties at Government House under Sir Shenton and

* N. G. Morris, C.M.G., M.V.O., Q.P.M., joined the Colonial Police in 1928, and became Commissioner of Police in Singapore, and later of the Bahamas. In 1958 he was Police Adviser to the Secretary of State for the Colonies.

Lady Thomas were always extremely enjoyable and well organized. The fare provided, the wine and the drinks, unlike some Government Houses which I visited in later years, were always lavish, and though Sir Shenton was not I think a naturally extrovert person he was well liked and respected by all sections of the community. I also feel he had a sense of humour which I did not appreciate at the time.

Looking back it seems difficult to believe there was a time when I was unable to afford enough food to live on in my quarters – usually a small house in the compound of the Divisional Police Headquarters of which I had charge. This was, however, very much the case, and for long periods I lived virtually from dinner party to dinner party. If I was fortunate enough to be invited to dine at Raffles Hotel I had an arrangement with the Maitre d'Hotel for any left-overs to be wrapped and to be handed to me surreptitiously on leaving! – this must have been the precursor of the "doggy-bag" which has become a way of life in the United States. In those days there was no "doggy" – just an impecunious hungry young officer. An invitation to dinner at Government House was therefore a much sought-after treat as far as I was concerned, and with John Parks, my colleague and closest friend as the Aide-de-Camp, I became a fairly regular attender at Government House dinners, although, as I discovered, not an entirely welcome one. . . . It appears that His Excellency, who had to see the list of guests at every function, submitted to him by the A.D.C. for signature, became slightly tired of finding my name so often on the guest list – allegedly to "make up numbers". On a couple of occasions he crossed it off and took the A.D.C. to task. A period of enforced dieting ensued until some months later, when, to my joy, I received an invitation and assumed that the ban had been lifted. The day following the dinner party John Parks was summoned to the presence and H.E. demanded to know why I had been at the dinner, as he had definitely not approved any list with my name on it. The A.D.C. respectfully assured him that he had initialled his approval whereupon H.E. called for the list. All the names of the guests were normally on the front of the card, which was in fact initialled by the Governor who triumphantly pointed out that my name was not there. John Parks then explained that there was insufficient room on the front of the card for all the names, and on the back of the card was one name – mine. This marked the end of my free dinners at Government House, and shortly thereafter I went on leave to the U.K.

In time there were few regions for which he was responsible that Shenton Thomas had not visited, though surprisingly he never went to Christmas Island or the Cocos and Keeling Islands, so eloquently described by Victor Purcell in his book *Memoirs of a Malayan Civil Servant.* *

* Cassell, 1965.

His purpose on tour was not just to impress by attending Legislative and Executive Councils, the sessions of the Federal Parliament, or to visit Malay rulers and preside at Official functions and formal, or informal, social occasions. His object was to get to know the way of life, the aims, aspirations and national characteristics of the various races and communities. Racially there were five main groups – Malay, Chinese, Indian, Eurasian and white (British and European). The last group held the reins of power, but they were all expatriates, whether officials, planters, or businessmen; and here the Governor's long experience in Africa exerted its influence. He believed that the land and the products of its soil belonged to the indigenous races not to the expatriates, who did *not* hold their power in perpetuity; their factual possession, political or otherwise, amounted to trusteeship, not to ownership. Thus the influence of that indirect rule which Shenton Thomas had first learnt and practised in tropical Africa now made its mark again in a new setting. Later we will see how this influence affected the conduct of his administration.

On mainland Malaya and in Borneo the Malays predominated; they were the rural community and the farmers of the land. "A delightful people, colourful, gentle and with a great sense of humour and of the ridiculous," wrote Cecil Lee, who spent much of his professional life in the service of the great rubber plantation agents Harrison & Crosfield.* He went on:

> In those days it was "de rigueur" to join the local volunteers, and there were battalions in the Malay States, and in Singapore and Penang, which always had regular British non-commissioned officers or warrant officers as permanent staff instructors. . . . I was one of a detachment of Volunteers who marched in the procession at the State Funeral of the Sultan of Selangor at Klang in 1937. Afterwards we fell out for drinks at a booth near the burial ground, and I asked the sergeant-major, of the Royal Sussex Regiment: "Who was it that provided this pleasing refreshment?" He replied in Malay: "*Sultan punya kira*" ("It's all on the Sultan"). This caused a great burst of laughter from the crowds of Malays attending the solemn ceremony! . . . The Malayan civil servants (the M.C.S.) were all able, liberal men who were concerned to protect the Malays, the pleasant easy-going Malays, from the encroachment of European entrepreneurs, and the more pushing and forceful Chinese or Indians.

Malaya had been a legacy from the East India Company and the

* From *Malayan Tales of a Grandfather* (1934–1942) – published privately.

Indian Civil Service, whose way of life was high, and Professor Heussler* writes:

> There can be no doubt that the Malayan Civil Service (M.C.S.) became one of the best-paid services in the Empire, so much so that senior officers were reluctant to accept higher-ranking posts elsewhere. . . . But the M.C.S. should be seen, not by contrast with other colonies but in its own local context where business and professional men lived far better than government servants, who were expected to be on close terms with the former in order to do their job.*

Lee's unsolicited testimonial to the M.C.S. is appropriate because, as Thomas found, the labour force employed in the Malayan tin mines was mainly Chinese, while Indians, generally Tamils from southern India or Ceylon (Sri Lanka), worked on the rubber plantations as tappers. The Indian population was never more than three-quarters of a million; that of the Chinese in the late 1930s exceeded two and a quarter million. It was the sheer importance of rubber to Malaya's economy that made its production a key factor in Sir Shenton's administration. Professor Heussler summed it up thus:

> All the way down the ranks (of the M.C.S.), through Residents to district officers, the central importance of rubber was a daily reality. Despite the industry's dependence on big estates, thousands of small-holders – Malay, Chinese and Indian – also vied with one another for land on which to plant rubber. Rubber, indeed, clashed with food crops.*

The M.C.S. in the 1930s was responsible for an economy based on tin and rubber, operated mainly by Chinese and Indian labour, while the Malays produced most of the food. Over all the white man presided, with ultimate political power. Eurasians generally provided clerical staff. Finally there was a rich opium trade – grown, processed and retailed chiefly by the Chinese. Sir Shenton, as head of the M.C.S., had to make this strange amalgam a vehicle for success, though he had no previous knowledge or experience of the Far East.

He soon saw that probably his most important task was to convince the M.C.S. at all levels that he was a man they could trust. On the face of it he was handicapped by a fact that could not be denied: he had never served as a district officer. Professor Heussler, whose book is generally regarded as the authoritative history of the Malayan Civil Service, wrote at length on the matter:

* op cit.

Generally speaking, everyone served at one time or another in both Secretariat, or *Ulu* (up-country) posts, the theory being that knowledge of both was *necessary* (author's italics) and that a good man could manage either without difficulty. It was thought that too much or too little of each would leave men's records improperly balanced. . . . Malaya was not immune to the prevailing mystique of the Colonial Empire, that the romance and the morality of European rule in tropical countries was centered on outstations run by omni-competent district officers, whereas the Secretariat was the home of the effete, the ambitious, and the not quite respectable. Inveterate *Ulu* types could be depended on to pour scorn on bureaucracy and all its works. Saddled on one occasion with a hopelessly incompetent young assistant, a senior M.C.S. officer, when asked for his advice as to where the hapless junior's talents could be more advantageously employed, replied at once: "In the Secretariat or the Museum." Even Sir Richard Winstedt (an acknowledged authority on the M.C.S.) with his quite different, scholarly temperament, could not help smiling at those who got on in the service by staying in Secretariats and writing equivocal dispatches to London. One ex-Governor of Malaya went so far as to insist that the essence of administration was to be learned *only* in districts.

The prospect for Shenton Thomas, against this assertive background of civil service opinion, cannot have looked promising, and if he needed further evidence of disparagement about himself, he probably knew that his detractors were calling him "Tom-Tom", to emphasize the uncivilised nature of his service in the African bush!

Before we see how Shenton fared let us look at Professor Heussler's last words on this matter:

When it is asked who got on in the service, who did not, and why in both cases, the answers present a similar picture of generalization and diversity. For most the key to success was the same quality of gregariousness and ability to work happily with one's fellows that opens doors in any field. . . . Social acceptance in all the myriad inter-racial and government-commercial settings of Malaya counted far more than specific attributes of character, not to mention particular qualifications such as language facility. . . . Reviewing the comments of Governors on M.C.S. officers, one finds that in all cases men were good, bad or indifferent. . . . it all depended on what a man was, and how he had done.

Some readers may prefer Cunyngham-Brown's* formula for

* J. S. H. Cunyngham-Brown, C.M.G., joined as a cadet in 1930. He rose to high rank and lives in Penang to this day as an honoured citizen. A distinguished author, few people are better qualified than he to speak for the M.C.S.

advancement in the M.C.S. Short, simple and to the point, he recommended: "Bowing at the doors of the mighty, marrying a nice girl, seeking a post in the central Secretariat, and becoming a Free Mason"! Yet what stands out in any assessment of the Colonial Service of the British Empire is the sheer devotion of the officers to their job. A prime requirement was a sustained sense of humour as is shown by the following experience of a British Adviser in Kelantan. The High Commissioner was coming on tour to Kota Bharu and the Adviser had to see to the preparations for his reception by the Sultan. A day or two beforehand he got a message from the Private Secretary, telling him to make sure that lavatory accommodation was available for the ladies of H.E.'s party. What happened is best told in the Adviser's own words:*

> I called at the Palace, a large wooden structure at the foot of a hill . . . and was shown the "arrangements". I was conducted along a labyrinth of passages hung with gorgeous silks . . . to a small room in the middle of which, on a wooden stand and supported by a bright yellow cushion, was one chamber pot. "This is the place for the mems" I was told with pride. They had gone to immense trouble and I left it at that, and hoped for the best!

The Adviser went on:

> Thinking that a twenty-one gun salute was required for the occasion, the Sultan's guard had set up a brass muzzle-loading cannon on the hill above the Palace, aimed to fire directly over the roof. The first few rounds went off normally, after which rain dampened the powder. The banquet began: curried goat and rice, with warm creme de menthe. As the High Commissioner rose to speak – the rain having stopped and the powder having dried – the salute was suddenly resumed, each salvo bringing down a shower of dust and lizards from the shaking timbers above on to the banquet table below, where H.E. was struggling in vain to make himself heard. Responding to an agonised look from the A.D.C., the Adviser hurriedly left to stop the bombardment. When he returned the farewells were being said – all was quiet and smiles.

It was not long before Shenton Thomas became aware that his initial popularity was on the wane. He believed in building up strong monetary reserves in both the Straits Settlements and the Malay States, and followed a strict and cautious financial policy during his first years in office. In time this policy brought successive years of financial sur-

---

* Heussler p. 210.

pluses in the four Settlements and the F.M.S., and was no doubt popular with the Colonial Office in London. But those who earned the money wished to enjoy the profit they made and not see it ploughed back into reserves. The *Malay Mail*, voicing the general dissatisfaction, said: "During the past two or three years we have been told that the Government has been accumulating large reserves . . . but if at the slightest threat of adversity Government is determined to put up its shutters we do not see the necessity for accumulating such reserves."* Shenton countered this by declaring: "I do not want it thought that we are going to harm the community at large by putting away all this money. On the other hand we are going to help them by providing, in the bad times which are coming one day, the occupation which will keep them employed."**

At this same time he was criticized for his educational policy. One critic was heard to say, "I wish he wouldn't keep ramming that Gold Coast University down our throats!" Some M.C.S. officials also complained about "H.E.'s proneness to write long essay-like minutes, though they are always beautifully written, and in red ink"! Readers may notice how the practice of recording important decisions in manuscript, not in typescript, was still prevalent in Colonial governments even in the 1930s.

But Andrew Gilmour,*** who joined the M.C.S. in 1921 and has written much about Malaya, has this to say about Sir Shenton Thomas:

> The Governor's *unforced* affability was a valuable asset, which he combined with the necessary modicum of dignity; while other lesser men felt compelled to create an atmosphere of awe, he set one at ease immediately. My first meeting with him was in the mid-1930s, when he paid an official visit to my district up-country in an Unfederated Malay State. I had brought down for the occasion a band of Temios (aborigines) straight from their jungle home. Incredibly swiftly they roofed with special leaves a large reception area covering the greater part of our lawn. The Governor recorded all this on his cine-camera, moving happily amongst them and taking great interest in their prowess with their blowpipes. Their women were *not* overdressed, jungle flowers being their main apparel, and my straitlaced old Chinese amah remarked reprovingly to my wife: "The *Tuan* Governor took a very close look at those girls."

---

* *Malay Mail* 24 October, 1936.

** Speech at Federal Council Proceedings, Kuala Lumpur, 1937.

*** Andrew Gilmour, C.M.G., who served with high distinction in M.C.S., and elsewhere in the Colonial Service, from 1921–1956. Is currently Hon. Life President of the Singapore Cricket Club.

There is no doubt that Shenton's proficiency at cricket helped him a lot at Singapore; it was not often that a Governor was seen to lead his team on to the ground at the Singapore Cricket Club. Gilmour recalls one occasion when, in a match on Raffles College ground, Shenton hit two straight sixes over the screen, took a couple of neat slip catches and bowled a few tidy overs.

Probably his most difficult time was during the first two years when he had to settle cases left unresolved by Clementi. The latter's unpopularity had increased in particular over what became known as the decentralization issue. According to Heussler, practical men in the M.C.S. regarded the intellectual Clementi, and his rather difficult wife, as unsympathetic and ignorant of everyday problems. On one occasion, when Clementi's own officials in the F.M.S. Legislative Council threatened to join the unofficials in opposition to him, Clementi answered them in Greek, nearly causing an uproar! One British Resident said that the only reason he would like to go up in an aeroplane was so that he could spit on Government House! Clementi insisted that much more political and adminitrative power should be delegated to the Malay rulers and their state governments, thus reducing the power then held by the Federal Government at Kuala Lumpur on behalf of the High Commissioner in Singapore, and he insisted that this be brought into effect quickly, ignoring the fact that such sweeping changes required time and consultation. This insistence soon brought trouble.

Clementi also left Thomas a problem with the Ruler of Selangor over the question of which of the Sultan's three sons should succeed him. The Sultan entirely agreed that his eldest son was clearly unsuitable, being extravagant, heavily in debt and irresponsible, and said that his second son should be appointed his successor. However, Theodore Adams, British Resident at Selangor, maintained that the second son was even worse than the eldest, and therefore decided, in opposition to the Sultan's own preference, that the third son should succeed. It was at this stage, in February, 1934, that Sir Cecil Clementi returned to England, ostensibly on leave, but in fact to be removed from office, leaving the whole problem to be resolved by the new High Commissioner. There was also that question of decentralization to be settled, the Malay rulers being hostile to any change in their "royal" prerogative, especially when presented to them by the High Commissioner as *faits accomplis*.

Theodore Adams, like Clementi, was a public school and Oxford man and had had a distinguished career. He was notoriously pro-Malay and a keen advocate of having more Malay officers in the M.C.S.

Now he sought to overrule the wishes of his Sultan in the matter of the succession. Sir Andrew Caldecott, who was Acting Governor until Shenton Thomas arrived, was as pro-Malay as Adams. The case quickly grew into a *cause célèbre*, eventually involving the Colonial Office and the King and Cabinet in London. Shenton Thomas favoured Adams's views, but as High Commissioner he could not support the Resident against the Sultan, and Adams had to be got rid of! What happened next has been told by Heussler: "The Governor was masterful. Adams's candidate was made heir apparent, and the other sons were compensated appropriately. Furthermore, the Sultan and his defenders were appeased by the removal of Adams, who left the country but was consoled with a knighthood, and made Chief Commissioner of Northern Nigeria!" Heussler added the following comment on Sir Theodore Adams, with which I venture to disagree: "He was a lifelong bachelor, very courteous to ladies in company, but seldom seeking this." The truth is that Adams was not a would-be lifelong bachelor. He was a cousin of my family and I recall him well, particularly because he tried his very best to marry my sister and pursued her for many a long month. He had a fine presence, somewhat awe-inspiring, was highly intelligent and hard-working and very keen on cricket. But my sister, Winsome, would have none of him!

I was surprised when I was told* about the eventual solution to the decentralization problem. In reality Shenton Thomas agreed with Clementi's policy that more political power ought to be given to Malay nationals. Clementi lost his job because his methods, his sense of timing and his personal qualities – and those of Lady Clementi – made it impossible for him to succeed. Shenton Thomas, on the other hand, was popular and said little but got on with the job. His wife was always composed, tactful and charming to her guests. His speeches clearly show how he went about it when he first met the problem officially, at a meeting of the Federal Council in Kuala Lumpur in January, 1935.

> With so short an acquaintance with this country and its problems, you will not expect me to speak in detail on the question of decentralization. But there are one or two points of policy on which I am glad to take this opportunity of expressing my views. . . . I do not wish to intervene unduly or to attempt to centralize the government in the office which I hold. . . . In dealing with matters which come up before them I hope that the States will remember always that their individual prosperity is bound up with the prosperity of the country as a whole. . . . We have embarked this year on a new policy, a policy which has my complete sympathy and

* Tan Sri Dato Mubin Sheppard to the author at Kuala Lumpur, March, 1982.

support. . . . Provided that it is not developed hastily, and provided that the broad principle of common interest is kept constantly in view, I believe that the policy has every chance of success.

I have said that Shenton Thomas was popular but have given no evidence to support that view. A letter from Mr G. L. Bayliss of Chilliwack in British Columbia, Canada, provides it. He wrote:

In 1935 I was Acting Principal of Raffles Institution, Singapore. . . . The Inspector of Schools instructed me to ask H.E. to honour the School Speech Day with his official presence. I did so and to everyone's surprise he readily agreed. We made very careful preparations for the day . . . and in my opening speech I drew attention to the inadequacy of our ancient building and strongly hinted our hope for better things to come from H.E. Our hopes were fulfilled, and H.E. said that provision of a new building would be seriously considered. The next day the newspapers printed banner headlines "GOVERNOR PROMISES NEW RAF- FLES INSTITUTION". But it was not to be! Instead of a new school a new Prison was built at Changi in 1936, where, with said irony, Sir Shenton and many British civilians were confined by the Japanese in 1942. Nevertheless Sir Shenton was a man of considerable charm. He made an obscure person, like myself, feel that his work was important and that he, as Governor, was closely concerned with it and interested in it.

In the Malay Civil Service officers normally took U.K. leave every two years and the Thomas family, including Bridget, returned to London by sea early in 1936; this was soon after King George V died and Daisy wrote, "We all had to have black dresses made for our arrival in England just in time for the royal funeral!" But the main reason for their leave was the marriage of their daughter Bridget to Captain Jack Lotinga of the Royal West African Frontier Force. Jack had been Shenton's A.D.C. in the Gold Coast and remained in West Africa when the Thomases went to Singapore. The family rented a flat in Berkeley Street for the wedding, which took place at St Margaret's, Westminster on 9 June.

It is now 1938, the year in which Hitler invaded Austria and took the Sudetenland from Czechoslovakia. However, in the Far East things remained outwardly calm. Since 1930 people had got used to the spectacle of Japanese military expansion in Asia. Having taken Man- churia from China and renamed it Manchukuo, she had encroached on Shanghai and, since 1937, had been waging active war on Chinese soil.

But one military event of 1938 which attracted world-wide attention was the completion of the British Naval Base on Singapore Island.

This great project had been accepted as an essential measure for the protection of the British Empire's Far Eastern interests as far back as 1922, following our abrogation of the Anglo-Japanese Alliance the previous year, which historians nowadays tend to regard as an ill-advised act. The project for the Base was immense in its scale, and, due to political uncertainties and changes in defence policy, took sixteen years to complete at a cost of sixty-three million pounds. The following description of the Base is taken from *Seventy Days to Singapore* by the American author Stanley Falk:

> North of Singapore, on the Strait of Johore, was the great naval base, twenty-one square miles in area and capable of sheltering an entire British fleet. . . . Amidst the piers, cranes, store-sheds, repair-shops, power stations, and other structures, two great 50,000-ton dry docks caught the eye. One, the King George VI Graving Dock had only recently been completed in 1937. The other, a huge floating dock, had been built in England in 1928 and towed half-way round the world to Singapore – an outstanding feat of seamanship. . . . The primary defences of the base were sited to protect the base against amphibious attack. They included five great 15-inch naval guns, six powerful 9.2-inch guns, eighteen 6-inch guns, as well as secondary armament.

The Base was formally opened by Sir Shenton Thomas, accompanied by Lady Thomas, in the presence of a large gathering of high-ranking service and civilian representatives from Great Britain, and other member states of the Empire, on 15 February, 1938. None of those present could foresee the irony of the fact that this event occurred precisely four years to a day before the British destroyed the base and surrendered Singapore to the Japanese.

In every Colony and Protectorate of the British Empire there was a Defence Committee, or similar body, generally presided over by the Governor and Commander-in-Chief, assisted by the Defence Secretary who was normally, but not invariably, a senior officer from the local armed forces. This was the practice in Malaya until, in that same year, 1938, Air Vice-Marshal A. W. Tedder*, then A.O.C. Far East, wrote to Shenton Thomas suggesting the need for a change in this procedure. Tedder had begun his professional career in the Colonial Service in Fiji before 1914, and he now recommended that in future the Defence Secretary at Singapore should be appointed from the

---

* Later Marshal of the R.A.F. Lord Tedder, G.C.B.

Malayan Civil Service, preferably an officer with long term experience of the country's problems; he argued that this would give much needed continuity by avoiding frequent changes in the holder of the appointment, due to the short tours of regular staff officers. Shenton Thomas acted at once on this advice with important and far-reaching results, both for himself and the strategic defence of all his territories.*

The first civilian Defence Secretary for Malaya, appointed by Sir Shenton Thomas in December, 1938, was Mr C. A. Vlieland. This officer already had twenty-six years' service in the M.C.S. and had a reputation for efficiency and a thorough knowledge of the country and its problems. He was not, however, renowned for tact, and certainly made no attempt to curb his intolerance of inefficiency or ignorance, wherever in his view either existed. Vlieland began by announcing that certain opinions long held by strategists in Whitehall, and often reflected overseas, were entirely fallacious and should be rejected. In particular he repudiated the idea that the dense jungles north of Johore would form a secure bulwark against any attack on Singapore from the Malayan hinterland, and therefore the primary role of the army in Malaya would be to provide for the close defence of the Naval Base itself. His own views on defence strategy for Malaya are paraphrased below from a Memoir** that he wrote later.

Vlieland was convinced that Singapore, though of great economic importance, and thus a valuable prize for the Japanese if they could capture and hold it, had no significant strategic value. In his view the base, completed barely ten months earlier, was *useless*, as there was never any likelihood that the Japanese would attempt to capture Singapore by direct sea-borne attack. This was strong meat, difficult to swallow by those who had acclaimed the base as a vital defence measure, well worth the £63,000,000 it had cost! That later events proved Vlieland right in this forecast shows just how prescient he was. He did not join in the later accusation that the big guns at the base were pointing the wrong way and could not be fired against a land attack from the north. He knew that the 15-inch guns had a 360-degree traverse, and the 9.2-inch and 6-inch guns could traverse through 180 degrees; the fault lay in their ammunition, which was all naval armour-piercing shell for use against warships and not suitable for the land battle.

Vlieland firmly believed that as long as we held the whole Malay

* Letter from Andrew Gilmour to the author January, 1982. Shenton showed Tedder's letter to Gilmour before acting on it.

** Memoir by C. A. Vlieland, lodged in the Liddell Hart Archives at King's College, London University.

Peninsula there was no need to fear. He repeated that Singapore was almost certainly not a main *strategic* objective of the Japanese in their war planning. If so, this again proved how useless the base was as we could make no effective use of it! *Ergo* Singapore could never be, and never was, a fortress in the way Churchill in particular looked upon it. The Japanese aim was to acquire an Empire in the South Pacific seas, at the heart of which would be the very wealthy and advanced, but under-populated, Malay Peninsula. The Japanese wanted the valuable rice-growing lands of Burma, Indo-China, Thailand and Indonesia, with of course the oil of the region. This was the political and strategic philosophy of the Japanese, which they would pursue relentlessly. With this forecast in mind Vlieland continually urged the need to regard the defence of the Malay Peninsula as the only effective means of preventing a Japanese occupation of Singapore Island, *by land attack from the north*.

Sir Shenton Thomas thoroughly approved all Vlieland's views and gave him his full support. So much so that Vlieland wrote:

> In December, 1938, I was appointed Secretary for Defence, Malaya, with a mandate from the Governor which gave me practically a free hand to pursue my aims. . . . I had acquired a considerable knowledge of the varied terrain of Malaya by hunting game in its forests, shooting over its open countryside and round its coasts. . . . I knew men up and down the land who were, so to speak, my eyes and ears. There were planters, miners, prospectors, foresters and game rangers who could send word of strange things which were happening in odd places; there was an old Malay tracker friend who brought me news of Japanese activities in the northern frontier region of Malaya. . . . The best and most detailed *forecast* of the eventual disasters in both Hong Kong and Malaya that I ever heard came from a Chinese servant who had worked for British masters in both territories for thirty years.

The foregoing is, I hope, a sufficient vignette of the man to whom Shenton Thomas gave his entire support in defence matters during those vital ten months before the outbreak of the Second World War. Evidently this set-up prospered well, for Vlieland referred to "Plans worked out between Sir Shenton, Sir Alexander Small, the then Colonial Secretary, and myself . . . with the full co-operation of General Dobbie,* then G.O.C. Malaya. . . . The A.O.C. Far East (Air Vice-Marshal Babington) was all in favour of my appointment, and the

---

* Major-General W. G. S. Dobbie, G.O.C. Malaya 1937–39. Dobbie's senior staff officer was Colonel A. E. Percival, to become G.O.C. Malaya from May 1941.

Senior Naval Officer in Singapore was pleasantly cooperative with the rest of us."

In Whitehall, too, Vlieland's planning was apparently well received at this time. The following passage appears in the *Official History of the War Against Japan*, Vol. I (The loss of Singapore), published by the Cabinet Office in 1957:

> It was, however, becoming apparent to both the army and air commanders in the Far East that the defence of the Naval Base at Singapore, on which attention had been concentrated for so long, did in fact involve the defence of the whole of the Malayan peninsula. . . . The G.O.C. Malaya (Major-General W.G.S. Dobbie) examined the defence problem from this new angle. . . . He reported to the War Office that landings on the east coast of Malaya were possible during the north-east monsoon (October to March) . . . and in his opinion were indeed probable, since bad visibility at that time would seriously limit air reconnaissance. . . . In 1938 he gave a warning that an attack on Singapore from the north should be regarded as the greatest potential danger.

Thus defence planning continued in a climate of exemplary civil and military relations, until August, 1939, when General Dobbie was relieved by Major-General L. V. Bond. The latter's strategic concept for Malaya's defence differed markedly from that of his predecessor, with significant results for conduct of preparations for the war with Japan, as yet two years ahead.

About this time also Shenton Thomas was thinking seriously of the need for up-to-date scientific advice in order to preserve the fauna and flora of Malaya, particularly the creation of game reserves. He therefore applied officially to the Government of Kenya for the temporary services of Captain Archibald Ritchie, Chief Game Warden of Kenya, whom he hoped would come to Singapore and advise the Government. Captain Ritchie and his wife duly arrived, and very soon the Governor, with Ritchie and Mr E. J. H. Corner*, a British officer of the M.C.S., then Assistant Director of the Gardens Department of the Straits Settlements, made an extensive tour of the Malay Peninsula. It was a difficult and prolonged expedition during which they climbed to the summit of the highest mountain peak on the mainland. Afterwards Ritchie's advice provided the basis of a report from which the Game Laws of Malaya were first drafted.

---

* Now Professor E. J. H. Corner, C.B.E., F.R.S., Professor Emeritus of Tropical Botany at Cambridge University.

This tour was interesting also for Shenton, as it was his first meeting with Mr Corner who appears again in this biography.

Shenton Thomas had now been more than four years in Singapore. He had just passed his 59th birthday and it is therefore appropriate to look at an assessment of his standing and professional reputation; at that age it could not fail to be his last job.

The salient fact is how he had confounded the critics, who maintained that no professional officer could rise to the top unless he had been a district officer "up-country". But Shenton had already been a Colonial Governor for ten consecutive years. Here is Professor Heussler's final opinion of him:

> Thomas prided himself on being affable, down-to-earth, able to get on with all sorts of people. As Governor of the Gold Coast he had an ideal conditioning for Malaya; a mixture of bustling commerce and back-country traditionalism: *evolués* and dignified native chiefs: European moguls and sharp middlemen who were neither native nor British. . . . If after the slump Malaya's job was to provide the Empire with a "dollar arsenal" Thomas was the very man to preside over it. Officers serving under him approved, finding the Governor straightforward, competent, and anything but Olympian in his ways. If he lacked the gubernatorial presence of Clementi that was the acceptable price to pay for peace and for the smooth, efficient running of the machine.

But the Second World War was soon to give every man, in all walks of life, a stark and frightening test of his capacity. In September, 1939, Daisy Shenton Thomas wrote:

> I shall never forget that Sunday when we knew war had broken out at home. Of course there had been rumours for some time – but that awful day came when we knew it was true, and there was hardly a soul in Malaya who had not relations and friends at home.

V

TWILIGHT WAR
3 September, 1939–8 December, 1941

Colonial Office
Downing Street
18th October, 1939

PERSONAL

Dear Thomas

I have been giving consideration to the question how far prospective changes in governorships should be affected by the new conditions which war has thrust upon us. You will be coming home on leave early next year with a view to retirement after your leave, when you will have completed the full term of your appointment. . . . If, however, you feel that you can manage it I should be relieved to think that you would remain in Malaya for a longer period. I have complete confidence in your handling of the many difficult political and economic problems which arise particularly in war, and I would like if possible to avoid a change in the command while the war is on.

Perhaps you will write and tell me how you feel about this? Please do not hesitate to be quite frank. . . . I assume that in any case you will require to take some leave next year. . . .

Yours sincerely,
Malcolm Macdonald
(Secretary of State)

Sir Shenton Thomas, G.C.M.G., O.B.E.

Shenton replied saying that of course he would be glad to remain at his post for as long as he was required, and later *The Times* reported that the Secretary of State had requested "Sir Shenton Thomas to continue to hold office for the duration of the war, provided that his health permits". In January, 1940, Shenton asked Macdonald for permission to leave Singapore in April "for such leave as you may approve". He added that he felt he should be away not less than six months, "considerably more is due to me".

In the late 1930s Malaya, by and large, was a happy, wealthy and loyal land, made so by the industry of civilian private enterprise and sound government practice. The standard of living generally was high, and there was a rich and cultured Asiatic community, many of whom were highly trained in business matters. About half the prosperous rubber industry was Asiatic-owned, the majority by smallholders farming 100 acres or less. One-third of the tin mines were Chinese-owned, and other large industries, such as canned pineapples, that provided 90% of the total consumption in the United Kingdom, were generally under Asiatic control: the oil and palm oil trades were mainly European-owned and managed.

These details were important as they ensured there was no economic closed shop in pre-war Malaya, and relations between the various racial communities were cordial. In the theatres and amusement parks, at race meetings and games, there was no racial discrimination; it was noticeable that in lawn tennis and athletic championships the Chinese and Malays, less commonly the Indians, were successful as often as not. In the social round of club life, however, there was definite segregation, and the representatives of the M.C.S., the services, and the great European mercantile firms always had their "Club", which the "coloured" communities did not join, or attempt to join. Certainly for many British the "Club" was the centre of their social life. Cecil Lee well described it, as seen by a young civilian on first arrival:

> How can I sum up those placid, peaceful Pre-war years in Malaya? From the time when I stepped off the steamer in Penang, and inhaled for the first time that pungent, spicy odour, so distinctive to the Far East, took a siesta in the gaunt high-ceilinged Penang Club, resting on a long chair with great swinging arms for one's legs, and a slot for one's *stengah* (whisky and water); watching the Chinese "boys" padding unobtrusively through the carpeted rooms, silent except for the occasional call of "boy" – or raucous laughter. The breakfast of papaya, and the journey to the office in a rickshaw clad in new white drills; and from the office window the sight of a Malay fisherman casting his net in the yellow silted waters at the confluence of the rivers Gombok and Klang – hence the name Kuala Lumpur (Muddy Mouths).

Meanwhile the British Raj reigned supreme, paternalistic maybe, yet secure in its position, in spite of the beginnings of Malayanization, including that decentralization progress mentioned in the previous chapter.

At the start of war in September, 1939, the Defence Committee at once became an expanded War Committee. The Chairman was the Governor, with Vlieland and senior departmental officers as civil members, together with the heads of the three fighting services.

This was the period of the "phoney" war in Europe, 10,000 miles away from the Far East where actual war conditions seemed very remote, and the habits and customs of day-to-day life in business and

social circles did not change overmuch, at any rate for civilians. At
Government House large state dinner parties were still held; the guests
still assembled for cocktails in the ground floor reception room, and
were "marshalled" there by the Private Secretary before H.E. and
Lady Thomas, with the A.D.C., came down the grand staircase to meet
their guests; each male guest had met the lady he knew he was to take
into dinner, and had been given a printed table plan with the order of
entry into the dining room. On such occasions formal precedence was
very important; for instance at G.H. Singapore, which was a colonial
possession, Sir Shenton was served first at the table, ahead of the ladies
beside him because he represented the King. Not so, however, in an
Unfederated Malay State where H.E. would be the High Commissioner and the Sultan would have precedence over all.

Looking back it may seem strange now that life should have been
allowed to continue thus after war had begun in Europe. But in that
Malaya was certainly no exception, and in India, and in the colonies
generally, life followed precisely the same pattern. On the other hand in
certain spheres the tempo did quicken enormously. For Malaya was a
treasure house for the accumulation of foreign exchange; in 1939 the
U.S.A. bought from Malaya twenty-five times as much as the latter
bought from America. Equally important, H.M.G. required Malaya to
give top priority to the production of tin and rubber which, apart from
their economic value, were essential war commodities.

Although official entertainment had to continue at Government
House, Daisy Thomas recorded the very great increase in other
activities that war brought to the calm of the Governor's residence:

> I felt we must do all we could to help. The day after war began I called for
> a committee of the wives of *all races* in the Government, and we set up
> what was known as the "Malaya Patriotic Fund". I had never started
> anything so rewarding. Money poured in, enormous sums, from every
> part of the country. We arranged that a committee from each racial
> community should organize the making of socks, jerseys and every form
> of clothing for the armed forces. All these items were sent to Govern-
> ment House, where the staff made their contribution to the war the
> packing and labelling of everything for dispatch to the Forces at war, or
> to the Red Cross.

At this time a setback occurred when Major-General Bond arrived
from London in relief of General Dobbie. The change did not have
immediate effect, but developed gradually, as recorded by Vlieland in
his Memoir:

It was clear from the first that General Bond's briefing by the War Office, no less than his own point of view, were going to make things very difficult . . . . He clearly considered that my functions should be strictly confined to "civil defence", and that defence policy and military strategy were no concern of mine, or even of the Governor. But worse than all this was that he told me specifically, at his first interview with me, that his orders were to defend Singapore and did not permit him to concern himself with the peninsula. All this was more than tiresome, but it did not, for the time being, impede our progress towards real preparedness for war in Malaya. Until Sir Shenton went on leave in April, 1940, the balance of power in defence councils was secure. The Naval C-in-C was still in Hong Kong, and the senior naval officer in Singapore gave no trouble. The Air C-in-C was wholeheartedly on the side of the Governor and myself, and determined upon the defence of all Malaya; and I had Sir Shenton behind and with me all the way.

This embarrassing divergence of view between the Governor and his army commander bedevilled the war planning in Malaya; yet in all fairness to Bond it is clear that both Shenton and Vlieland failed, or did not try, to appreciate Bond's personal position. Lionel Bond was a professional soldier, an experienced regular army officer, and who can blame him if he objected strongly to the civilian members of the War Committee trying to teach him defence strategy? Nor did it help him when he found that the Air C-in-C in Malaya (Air Vice-Marshal Babington) favoured relying primarily on air power for defence, and therefore strongly supported the Governor's view of the need to hold all Malaya by air forces operating from the northern airfields from which they could attack Japanese invasion attempts.

However, it is clear that Bond did appreciate that the Japanese invasion, if it came, would come from the north, but he realized that he just did not have the financial or military resources to defend the northern airfields in Kedah, Kelantan and Kuantan. But there his logic seems to have failed him, for he omitted to use even those resources which had been left him by Dobbie*. General Bond is dead but his foremost critic has been the official historian, General Kirby, who said of him: "Although a man of sterling worth and character, he was lacking in personality, kept himself aloof and was inclined to exercise control from his office chair. He seldom, if ever, studied his problems on the spot." Certainly Thomas and Vlieland agreed with this view.

---

* In 1939 Dobbie had been granted £60,000 for fixed defences in Johore to prevent artillery bombardment of the Naval Base; of this only £23,000 was spent, but the balance was never used by Bond. *Singapore* by Ivan Simson, Leo Cooper, 1970.

In these conflicting circumstances Shenton Thomas decided to frame his own appreciation of the Japanese threat to Malaya and the essential precautionary measures that should be taken. After the war the *Official History* published the gist of his long despatch to the Colonial Office, dated 27 January, 1940, the main points of which follow below.

He began by saying that, in his discussion with General Bond, he found it increasingly difficult to decide whether the claims of national defence should have preference over, or be subordinated to, the huge economic contribution which Malaya was required to make to the overall war effort. He added, "I conceive it to be our duty to give absolute priority to the claims of industry." As regards positive military measures Britain was not at war with Japan and, though it would be foolhardy to assert she would not be, there were signs this had become less likely. He thought that the Japanese, if they attacked, would need first to establish an advanced air base within striking distance of Singapore. (In the event, and paradoxically, how right he was!) So the Governor looked to the R.A.F. for primary defence of Malaya and urged that the air capability should be increased appreciably.

Simultaneously the Air C-in-C sent his own very similar views to the Air Ministry in London. He also strongly supported relying on strong air forces for Malaya's defence, adding that, "Should the Japanese gain a foothold in Malaya, the fate of Singapore would be sealed." Again, how right he was!

On 10 March the Cabinet Sub-Committee met to consider Shenton's appreciation; and how delighted he would have been could he have known that at this meeting, attended by the Directors of Plans of the three armed services, with representatives of the Foreign Office, the Colonial Office, the Treasury and Ministry of Home Security, his opinions were strongly favoured by the Foreign Office, which held that economic considerations should outweigh strategic requirements in Singapore; the Foreign Office maintained that the threat to Singapore should be regarded as remote, and measures to guard against it should not be allowed to interfere with the economic effort of Malaya.

Looking back now at what actually happened, it may seem extraordinary that responsible officials in Whitehall should have accepted the view put forward by the Foreign Office. But it has to be remembered that it was March, 1940, that the war was still confined to Europe and that the major concern was the safety of Britain. Hitler had not yet invaded Denmark and Norway, and the Far East, everyone hoped, would remain quiet. Neville Chamberlain was still Prime Minister. Perhaps not surprisingly, therefore, the Cabinet (Defence) Sub-

Committee replied to Shenton Thomas's despatch in terms which today we should regard as a non-event:

> The Committee, having carefully considered the views expressed by the Governor, accepted that the security of Singapore was so vital for the safety of the British Commonwealth in the Far East that any matter relating to its fundamental defence policy was of the highest importance. Nevertheless, with the full scope of the general conflict not yet revealed, it was, they thought, out of the question to make any change in the existing policy.... There was in fact no immediate possibility of effecting such an increase [in the R.A.F. in Malaya] that the Governor had requested, or even of bringing the existing squadrons up to their wartime establishment.... The Committee ... recognized that the economic contribution of Malaya was of the first importance and should not be interrupted.

This reply reached Singapore early in April and prompted Shenton, supported by Bond and Babington, to ask the Colonial Office for an opportunity to discuss Malaya's defence problems and priorities personally during his forthcoming visit to London.

Finally we see General Bond staging a remarkable *volte face*. In an appreciation which he forwarded to the War Office on 13 April, and which he said was agreed generally by the Governor, the Air C-in-C and the Rear-Admiral, Malaya, the G.O.C now agreed that the Japanese could effect a landing *at any time* on either the east or west coasts. In these changed circumstances the whole of Malaya would have to be held, particularly as Whitehall had declared that, in the event of a Japanese attack, the garrison would have to hold out for at least 180 days before the arrival of a British fleet at Singapore could be expected. If therefore, as the G.O.C. feared, no appreciable military reinforcement for Malaya was possible (he had already requested a further three equivalent divisions) then he accepted that the only solution, as inferred in the Governor's appreciation, lay in utilizing the R.A.F. to the fullest possible extent.

It is now mid-April, 1940, and Shenton and Daisy are about to leave Singapore by sea for England for a period of leave approved by the Colonial Office. It was the official view in Malaya, and indeed throughout the Far East as well as in London, that war with Japan was possible though improbable. It was also widely held, in spite of contradictory reports from British sources, that there was little to fear from the Japanese armed forces: their military prowess was discounted.

In accordance, perhaps, with this complacent view, the strength of our armed forces in Malaya was very thin on the ground and certainly

gave no confidence to serious professional soldiers. The Singapore
Naval Base was complete but there were no sizeable fleet units
stationed there; most of the warships available to the C-in-C China
Squadron were deployed for protection of convoys and sea communications in the Indian Ocean. The Air C-in-C Malaya had fewer
than 100 first-line aircraft, mostly obsolete, with no fighter aircraft at
all. The G.O.C., General Bond, had at his disposal only one infantry
brigade of five regular battalions (three British, one Indian and one
Malay) plus the local volunteer forces (territorials); the supporting
arms were confined to coastal defence and anti-aircraft artillery with
Fortress squadrons of Royal Engineers.

Meanwhile, there was apparent unanimity in the War Committee at
Singapore as to the nature and scale of the reinforcements that were
urgently needed for the defence of Malaya. The plan being to rely
primarily on air power for defence, Air Vice-Marshal Babington had
sent his requirements to the Air Ministry. The Governor was to discuss
the whole matter of Malaya's defence and her contribution to the war
effort with the authorities in London.

That was the overall position when Shenton and Daisy sailed from
Singapore. However, the Governor was not so content with the
position in the War Committee as officially appeared to be the case.
Vlieland wrote as follows on the day that the Thomases sailed:

> I think I should place on record Sir Shenton's parting words to me
> before he boarded the liner on which he sailed from Singapore in April
> 1940. These were: "Remember, Vlieland, I rely on you to hold the fort
> while I am away and not to let Bond get away with it. Jones [the Colonial
> Secretary who was to be Acting Governor] knows very little about the
> defence side, and you'll have to keep him straight".

The voyage to England in wartime involved sailing via Colombo,
Bombay, Mombasa, Durban, Cape Town and West Africa, but not in
convoy. They were in the old *Empress of India*, a fine P. & O. ship, and
though there were blackouts at night the voyage savoured of the old
order of sea journeys for officers returning from tropical service.

When the Thomases reached England they needed a temporary
home, preferably near their daughter Bridget, who was then living in
The Steward's House at Broome Park in Kent. They were fortunate to
be able to rent a lovely country house called Littlecote, at Littlebourne
near Canterbury, which they occupied for the whole of their leave.
Meanwhile the war situation, which had seemed so remote in the Far
East, had changed very considerably for the worse.

Hitler had invaded the Low Countries in May, on the 10th of which month Churchill replaced Chamberlain as Prime Minister; the Dutch Government had been forced to move to London, and in June France had collapsed, leading to Dunkirk and the British evacuation of France. These developments deeply affected the political scene in the Far East and one could not look at the map of South-East Asia without seeing the serious dangers to British interests. French Indo-China was now a satellite of Vichy France and could no longer be regarded as friendly, while the Netherlands East Indies had lost their parent government in Holland. Thailand's neutrality must now be in doubt, and Japan, in the light of the fall of France and Holland, might well see these events as an opportunity to make herself master of the south-west Pacific. Worse still, Italy had joined Germany and Britain now stood alone against the power of Hitler, who controlled virtually all central and western Europe, except for Switzerland and the Iberian peninsula.

One may well ask why the Governor did not apply at once to the Colonial Office for facilities to enable him to return to his post. In fact this very question was asked by Admiral Sir Percy Noble, C-in-C China Station, who took the view that the Governor "would quickly return to his post, and he was horrified and alarmed when July passed and it become obvious that Sir Shenton had no intention of cutting short his leave".* At that stage Admiral Layton relieved Noble who returned to London, where he reiterated his disquiet about the Governor's absence to Lord Lloyd, recently appointed by Winston Churchill as Secretary of State for the Colonies. In the event no action was taken because Lloyd died shortly afterwards. But this intervention by Admiral Layton is also interesting because he recommended to Lloyd "that both General Bond and Air Marshal Babington should be replaced as soon as possible by experienced younger men who could cooperate with each other, but that Sir Shenton Thomas should remain as Governor, since he had a detailed knowledge of the very complicated administrative set-up in Malaya".**

As we have seen, Shenton had applied to see the authorities in London in order to present the case for far greater interest in Whitehall in Malaya's preparations for war, particularly the urgent need for considerable reinforcement of the R.A.F. He reached England late in June, 1940, and subsequently wrote this letter to the Colonial Office:

* See *Singapore, The Chain of Disaster*, by S. Woodburn Kirby, Cassell, 1971. Kirby was a persistent critic of Thomas.
** Kirby, page 53.

I submit it is necessary to decide now what action should be taken in the event of war with Japan. Apparently naval reinforcements are not possible. . . . It is only by preventing an army from landing that Malaya can be preserved, and in the absence of the Navy, the R.A.F. is the only source of help. In my opinion it is also the best source. . . . If, then, it is decided to defend Malaya by means of the R.A.F., such equipment, spares and stores as cannot be transported quickly should be laid in *now*; maintenance personnel should be sent out before an emergency.

I know it will be said that sufficient forces of the R.A.F. cannot be spared today. If, then, Malaya should be attacked by Japan within (say) the next two months, is the territory and Singapore to be left to its fate? If so, let us be told, and we will do the best we can: but if not, let a decision be taken at once as to the size and nature of the relieving air-force, and let all preparations for receiving it and enabling it to function with the maximum efficiency be put in hand now.

After the war Shenton wrote as follows about the reaction in Whitehall to the letter quoted above:

I was allowed to put my case personally before the Joint Planning Sub-Committee of the War Cabinet on August 1st 1940. The Sub-Committee found themselves "generally in full agreement" with my views but felt that no change of policy was practicable for the moment. So matters rested until the Japanese attacked.

Against this background it appears significant to the timing of Shenton's personal interview at the Cabinet Office that one week later, on 8 August, the War Cabinet met to consider Far East War Strategy. At this meeting the Chiefs of Staff acknowledged the need to defend the whole of Malaya and admitted that current R.A.F. strength in the region, under 100 first-line aircraft, was well below the minimum needed (336 aircraft, with 168 in immediate reserve). They also noted General Bond's plea that army strength should be increased to at least the equivalent of three divisions. So far so good, particularly as on 28 August the War Cabinet formally accepted the Chiefs of Staff's recommendations, leaving Shenton Thomas with every reason, at that stage, to be pleased with his intervention in Whitehall. The more so as the Chiefs of Staff, a week later, on 4 September, informed the Prime Minister of their intention to send the 7th Australian Division and two Indian infantry brigades to Malaya, as the first move in their reinforcement programme.

For reasons that appear later, I believe it is safe to assume that, before he returned to Singapore, Shenton must have been told of the final unfortunate end to these efforts to help Malaya. The Prime

Minister, Winston Churchill, flatly refused to allow the 7th Australian Division to go to Malaya, thus overturning the decisions made in August. Almost worse was Churchill's firm belief that the main defence of Singapore must be the Fleet, and that the policy of trying to defend the whole of Malaya had no merit. Professor Callahan* has summed up British war strategy for the Far East at this time:

> There were really two strategies for the Far East. The official one was contained in the Chiefs' of Staff paper; Churchill's personal policy consisted of relying on America and hoping for the best.

Having had his say in Whitehall Shenton made his plans to return to Malaya, but that was easier said than done. The sea voyage round the Cape now took 2–3 months and air passages for civilian officials, however high-ranking, were seldom available. Eventually in September, before Hitler formed the tripartite Germany-Italy-Japan axis, he and Daisy were routed by air to Lisbon; thence by Pan-American Airways to Canada, and from there across the Pacific to Australia, finally arriving on 5 December.

Looking again at the timing of Shenton's movements in 1940, it is easy with hindsight to be critical of his *apparently* long leave. But in fact he was in the United Kingdom just three months. He was 61 and had served in the hot, humid, and enervating climate of Malaya since 1934, with only one short period of U.K. leave. In these circumstances no charge of slackness or undue delay can fairly be laid against him.

At this time the authorities in Whitehall made one very considerable change in the command structure in the Far East. This was the appointment of a highly distinguished officer of the R.A.F., Air Chief Marshal Sir Robert Brooke-Popham, G.C.V.O, K.C.B, C.M.G., D.S.O. A.F.C., to be Commander-in-Chief The Far East. This appointment was made not only for professional military reasons, but also to ensure the best possible co-operation and good will between the armed forces and the Governor, the M.C.S. and the civilian community generally, particularly on account of conflicting priorities. Whitehall had given Malaya two urgent and very different requirements. The armed forces were to prepare for war against Japan while the Governor and the civil servants were to ensure maximum production of tin and rubber. The intention underlying Brooke-Popham's (B.P.) appointment was admirable; unfortunately in its implementation, it achieved very little.

---

* *The Worst Disaster*, Raymond Callahan, University of Delaware Press, 1977.

Although styled C-in-C The Far East, B.P. had no authority or control whatsoever over the Royal Navy, nor even ultimate command over the Army and the R.A.F. General Bond and Air Vice-Marshal Babington continued to be responsible to their own Service Heads and Ministries in London, while Shenton Thomas took orders only from the Colonial Office in Whitehall. Had B.P. been appointed a Supreme Commander with absolute formal control over all military and civil authorities, including the Governor, then his appointment *per se* would have been admirable.*

Most writers on the Malaya War have strongly criticised Brooke-Popham for lack of decision or direction to his subordinate commanders, but the fact is he was given a virtually impossible task. He was supposed to command the armies and air forces in Burma, Malaya and Hong Kong, with control and direction of training in Ceylon; but he had only a staff of seven officers. Although charming, with a highly distinguished appearance, he was already over 62, too old for such a strenuous and demanding task. He had retired from the R.A.F. in 1937 to become Governor of Kenya, until recalled to service on the outbreak of war. He had an unfortunate habit of dropping off to sleep during a meeting, or at a formal dinner party at Government House! He received his directive in London on 22 October; it took him four weeks to reach Singapore on 18 November.

Shenton Thomas always enjoyed very cordial relations with Brooke-Popham, and after the war he took care to record this in his comments on the draft of the *Official History*:

> The C-in-C Far East and the Naval C-in-C were members of the War Committee. . . . There was no important war matter falling within the preview of the civil government which was not accepted by me after due discussion. . . . To speak of trouble, lack of co-ordination and dissension, in civil and military relations (as the *History* so often does) is wrong. There was, however, one exception to this.

This exception centred round the case of the senior civil officer, Mr C. A. Vlieland, whom Shenton had appointed as Secretary for Defence.

While the Governor was in England, Vlieland had been experiencing the very difficulties which B.P.'s appointment was supposed to avoid, and which Shenton had mentioned to Vlieland before he sailed from Singapore. Vlieland described this in his Memoir:

* The first supreme commander *proper* in the British Commonwealth was Admiral Sir Geoffrey Layton who held supreme authority in Ceylon 1942–45.

During Sir Shenton's absence, General Bond, with the support of Mr Jones [Acting Governor], had it all his own way, not only to the exasperation of the Air C-in-C and myself but to the bewilderment and perturbation of the general public of Malaya. G.H.Q. (B.P.'s H.Q.) saw no necessity to consult me over any measures they could take without express governmental sanction or assistance. . . . I always made it clear that Singapore alone was defenceless against an overland attack and therefore, unless the peninsula was firmly held, the naval base would be unusable.

On 13 December, 1940 Shenton chaired a meeting of the Malaya War Committee. Vlieland described what happened:

> When I entered the council chamber and took my old seat at his right hand, Sir Shenton did not greet, or even look at me. He opened the proceedings by inviting B.P. to speak. The C-in-C Land and Air then made a savage attack on me. It was, in effect, more of an attack on Sir Shenton's previous régime than on myself. No one else said a word. Bond and Layton nodded their approval and my friend the A.O.C. could not rally to my support in defiance of his Air Chief Marshal. Sir Shenton remained silent with bowed head.

One is at once struck by Thomas's apparent complete *volte face* in comparison to his friendly words to Vlieland when he left Singapore eight months earlier. There must be an explanation for this, and I am convinced that it lies in the briefing that he was given in Whitehall, either at or after his meeting with the War Cabinet Sub-Committee on 1 August. He must have been told that it was useless to press for more aircraft for Malaya and Singapore as long as the Prime Minister took an entirely different view, and that Vlieland and Babington should be told to "pipe down". This would also account for his subsequent statement about the "one exception" to cordial relations between civil and military in the War Committee.

> Bond and Babington held totally different views on the question of defence, and friction did arise. The civilian official [Vlieland] who was dealing with defence allied himself with Babington, and the matter came to a head while I was on leave *in 1940* [my italics]. On my return Brooke-Popham spoke to me about it, and the civilian officer went home on retirement in February, 1941.

Thus ended the tragic case of Mr Vlieland, who was doomed, so it appears, by Whitehall, where the military authorities no doubt regarded him as an upstart civilian who had no right or reason to teach strategy or tactics to professional officers of the armed forces! And tragic his case really was for his prescience was quite remarkable. In July, 1940, he had written his own appreciation of the likelihood of war with Japan, in which he forecast with almost uncanny accuracy the timing, scale, direction and targets of the eventual Japanese invasion of Malaya. However, this most unusual document never became an official paper, for the Acting Governor (Jones) refused to read it and asked Vlieland not to submit it *officially* – "as it would only make the General (Bond) angry and could do no possible good"! All this, I believe, lends credence to the view that Vlieland's departure was decided in Whitehall, probably on the advice of Brooke-Popham. Certainly in the next two months Whitehall also got rid of Bond and Babington, the former being replaced by General Percival and the latter by Air Vice-Marshal Pulford.

We are now in 1941 and Shenton and Daisy are caught up in the quickening tempo of war conditions, particularly the arrival of considerable reinforcements, notwithstanding controversy about their quality and training. Two brigades of Indian infantry had arrived and now the Australians (the 8th Infantry Division commanded by Lieutenant-General Gordon Bennett) were coming. Shenton writes in his diary:

> *Feb. 18 1941*
> Lunch with Admiral and Lady Layton, and then watched *Queen Mary* arrive with 6,000 Australians. All splendidly fit. 8 to stay at G.H. for a few nights.
> *Feb. 19*
> I broadcast re Australian Imperial Force arrival. Dinner for about 50 including General Bennett and 25 more Australians. Hot and sticky.

Evidently Government House is to be used for dances for British and Australian troops, for Shenton wrote:

> *Feb. 21*
> First of our 2 troops dances. Rather over 700 and quite successful.

Then in July a sinister note appears in the diary:

> *July 24*
> Japan is moving into Indo-China.

Yet, strangely, this does not appear to have been taken seriously, any more than it was in London where, as late as midsummer, the Far East situation was not rated as urgent.

Much more important for the Governor personally was the arrival in September of the Duff Coopers – Alfred Duff Cooper, protégé of Winston Churchill, with his famous wife Lady Diana Cooper, star and socialite of the 1930s. His brief in September, 1941, was to ensure better coordination and control of policies in the Far East, which by then it was clear Brooke-Popham was failing to do. The Prime Minister had therefore sent Duff Cooper to Singapore on a "mission of inquiry".

Many books have referred to the differences of opinion that developed between Sir Shenton Thomas and Duff Cooper, and Shenton's own record of those events will appear in a later chapter. But it has to be said that until the invasion relations between the two men were cordial enough, though Daisy and Diana certainly never had anything in common! The Duff Coopers arrived on 9 September and the first reaction of the locals was amazement at the amount of their personal luggage, some 100 suitcases, which was considered inappropriate, to put it mildly, for any wartime mission! However, Duff Cooper began by touring widely, with his wife, throughout the Far East, including visits to India, Burma and the Philippines, so was seldom in Malaya until December.

Nevertheless Shenton Thomas had a difficult time, in official circles and with the Singapore press, trying to explain the reason for Duff Cooper's arrival. He expressed his own feelings as follows:

> The news of Duff Cooper's appointment to the Far East had been received with little enthusiasm. He had not been successful as a Minister of Information and had been demoted to be Chancellor of the Duchy of Lancaster. We felt we were being landed with a failure. We remembered Sir Stafford Cripps' description of him as a "petulant little pipsqueak"! Otherwise the chief criticism was that at such a time the appearance of Lady Diana was improper; why should she be sent round the world at public expense? I stopped this by a letter to Seabridge [of *The Straits Times*] in which I denied the anonymous inaccuracies that he was publishing and pointed out that a representative of His Majesty's Government charged with such a mission might fitly be accompanied by his wife.

Meanwhile, at Government House, visitors came and went and had to be entertained. I was, however, surprised when I discovered that a distinguished Soviet statesman had visited Singapore and stayed at G. H. late in November, 1941. In the Visitor's Book there is a photograph of Maxim Litvinov with an entry showing he stayed there from 28–30 November. Litvinov had been the Soviet Minister for

Foreign Affairs only two years earlier, until he was replaced by Molotov. Russia had already been invaded by Germany and it is interesting to speculate why such a senior Soviet ex-Minister should have been allowed (or sent?) to visit Singapore just a week before Japan attacked Britain and the U.S.A. Before he left Singapore he wrote the following letter to his hostess, which shows not only that apparently he liked her, but also that he had used reams of G.H. stationery!

Government House
Singapore

Dear Lady Thomas

I couldn't sleep all night – not a wink! Thinking, thinking, going over and over again in my mind all the troubles and griefs of our life now. I tell you this, because by your dearness to me you have been more than just a passing hostess.

At last after 3 I got up and wrote an endless letter to my daughter. Oh, how sorry I am I didn't show you her photo, my pretty one – when shall I ever see her again? Because of course about daughters you and I can understand one another.

Yes and by the way I used up *reams* of your good stationery. Please forgive!

I will never forget you – and don't forget me!

Yours sincerely (very)
M. Litvinoff

The eighth of December, 1941, is now very near, yet it seems extraordinary that so few officials were worried about the possibility of an imminent Japanese attack. From the many books already published about ULTRA it can surely be accepted that by mid-1941 the Americans were reading the Japanese diplomatic cypher, and so must have had a mass of information making it perfectly evident that the Japanese were preparing for a *major* war. If this is true, why were the Americans caught unaware at Pearl Harbor?

As far as we are concerned, we need to know (a) were we ourselves also reading the Japanese diplomatic signal traffic in 1941, and (b) how much, if at all, was Washington sharing with London the intelligence it derived from this source? This is the mystery to which we still do not have the answer, and we can extend Singapore's connection with the mystery by asking ourselves: "Presumably American Naval Intelligence was in direct contact with the Far East Combined Bureau [Singapore's Intelligence Centre] and would have warned the Bureau that war in fact was very close?" All we know for certain is that at Pearl Harbor and Singapore there was no fear of invasion on the Saturday night of 7 December, 1941. In both cities the lights were blazing, people were dining and dancing and there was no thought of tomorrow, except that it would be a holiday. Nobody thought of blackouts or air raid precautions.

Yet there was one place in Singapore where nightwork was certainly going on, where people were thinking only of approaching aircraft and bomb attacks. This was the Radar Filter Room, established early in 1941, with four or more outstations on the island and the peninsula. These radar outstations spotted and then plotted the track of aircraft approaching Singapore from any direction, while simultaneously transmitting their "plots" to Radar Headquarters, then at Seletar airfield close to the great Naval Base. No aircraft could enter these "floodlit" sectors of radar search without detection. All these reports were received first at the Filter Room near Kallang airfield. Here they were "digested" and coordinated and then passed immediately to the Fighter Control Room next door, where all necessary operational action was taken; this included orders to fighter aircraft to scramble, then directing them on to the incoming radar track, informing higher authority and so on. The Filter Officer decided whether an incoming aircraft was hostile or otherwise; if the former he had also to alert A.R.P. Headquarters for air raid warning action.

At about 0320 hours on Sunday morning reports from the radar station at Mersing reached the Filter Room indicating that aircraft had been detected over the sea 75 miles north-east of Mersing, flying south. They continued flying south, plotted subsequently by all four radar stations and still over the sea, until they were east of Singapore. Then they turned west, directly towards Singapore. It must have been a tense moment in the Filter Room, at that early hour in the complete darkness of a tropical night, and the scene is worth describing.

On the Filter Room floor there was a large table painted with an outline map of the area, superimposed on a grid with 10 km. squares. Seated round the table were the plotters, wearing headphones through which information came from their outstations; with holding clues they moved the position counters on the table. Sitting in an observation gallery looking down at the table was the Filter Officer in command. He had to be able to assess a complex technical situation and reach a decision accurately and quickly, and for this reason many of the people initially recruited as Filter Officers had been stockbrokers in civil life, specializing in international arbitrage. A teller passed the information, as directed by the Filter Officer, to the Fighter Operations Room.*

---

* Dr T. C. Carter to the author, 1982.

The Filter Officer that morning was Flight-Lieutenant Harry Grumbar, who until 1939 had been a broker with his family firm on the London Stock Exchange. Fifty-five minutes elapsed between Grumbar's first plot, passed to the Operations Room, and the first bomb drop on the city. Grumbar's account of what happened at Radar Headquarters during those fifty-five minutes before war came to Malaya is most interesting. It has not been published before:

> I labelled the plot of these incoming aircraft, seventeen of them as it transpired, as "X" (unidentified) because I knew we were not at war and so had not yet got an official enemy. My "X" track on the Filter Room table would have been automatically plotted on the Operations Room equivalent as I composed it. I recollect that I also telephoned A.R.P. Headquarters, which *was* manned, on my direct line; but I was told that they were powerless to sound the air raid sirens because their Chief Warden was at the late night cinema (some cinemas in Singapore had all-night viewing), and only he had the keys that controlled the Alarm switch. I also tried to get the city lights extinguished as a first priority, but with equal lack of success.
>
> I made no more 'phone calls as all further action was now out of my hands. But I remember leaving the Filter Room to enter the adjacent Operations Control, in order to give my personal opinion to the officer there. There was not a shadow of doubt, in my view, that this was an enemy raid, even if we were not actually at (declared) war. The pattern in the radar track I had plotted was so similar to that of hostile aircraft appearing in the English Channel during the 1940 Battle of Britain.*

Grumbar's story is important because of the *Official History*'s account of this first raid says: "Warning was at once passed to all service establishments and formations on the island, and the anti-aircraft gun defences were brought to instant readiness. It was not possible for similar warning to be given to the civil defence authorities, as the Headquarters of the Air Raid organization was not manned". We now know that the A.R.P. Headquarters was manned because all Head-quarters, military and civil, had been brought to the state of First Degree Readiness some days earlier; that the Chief Air Raid Warden was at the cinema is another matter! After all in the United States even expert orientalists, *at the same date*, were caught napping. The following quotation from Ronald Lewin's recent and most revealing book makes this very clear:**

* Harry Grumbar to the author, 1982.
** *The Other Ultra*, Hutchinson & Co., 1982.

On the morning of December 7 (Dec. 8 Tokyo Time) the Institute of Pacific Relations met in conference at the Country Club in Cleveland, Ohio. The director divided this body of Far Eastern experts into two groups which then, independently, assessed the possibility that Japan might take military action against the United States. About two o'clock (p.m.) the groups re-assembled. Each announced the same conclusion: the Japanese *would make no move for a year or more.* As discussion continued Kay Halle, who was covering the conference for a local radio network, was handed a slip of paper to pass on to the director. It was the announcement, just released by President Roosevelt's press secretary, that the Japanese had bombed Pearl Harbor. If professional Orient-watchers could be taken so humiliatingly by surprise, how much greater the impact on millions of ordinary citizens.

Maybe then we should not be surprised that the Chief Air Raid Warden was at the cinema!

VI

THE CAMPAIGN

On 10 September, 1940, Colonel T. Tanikawa, planning chief of Japan's Imperial Army Headquarters in Tokyo, arrived in Singapore. He was accompanied by Major Kunitake, a staff officer of the 25th Army under General Yamashita, which in December, 1941, attacked Malaya and Singapore; both men wore plain clothes.

These two officers wanted to travel round the Malayan coasts, east and west, their purpose being to investigate the condition of the beaches, and I had been requested to take them there. . . . I was not, of course, a spy for Japan. I was a press attache in the Consulate General.

First we toured Singapore city, travelling along the coast road through Katong, Siglap and Changi, to Pasir Panjang. We skirted Tengah Air Base then still under construction, and drove down Bukit Timah Road to Johore Bahru, going on to Kota Tinggi, Mersing and Endau.* The next day we went to Malacca.

On 13 September we returned to Singapore, to the house of Mr Yamakawa who had been a Japanese Army Captain. At Yamakawa's a map was spread out before us, and Colonel Tanikawa declared: "It is impossible to attack Singapore City from the sea, that is from the east, south or west; attack is possible only from the Johore Strait north of Singapore". The next day the Japanese military officers returned to Tokyo.

Thus Mamoru Shinozaki, an official in the Japanese Consulate General at Singapore, in his book *Syonan – My Story*.** However, Mr Shinozaki did not know he had been shadowed by detectives from Singapore Special Branch, under Mr A. E. G. Blades, a Japanese-speaking officer who knew of his involvement in assisting two Japanese officers to obtain "information which might be useful to a foreign power". Despite the protests of Mr Toyoda, the Consul General, Shinozaki was prosecuted in the Singapore Supreme Court and sentenced to three years' hard labour. He was confined in Changi Prison where, according to his book, he suffered privation and

* Geographically, the route seems illogical, to say the least; but this is what he wrote.

** Published by Times Books International, Singapore 1982. The book describes the Japanese occupation of Singapore, 1942–1945.

hardship until he was released on the evening of 15 February, 1942, by the arrival at the prison gate of two Japanese officers, who called out, "Any Japanese inside? The British have surrendered."

Mamoru Shinozaki then joined the Japanese Military Administration of Singapore Island, and we shall meet him again in this story, to see in particular the good work he did for the British and Chinese in Syonan – the new Japanese name for Singapore.

This brief reference underlines the scale of Japanese espionage and other preparations for the invasion of Malaya, long before they began their 70-day campaign. Colonel Tanikawa and his companion were able to report every detail of military interest on Singapore Island.

On 8 December, 1941, Shenton Thomas began writing his war diary, on foolscap-size paper and covering every day until the final entry on 14 February, 1942, the day preceding the capitulation. He wrote it as usual – all 68 pages – in pencil in his neat and legible handwriting, with the following title page:

GOVERNMENT HOUSE
SINGAPORE

My War Diary
Dec. 8 41–Feb. 14 42
The complete diary is the pencil copy below
T.S.W.T.

It has been stamped as received in the Colonial Office on 13 April, 1942.

This diary well shows the involvement of the Governor with military commanders in the controversial conduct of the campaign, including Shenton's personal opinion of General Percival and the other service leaders. The extracts that follow provide, as it were, a picture book of the Governor at war, with captions furnished by the comments and quotations below each entry.

The War Diary

December 8   1.15 a.m.
Percival telephoned that Japanese were shelling beaches at Kota Bharu. I telephoned Police to collect all Japanese for internment and also to put in force the scheme for seizing Japanese power boats in harbour. Both done very successfully and without incident. At 4 a.m. Pulford (A.O.C.) "phoned approach of hostile aircraft. I asked how far and he said 25 miles. I had just time to phone Rodgers of Harbour Board and Jeans (head of A.R.P.) before they appeared. Brilliant moon and we had all our lights on. One lot went for the Base area and met lots of wild anti-aircraft

fire. The other, about 6–8 machines, dropped bombs in Raffles Square, near Chinese Protectorate, in the water and towards harbour. All over in a few minutes. No fires but about 60 killed and over 100 injured.

　　Legislative Council today. Drove down during alert. Streets very full. Another alert during Council. No bombs. We inflicted heavy losses off Kota Bharu but our aerodromes in the north were rather badly bombed and several machines destroyed on ground.

I wondered why Shenton did not mention that vital conference at the Naval Base which he had attended at 2.30 a.m. on 8 December (see Chapter I). That he was present can not be in question in view of the evidence of Captain McClelland who had been instructed by Admiral Layton to record the conference unofficially. McClelland knew and recognized the Governor and wrote down verbatim all he said. The actual words Shenton used, particularly his remark about tribal war, are so typical of the man that they could scarcely have been spoken by anyone else. Shenton knew that the meeting was highly secret and that Admiral Phillips did not wish any *official* minutes of it to be taken, which presumably accounts for lack of any reference to it in his diary. Finally, with the time and distance involved, he would have had no difficulty in driving from. G.H. to the Naval Base for the meeting and returning in time to receive Pulford's telephone call at 4 a.m. This explanation is necessary as critics could argue that the Governor could not have attended the conference! McClelland added that "the conference started between 0300 and 0330 hrs, but I could not see my watch as it wasn't luminous and I was in the dark; the 'Air Raid Warning Red' was announced at 0400 and the meeting broke up at 0440." On those timings the Governor certainly could not have returned to G.H. by 4 a.m. I believe then this matter, a question of timing on which great issues so often depend, must remain an enigma. Definite proof probably lies in the top secret cypher telegram that the Admiral sent to Whitehall through McClelland, immediately after his conference, and which is still withheld from public access. That the signal was sent and received in Whitehall is beyond doubt; the plain language office copy lies with the *Prince of Wales* at the bottom of the South China Sea.

All in all it must have been a night of high tension for the Governor, including two drives across the island between G.H. and the Naval Base, followed by Pulford's warning of the near approach of hostile aircraft. That entry in the diary "I had just time to 'phone Jeans (A.R.P.)" underlines the fact that the street lights of Singapore were full on when the bombs fell; it was the first indication to the citizens of Singapore that war had begun. Although we have seen that the actual reason for the illumination was the temporary absence of the Chief

Warden, some writers have severely criticized Shenton Thomas for permitting a state of non-alert on that first night of war in the Far East. Later in this story I have therefore included an assessment of the Governor's part in the civil defence of the Malaya Peninsula.

December 9
Enemy reinforcing in Kelantan and State Government moved to Kuala Krai. Aerodromes in Kelantan, Alor Star, Sungei Patani and Kuantan badly bombed. More machines gone. Singapore quite composed and all first aid posts fully moved. All very reassuring.

The Governor's last sentence referred only to first aid, and not to the true state of the Imperial Army in Malaya, about which he was clearly unaware. As Governor he had inspected many of the regiments and corps, but, as the King's Representative, he would be shown only their "parade" appearance, always admirable for His Excellency. He did not see the reality of the military situation in terms of a soldier's professional knowledge, training, experience and ability to fight long and hard in extremely exhausting battle conditions.

The total number of troops on each side during the short campaign was about the same – at 80,000; but there was no equality otherwise. The Japanese army was homogenous in race, language and customs, thoroughly trained and experienced in jungle warfare and fully equipped with modern weapons, particularly artillery and tanks; their infantry at that time was among the finest in the world. By contrast our army in Malaya consisted of British, Australian, Indian and Malayan troops, with no similarity in language, customs, rates of pay or standards generally. The local Malay territorial forces were inadequately armed and their low state of training made them unfit to take part in mobile warfare. The great majority of the troops were Indian Army units, with fine traditions and well-deserved reputations; but on account of great expansion and pressing needs in the Middle East campaigns they had all been severely milked of their senior, experienced British and Indian officers and other ranks, which had seriously affected their training and efficiency. The proportion of artillery to infantry was low and there was a general shortage of anti-tank guns, light machine guns, mortars and armoured carriers. There were no regular armoured regiments in Malaya; there was one Indian armoured-car regiment (3rd Cavalry), but it had no armoured cars and was equipped only with cumbersome 15-cwt trucks.

It was true that considerable reinforcements had reached Malaya during 1941; but their strength on paper did not match their real military value, for they were sent hastily from India where they had been training for war in desert conditions. They therefore arrived at Singapore ill-equipped and unprepared for jungle warfare, without time to re-train before they were sent into battle against the Japanese. This awesome fate befell the 18th British Division, nine battalions of magnificent fighting men, all territorials from famous East Anglian regiments, the majority of which arrived as late as 29 January, 1942. Unfortunately the division had not been tactically loaded in the troopships, in readiness for battle, and therefore disembarked without its transport, supporting arms or adequate maintenance facilities. So, many fine men in this formation, thrown into battle at the last moment, were either killed or became prisoners-of-war.

I have drawn this picture of the prevailing state of affairs in the army in Malaya because so many of the civil, non-official, population of all races, British, Malay, Chinese, Indian and Eurasian, were not aware of the true conditions. As civilians they had always been remote from professional military men and matters, and war was beyond their ken. Some far-sighted citizens, British planters and contractors, civil engineers and agents of great mercantile houses, kept diaries of what happened when suddenly war came and I was fortunate indeed when Mr Vyvyan Frampton, a highly qualified civil engineer with many years' service in Malaya, gave me the following extract from his diary:

> Before the war began I was in Kuantan, a charming little sea port about half-way up the east coast of Malaya. The European population there consisted of rubber planters, an M.C.S. District Officer, a banker, some independent traders, and a remote, but self-contained, community of tin miners at Sungei Lembing not far from Kuantan. We were well served by a Straits steamship coaster which collected our products, brought us everything we required and provided comfortable passenger accommodation for a pleasant trip to Singapore. We also had our club and golf course. In those happy peaceful days the Governor, H.E. Sir Shenton Thomas, with his wife, sometimes visited us in their yacht, and entertained us. Then one day the powers decreed that an R.A.F. station accommodating one squadron complete with landing ground, hangars, all ancillary buildings, bombing range, and barracks for the ground defence force, was needed urgently. Land (part rubber, part forest and scrub) was acquired and work started.
>
> I was the contractor's agent in charge, and my wife and I were lucky in having a charming old bungalow near the mouth of the Kuantan River, set back slightly from the palm-fringed shoreline. We spent many happy days there, were warmly received and from the outset were made to feel one of the community.
>
> In due course R.A.F. Station, Kuantan, was completed and occupied

by a squadron of Wildebeeste (bomber) aircraft – surely one of the heaviest single-engined planes ever to scramble off the ground, with a top speed of 137 m.p.h.; how slow that seems now!

Then suddenly Pearl Harbour happened. Hong Kong had fallen and the Philippines were attacked. Landings in upper Malaya began and Singapore was threatened; our two great battleships were sunk almost within range of Kuantan. But only two or three minor air raids on us were carried out by the Nips. No high explosive bombs were dropped capable of damaging the landing ground, or destroying the hangars or fuel depots; it seemed as if the Nips were making certain the camp should be complete and ready to be taken over, as they intended! Later, early one morning in Kuantan, I met a man I knew well who asked if I knew that the R.A.F. had skedaddled during the night. I replied 'Not to my knowledge'; so we both drove at once to the station where we found the main gate open, no guard, and no one in sight. All the aircraft were standing in the hangars as usual, labelled with the day's maintenance charts and instructions, etc. All doors were open; offices, stores, workshops, mechanical stores, canteens, bakeries, dining halls, all in good order and brand new – yet no one there. We had a beer. I took a mosquito net and a case of whisky, and returned to Kuantan to report the condition of the R.A.F. Camp to the civil authorities. Of course later I described the whole affair officially to Air H.Q. and asked if an aircraft could be sent to Kuantan, with sufficient pilots to fly back as many of the machines as possible. But I never heard what happened; for then war overtook us too.*

Reading Frampton's diary made me appreciate even more the gulf, professionally and socially, that kept the armed forces in Malaya apart from civilian thought and action. Then I returned to Shenton's War Diary for the third day of the hostilities:

December 10
First meeting of War Council with Duff Cooper as Chairman, both C's-in-C (Admiral Layton and Brooke-Popham), G.O.C (Percival), A.O.C. (Pulford) and myself. Discussed procedures, powers, etc. Duff Cooper seemed to think we were to run the war, but Brooke-Popham said he took his orders from Chiefs of Staff and I that I took mine from Secretary of State for Colonies. Duff Cooper became very aggressive and told Brooke-Popham that he had produced the worst example of the old school tie he had ever known. B.P. behaved splendidly, smiled sweetly and said, "That's not fair". Agreed that Duff Cooper should get the position clarified, but his behaviour was a revelation.

---

* Kuantan was occupied by the Japanese on 5 January, 1942.

Below is Duff Cooper's telegram to Winston Churchill, asking for this clarification, with Shenton's comments endorsed thereon in pencil:

DRAFT TELEGRAM   IMMEDIATE
To Foreign Office
From The Minister for the Far East*
12th December
Following for the Prime Minister
    Some doubts exist in the minds of proposed members of War Council as to scope of its activities. In my view, members, whilst retaining their own responsibilities towards their Service or Civil Chiefs and their own powers of decision should bring before the Council all matters and proposals affecting the conduct of the war and they should be freely discussed. A case in point would have been the decision of the Commander-in-Chief Far Eastern Fleet to take the fleet out on December 8th and the conditions in which that operation was conducted. Had the War Council been in existence at the time that proposal should in my opinion have been brought before it and the opportunity given for views to be expressed and warnings issued — a warning for instance concerning the mentality of the enemy and the likelihood of encountering a suicide bomber squadron. It would still have rested with the Commander-in-Chief to take the decision, having heard the views of his colleagues. Equally decisions on matters of local government still rest with the Governor but he also should when possible consult his colleagues in the Council before taking important decisions.

                              (It appears that this did not go, see
                              minutes of 12 Dec. There is no reply
                              on record.   T.S.W.T)

The above typescript is a fair copy of the original in Shenton's file, including the deletions made in pencil: it is not known who made them. Maybe no reply was sent because Whitehall fully agreed that Tom Phillips should not have taken out Force Z on 8 December!
Shenton's diary continues:

December 10
p.m. Admiral Layton who was to have sailed that morning 'phoned that *Prince of Wales* and *Repulse* had been sunk by air attack. He heard a few minutes before his ship sailed, so he threw everything off and came on

---

* The Council's full title was now WAR COUNCIL FOR THE FAR EAST with, as its chairman, The Rt. Hon. Alfred Duff Cooper, Resident Cabinet Minister at Singapore for Far Eastern Affairs.

shore. Admiral Sir Tom Phillips and Captain Leach gone, but no news of others yet. Japs reported to have landed at Besut in Trengganu, to have entered Perlis and to have attacked Kuantan. A grim day.

For Shenton Thomas a grim situation was indeed developing. The naval disaster alone was bad enough, but now he knew the Japanese were invading four of his Unfederated Malay States – Perlis, Kedah, Kelantan and Trengganu – and had evidently found little difficulty in seizing vital aerodromes. This was politically very serious, for the rulers of the Malay States would now realize that the British Government, which by diplomatic treaty had guaranteed the protection of their territories, was failing to do so. It can have given him little, if any, satisfaction on this day, 10 December, to receive the following telegram from King George VI:

IMPORTANT   GOVERNOR SINGAPORE   PERSONAL
I have it in command from the King to convey to you the following message from His Majesty. Begins. The storm of Japan's wanton attack has broken in the East and Malaya bears the first assaults of the enemy. At this fateful moment I assure you of my high confidence in your leadership. I am at one with you, and their Highnesses the Rulers and the peoples of Malaya, in the trial which you are sustaining. I know that the Empire's reliance on your fearless determination to crush this onslaught will be fully justified, and with God's help the devoted service of every man and woman in Malaya shall contribute to our victory. Ends.   Private Secretary.

I wonder if the Governor showed this telegram to Duff Cooper!

Meanwhile, as if there were not enough problems for one day, Shenton suddenly found trouble of an entirely different kind affecting his personal staff. Just after Admiral Layton had telephoned the ill news about *Prince of Wales* and *Repulse*, Lady Thomas wanted to see one of the staff on some urgent matter. Unusually, he could not be found and was not answering his telephone, so Daisy Thomas went herself to his bedroom in Government House. She was not altogether pleased and in a hurry, so, having knocked, she opened the door and went straight in. There, to her utter amazement, she saw the man in bed with his girlfriend!

Daisy Thomas had been strictly brought up, with all the taboos of a generation now long past, and any idea that one of the Governor's staff should absent himself from his duties in the afternoon, *and* be caught *in flagrante delicto*, quite horrified her! As she herself was reported to have said, "That he should choose this day of all days"! Anyway the incident could not be condoned, and the offender was promptly sacked!

> *December 11*
> We learn 2,000 saved from the ships. Billy Handcock, Lt. Commander Humphreys, Commander Norman and Lt. Commander Nelson arrived to stay with us. Handcock with bruised ankle, Norman with water on knee, and Nelson with very bad bruises at base of spine. As he jumped the ship heeled over and he landed on the bilge keel from 30 feet. He thinks others doing same broke their backs.
>
> Heavy raid on Penang: much damage to Beach Street, Georgetown, and many casualties. Population streaming out.

The Governor already knew of the unfortunate start of the battle for Northern Malaya. All British troops north of Johore were under command of General Sir Lewis Heath's III Corps, consisting of 9th and 11th Indian Infantry Divisions. Brooke-Popham had been given permission as early as 5 December to launch a long-planned, pre-emptive operation inside Thai territory, without reference to London, provided the Japanese invaded Thailand, or were advancing with the apparent intention of landing on the Kra Isthmus. This operation involved an *offensive* drive into Thailand (Operation "Matador"), with the aim of denying the Japanese the use of the port of Singora, the adjacent airfields, and the railway and road to the Malayan frontier; in addition there was an alternative *defensive* move ("Krohcol") to stop and hold the Japanese just inside Thai territory. Both operations were planned, above all, to gain time for simultaneous British moves to disrupt Japanese attacks, principally by air strikes from those northern aerodromes. It is now a matter of history how Brooke-Popham, unable to make up his mind, failed to make a decision either way until it was too late. Amazingly, it was not until 9 a.m. on 8 December, seven hours after the Japanese landings at Kota Bharu, that Brooke-Popham ordered Percival to cancel "Matador" and operate "Krohcol". These orders, for unexplained reasons, did not reach General Heath at Kuala Lumpur until 1 p.m.

Inevitably this long delay was fatal for all British plans; and, sadly, looking at the whole concept of "Matador" again, historians may well blame Brooke-Popham for his lack of boldness – "vision" is perhaps a better word – in not seizing the opportunity, say very early on 6 December, to take possession of those airfields in the Singora-Pattani

area. A staff officer* has aptly described the situation at B.P.'s Headquarters:

> We were at the first degree of readiness. Whitehall had said (telegram
> C.O.S. 50) they had American assurances of armed support, and our
> C-in-C could order the invasion of Thailand if he knew a Jap convoy
> was about to land on the Kra Isthmus; in fact our air reconnaissance had
> already spotted many Japanese war and merchant ships, some steaming
> west towards Malaya, and some north. Excitement ran high in G.H.Q.
> as we gathered round the big map, wondering if B.P. would now order
> the invasion of Thailand. He didn't, though 11th Indian Division were
> ready for "Matador", well trained and eager to go. If we had gone in,
> before the Japs landed, and had been in possession of, and able to use,
> the Singora airfields we could have given fighter protection to *Prince of
> Wales* and *Repulse* on the morning of December 10th – and probably
> saved them.

What a thought!

Whether or not "Matador" could have succeeded is debatable. What
is certain is that the lack of "Matador", together with the failure of
"Krohcol", allowed the Japanese virtually undisputed passage across
Thailand's southern frontier into the Malay States of Perlis and
Kedah; this brought them close to the vital airfields, and, equally
important, to those good, well-developed rail and road communications that led to South Malaya. Shenton had already noted the
successful Japanese advance in the states of Kelantan and Trengganu.
Briefly then, the position now was that the 11th Division in Kedah had
been severely mauled and was not in contact with 9th Division on the
eastern flank of the central mountain range. Overall General Heath's
III Corps was in bad shape.

Meanwhile in Singapore the War Council met every day at 8.45 a.m.,
and copies of the minutes, recording their discussions and decisions,
were distributed to all the members. Shenton kept his records of these
minutes (eight very bulky and now tattered files) alongside his personal
war diary, and comparison of the two shows, inter alia, the restraint of
the official minutes in contrast to the private opinions of the Governor.
There is also a separate file dealing with certain matters of Civil
Defence. I can only quote here important extracts from this mass of
material, while keeping in juxtaposition relevant entries from the
official and personal papers.

* Brigadier I. R. Graeme, C.B, C.B.E. (then G.S.O. 2 at B.P.'s H.Q.) to the author, April,
1982.

December 12

Another raid on Penang and much migration. Hard fighting in Kedah.

Minutes of the War Council meeting on the same day referred to the following:

(a) The hard fighting on roads and communications in Kedah; touch lost with two forward battalions and a possible breakthrough by enemy forces using tanks. Believed Sultan of Trengganu in communication with Japanese. The Governor wanted information immediately of anything affecting civil population.

(b) H.E. also raised the question of getting away 3,000 tons of tin from Butterworth and Penang by rail.

(c) Functions of Council. The Minister said he did not want to burden the Prime Minister at such a time. Brooke-Popham stressed he did not like the idea of using a lever behind the backs of the Chiefs of Staff in London. If the Minister sent a telegram to the Prime Minister, then he would have to inform the Chiefs of Staff accordingly.

The Governor's continued anxiety about the Rulers and their people is very clear, as well as his efforts to keep the flow of tin going, notwithstanding the military situation. B.P. seems to have got his own back following his quarrel with Duff Cooper on 10 December!

In those northern states the civilian population's normal life had been abruptly shattered; meanwhile the Malayan Medical Service embarked on a heroic task which has probably never had sufficient recognition. A young British doctor* kept an account of those days which aptly describes the impact of the fighting on his life and work.

When the campaign began I was a very junior surgeon stationed in Kulim Hospital in south Kedah. On Sunday 8th December 1941 Penang was raided by enemy planes. We saw them fly over Kulim and took them without thought to be ours on some sort of exercise. However, during the afternoon the truth that war had come diffused slowly into the minds of us all – Asians and British civilians. Then on Monday, Sungei Patani in central Kedah was bombed from the air, causing about one hundred casualties among its citizens, and I was told to go to the town hospital and deal with them. Off I went, taking my golf clubs with me and expecting to stay in Sungei Patani for whatever number of months, or perhaps weeks, were needed by our army to drive the Japanese out of Malaya.

* Henry McGladerry, O.B.E, F.R.C.S., to the author January, 1982.

The hospital was in good order with all its staff present – British and Asian – and we spent the next four days giving the wounded all necessary surgery and treatment without any difficulty; no further air raids on Sungei Patani occurred. I lived with Dr Routley, the Health Officer, in the bungalow of a rubber planter who had gone south, and we greatly enjoyed the comfort, though without servants, of a house in full working order, with food and drinks from his refrigerator, etc.

Then suddenly the scene changed. All British women, including my wife, were sent south to Johore and Singapore by road and rail, and soon too we British doctors were ordered south. The disheartening experience of constant retreat had begun. Yet the medical service survived, and we continued to treat and care for the injured and the sick; we must have saved life and limb of hundreds, perhaps thousands, of wounded civilians and soldiers.

I remember once we felt that now at last the Japanese would be stopped. But an artillery officer told me that we had no gun that would disable enemy tanks, and had no tanks of our own. By then I had treated very large numbers of army wounded, both British and Indian, and I had formed an admiration for the infantry which I still retain. They fight so well and risk so much in actual combat with the enemy. . . . I don't think we foresaw the end; our morale was good and we continued to work for the people of Malaya until practically the whole of the Malayan Medical Service were taken into internment, from the hospitals where they were still tending the injured and the sick.

We must now return to Shenton's diary:

December 13
More air raids on Penang. Decided in War Council that I should visit Kuala Lumpur, but later withdrawn on account of (false) report of Japanese armada en route to Singapore. I spoke about Penang and bad conditions. No one to bury the dead; water mains burst; fire engines out of action and fires still burning. Looting because people could not buy food, all shops shut. I asked whether we were going to defend the place or leave it. Percival replied that we shall defend to the last to the best of our ability. Decided that I should advise European women and children to leave and other Europeans who wanted to. That was the Council minute, but my own note at the meeting was: "The European women and children should be allowed to go if they wish. Policy is to defend Penang. Difficulties great but that is the fixed decision. European men also should be allowed to go if they wish, but any who desire to stay and help – let them." In fact my telegram on that day to Forbes (Resident Commissioner) said that: "European males should not, repeat not, be encouraged to leave, and to all who stay of whatever race I send my sincere thanks for their courage and determination and my sympathy in this time of trial." 'Phoned above to Forbes.

The minutes of the War Council for 13 December reveal for the first
time a depressing atmosphere, a presage almost of defeat; this gloomy
attitude was introduced by Duff Cooper who spoke in the following
terms:

> We should now ask ourselves is it possible with barely four divisions
> (mainly Indian), with only three squadrons of fighter aircraft not all
> properly trained, without command of the sea, to defend a country the
> size of England? The Japanese can reinforce quicker, land anywhere. If
> not possible, then we should consider change of plan. Real question is
> the defence of the Naval Base by holding Johore. . . . There is a need to
> withdraw to Johore and hold the island to the last.

This defeatist talk, by a Cabinet Minister to his service Chiefs, was
anathema to Shenton Thomas who expected servicemen, everywhere,
to exhibit courage, guts, stamina and a determination to win. But he
said nothing more until the following day.

In his diary for 14 December Shenton wrote at length about his
speech at the War Council that day; first about Penang and the very bad
moral effect of a withdrawal from the island. Percival had circulated a
memo setting out the pro's and con's of withdrawal but *no* final
conclusion or recommendation. However, the Governor did not feel
competent to oppose a military decision *if* it was thought right to
withdraw the Penang garrison in order to reinforce the Kedah troops.
He added that "most of the Island Police had disappeared and the dead
continue to lie unburied." Shenton went on to describe the measures
that he proposed to take with the Attorney General, to "buttress" Civil
Defence. The measures could and would be passed in one hour by a
special session of the Legislative Council; they would provide legal
authority for the courts to take new and stringent powers on the
following lines: Instant trial, without jury, for any kind of 5th column
activity, including death penalty on conviction; treachery and looting
would also carry the death penalty if proven. People showing lights
during air raids or emergency periods could be shot at, and any person
who did not halt when challenged by a sentry could also be shot.

The diary also illustrates the growing difference of attitude to war
measures generally, and particularly now over Penang, between Shenton and Percival, the Army Commander. For the Governor "defend to
the last" means exactly that, but the General qualifies it with "but only
to the best of our ability", though well knowing that his ability could not
be sustained. Percival tables "pro's and con's" but does *not* add his own
conclusion and recommendation. Increasingly from now on we see

Shenton Thomas *en rapport* with Lieutenant-General Sir Lewis Heath
more than with Lieutenant-General Percival; probably this was natural
and inevitable. Heath was typically a fighting soldier, an Indian Army
officer, and an experienced commander, fresh from his recent suc-
cesses in the African campaigns of 1940–41; he had not been to the
Staff College. Percival was essentially a highly experienced and brilliant staff officer, but quite untried as a commander and lacking the
drive and ruthlessness which the situation in Malaya desperately
needed; probably he was altogether "too nice" to be a successful
military leader in war.

The issue of Penang – stand and defend or evacuate and retreat –
dominated the diary and the War Council minutes. Shenton argued
strongly in favour of no racial discrimination in evacuation; anything of
the sort, he said, might well turn the population against the authorities.
Duff Cooper said he personally would give preference to Europeans
over all Asiatics, though he would not say so publicly! Shenton added:

> *December 15*
> The others gave me little support, being presumably swayed by purely
> service considerations. But my argument was that if we are going to win
> this war we must win it decently. Evacuation so far of European women
> and children only, from Penang, had already caused comment and
> comparison with Hong Kong.

Shenton's stand on his evacuation policy stemmed directly from his
long experience in Africa, with his belief in trusteeship and indirect
rule; this was really the key to his character, which in this respect never
changed. He left defence matters to the military authority, but his duty
was to the local people themselves and the land that they owned. All this
brought him problems.

> *December 16*
> Corps Headquarters in K.L. have ordered demolition of Penlaga Cable
> Station (Penang) so Government no longer have a direct cable link with
> India and U.K., except through old line via Batavia. Services have their
> own W/T to U.K. but already overloaded. Fraser [Federal Secretary]
> 'phoned from K.L. that Heath, instructed by Percival, has ordered all
> European women and children to leave Perak State. I told Fraser that
> this [military] order was entirely invalid as far as I was concerned, and
> should not be carried out, without reference to me.
> *December 17*
> Big row in War Council. I was told off by Duff Cooper who said that
> Heath's position would be impossible if I countermanded his orders. It

did not matter to Duff Cooper that there were no enemy troops in Perak, or that from the northern State boundary to the southern by road must be well over 100 miles. Eventually agreed that civil government will not order compulsory evacuation of civilians from any area, but if a military commander considers military situation justifies it he may order compulsory evacuation by the civilian population. Meanwhile evacuation of European women and children from such large area as Perak, far from the front line, *with no mention of Asiatics*, must have a deplorable effect.

It was on this day that Percival ordered the withdrawal of III Corps behind the Perak River, a very considerable distance, as Shenton noted. It proved that the battle for northern Malaya was lost, and with it the concept that defence of the country rested largely on the strength and efficiency of air power, relying on the ability to hold, and operate from, those northern airfields. As a result Percival had to rethink his strategy, which had been to contain the enemy in the north for at least two months until those much needed reinforcements arrived. Unfortunately the plain fact now was that, after only ten days' fighting, the Japanese had control of sea and air, and the 11th Division, weak and exhausted after suffering heavy losses, was in retreat and having to fight a delaying action along the vital communications on the west side of the peninsula. The defeat of 11th Division would leave open the main railway and road to Singapore, while on the east side of the central range the 9th Division was also withdrawing and could not cross the mountains to assist the hard-pressed 11th; the 9th had already suffered heavy losses in transport and weapons but was still a fighting formation.

The British were learning, and Shenton certainly did not appreciate, that, in jungle warfare over mountainous country with very few roads, motor vehicles, particularly heavy lorries, are a severe handicap and a positive invitation to air attack. The Japanese had learnt this lesson and their infantry made extensive use of cyclists moving along jungle tracks, with small, two-wheeled, very light handcarts, easily stripped down and re-assembled. By such means the Japanese largely eliminated the orthodox, slow-moving administrative "tail" that so hampered mobility, particularly in the jungle-clad mountains of the Malayan central range. A company of Japanese infantry, each man equipped with only his weapons, including explosives, a bag of rice and a medical first aid pack, could operate quite independently in the jungle for days on end. It was sub-units such as these that so often put up road blocks by infiltrating *behind* the line of withdrawal of retreating British units; the only effective remedy was to prohibit use of the words "front line" and adopt counter-encirclement tactics, aimed at attacking the enemy and cutting *his* communications.

> *December 18*
> We are to go back to the Perak river line owing to Japanese pressure from Grik, due east of Penang. There is only an indifferent road from Grik to the main road south which was prepared for demolition, but this was ineffective. Many men from Penang have arrived now in Singapore, and Grumitt came to stay with us.

The War Council Minutes for this day emphasize the depressing fact that the only reserves available to General Percival for offensive action were two Indian infantry battalions at Kuantan. It was on this day also that the last formal Allied War Conference was held in Singapore, attended by British, American, Dutch, Australian and New Zealand representatives, under the chairmanship of Duff Cooper. The Conference could do nothing except report to the Chiefs of Staff, by telegram from Duff Cooper, that the military situation in Malaya was urgent and very serious; the Japanese had reserve divisions available, and to meet this added threat further large-scale reinforcements of all arms were essential. If the enemy succeeded in taking the airfields in central or southern Malaya they would be able to attack the ship convoys which were due to bring the reinforcements to Singapore.

I have stressed the dangerous military situation on this day because Duff Cooper, without telling Shenton Thomas, simultaneously complained personally to the Prime Minister about the state of government in Malaya. He had sent a letter by air to Winston Churchill expressing his disquiet in regard to the efficiency of Malaya's defence preparations. He added that some senior civilian officials in Singapore did not appear to be able to adjust themselves to war conditions, and that it might later be necessary to make some changes.*

Looking back at this extraordinary scene, three developments now stand out very clearly. First the impropriety of Duff Cooper in writing to the Prime Minister behind the back of the Governor who was the King's representative appointed with the personal approval of the Crown. For Sir Shenton Thomas was ultimately responsible for the role of the civil government in Singapore and Malaya, in the period before, leading up to, and during the Japanese invasion. Next, and to be fair to all concerned, Duff Cooper was a classic case of responsibility without power. He had been "exiled" by Churchill to Singapore with a

---

* Woodburn Kirby (*Official History* p. 233).

vague commission to see what was going on, and to do anything which he thought might be useful. He had no control over the Colonial Government, or for that matter over the armed forces, and had no power whatever to overrule the civil administration. Finally Duff Cooper, although he was an active and intelligent man, totally failed to comprehend the delicacies of the political scene throughout the Straits Settlements and the Malay States; he did not understand the nuances of British relations with Crown Colonies, or the Federated and Unfederated States. This was perhaps his greatest stumbling block.

Meanwhile Shenton, unaware of Duff Cooper's private letter to the Prime Minister, was increasingly concerned at the way in which Penang had been evacuated by the military authorities. For him the loss of the island was another deplorable breach in the edifice of British colonial power and influence in the region for which he was responsible. Some of the Rulers and their peoples in the Malay States had already seen this happen; now it was the turn of Penang, with its largely Chinese population and the first of the Straits Settlements (a Crown Colony) to be lost to the enemy. Shenton recalled Penang with affection; he loved his residence there at the top of the funicular railway 2,600 feet above sea level, and set in a cluster of holiday bungalows and jungle verdure. The hundred or more Chinese (Buddhist) temples filled with images and clouds of incense were a feature of the island; whilst the architecture of Georgetown, with its old colonial mansions, parks and gardens, lent serenity and charm to Malaya's second city.

The Governor's War Diary for the next few days shows how deeply he felt about it all, particularly his sense of outrage at Duff Cooper's attitude to himself.

December 19
Dreadful stories about Penang. It is said that all the European civilians were evacuated on military orders, but they have left the Asiatics with no help. Jones [Colonial Secretary] sent me a note asking if he might attempt to reach Penang to do what he could there, and said that Jordan [Secretary for Chinese Affairs] and others were ready to go with him. But no use now; Japanese are across the roads on the mainland and no ship can get near the island. A most harrowing day. Once again I brought up in War Council the question of evacuation, pointing out that we cannot expect Asiatic morale to be worth anything if we [British] disappear at the first threat. Duff Cooper invariably takes the military view, and then administers severe admonitions to me!
December 20
Such grave forebodings about Penang that I had to meet representative Asiatics this afternoon. Had to tell them that I knew nothing of the

evacuation till it had been carried out, that I had instructed there was to be no racial discrimination, and *that some civil officers at least were expected in future to stay behind to look after their people*. It was the most difficult speech I had ever had to make. Goho, C.I.M.A.,* spoke and I am glad to say believed me; his theme was to forget the past and unite for the future. In War Council we argued about evacuation procedure.

December 21

Very difficult day in Council about discrimination in ordering civil movements. The Army Commander [Percival] and I had agreed on a draft Instruction, but Duff Cooper wouldn't have it. It is very difficult when men, who know something at least of the country and people, are obstructed by one who knows nothing. After the meeting I told Brooke-Popham that Duff Cooper's mission appeared to be primarily to take me, and all connected with me, to task. He agreed.

Report from Kuching that Asiatics in Sarawak are demoralised, and Raja Brooke severely criticised for his absence.

This is the first mention in the War Diary of the High Commissioner's territories in Borneo. The Raja of Sarawak was, perhaps conveniently, in Australia when the Japanese attacked Malaya and he did not return to Kuching until after the war.

December 22

Everyone horrified at Duff Cooper's reference to Penang (in a broadcast he made today) in which he said the majority of the population had been evacuated, whereas in fact it was the small minority of Europeans. He did not show his script to me – or to anyone perhaps? In War Council I finally got a draft on evacuation accepted. The military authority can require the complete *emptying* of an operational area, but in all other cases he will *advise* the civil authority; and there will be no racial discrimination.

Brooke-Popham, who has been relieved by Lt-General Sir Henry Pownall, today asked if I could find him employment – perhaps in the Passive Defence line; he hated leaving at this juncture, but had received no instructions. I said that of course I would gladly have him, until his orders came. He went on to congratulate me on my tactful acceptance of Duff Cooper's assumption of authority! Nice of him, and I responded by saying how well he had behaved when D.C. accused him of having a dreadful old school tie approach!

December 23

Tickled to death by a telegram from Colonial Office *confirming* that evacuation should be made *without* racial discrimination. I am sure Duff Cooper thinks I prompted it! Anyhow there can be no more argument but I am glad we won our point before the telegram came.

---

* Chinese, Indian, and Malay Association.

It is possible that the disputes over the thorny question of evacuation policy might have been avoided, or reduced, by the imposition of martial law. Duff Cooper always pressed for it, Shenton never opposed it, but wished to see the civil courts given all the necessary additional powers; but as late as 24 December General Percival would not have it. Probably as long as there was no single Supreme Commander, with complete authority over military and civil power, the entire suspension of existing civil law would have exacerbated a most difficult scene. Meanwhile Whitehall seemingly bent over backwards to aggravate the military picture by a directive given to General Pownall, on the departure of Brooke-Popham! For any professional soldier today this directive will surely appear as nothing but a contradiction in terms. Pownall was told that:

> He was to be jointly responsible with the C-in-C Eastern Fleet for the conduct of British strategy in the Far East, but it was not intended that he should assume operational control, or the administrative and financial responsibilities, and the normal day-to-day functions, exercised by the G.O.C.s in Malaya, Burma and Hong Kong, and by the A.O.C. Far East.

Meanwhile, let us look at the overall military picture in Malaya at this time, just before Christmas, 1941, from the viewpoint of General Yamashita commanding the Japanese 25th Army. So far he had found little difficulty in driving the British Army southward, and, to his surprise, he had been able to cross the Perak River virtually unopposed by the British 11th Division, which was now deployed covering Ipoh and Kampar. He therefore believed that the fighting ability of the British troops was so reduced that III Corps would probably offer serious resistance only at long intervals, and would rely almost entirely on destruction of bridges and communications to delay his own advance. His aim now was to capture Ipoh and then advance rapidly southward along the rail and road lines, with Kuala Lumpur in central Malaya as his next main objective.

Regrettably Yamashita's appreciation of the British Army's condition at this stage was not inaccurate. The losses through casualties in all British regiments, including senior officers, had been very heavy. General Murray-Lyon, commanding 11th Division, had been replaced by Brigadier Paris, an officer with considerable experience of bush warfare, but all the original brigade commanders of the division were in hospital and new brigadiers had been appointed; the cumulative effect of such changes could not fail to weaken the standard of command at all battalion levels. Perhaps most serious of all was the fact that in every unit of 11th Division the men were suffering from sheer fatigue, though their fighting spirit in all ranks, British and Indian, was never in doubt and they had fought magnificently against great odds. An eye-witness account, quoted in the *Official History*, recorded that:

> The troops were very tired. Constant enemy air attacks prevented them from obtaining any sleep by day. By night they either had to move, obtaining such sleep as was possible in crowded lorries, or had to work on preparing yet another defensive position. The resultant physical strain of day and night fighting, of nightly moves or work, and the consequent lack of sleep was cumulative and finally reached the limit of endurance. Officers and men moved like automata and often could not grasp the simplest order.*

The 9th Infantry Division of General Heath's III Corps, on the east side of the mountains, had also been forced to withdraw southward, into Pahang State. At this time the Division still controlled Kuantan and its important airfield and was deployed on the general line of the east to west road axis from Maran–Jerantut–Kuala Lipis–Raub. Possession of Kuantan and its airfield was very important, for without them 9th Division could not fulfil its role of protecting 11th Division, and its communications, from attacks from the east.

Meanwhile the island and city of Singapore were still a comparatively long way from the battle area. Kuala Lumpur was some 250 miles from Johore Bahru, and by Christmas Day the Japanese had not yet taken Ipoh. So the war, in spite of sporadic air raids and the flow of casualties and refugees that steadily encroached on the city, still seemed distant from the day-to-day life of the European civil community; a sense or appearance of remoteness from hostilities frequently led to ignorance of the real military situation, blended with a quite unjustified spirit of optimism, yet always a fine determination to win. This general attitude comes through clearly in the personal diary of an English lady, Mrs Savage-Bailey. She was the Librarian at Raffles Museum and in charge of the A.R.P. Station there, where many came to shelter during air raids, and later on from artillery bombardment. Her diary tells a very human story, frequently relying on hearsay, but probably a unique record of the thoughts of a civilian, aged about 45–50, at this time.

---

* The reality of retreat in war generally brings hardship like this. There is, however, one qualification which can govern the outcome, the calibre of the commander. In Burma the retreating army was commanded by Slim. In Malaya there was no Slim.

In the end Mrs Savage-Bailey got away in an evacuation ship on 12 February, but her vessel was sunk by the Japanese and she was drowned. She had this to say about Singapore at Christmas time 1941.

> Dec. 22. Brings news that fighting in Kedah is going strong, and raiders have been shot down over K.L. Everyone here is having shelters dug, a bit late, but better late than never. Nine more enemy aircraft also shot down, otherwise nothing much is happening in the north.

In fact the news from K.L. was very bad, and the following day the A.O.C. gave orders to begin evacuation of its airfield.

> Dec. 25. Xmas day, and what a day! Hong Kong has fallen. More speeches to the Malayan population that "help is coming", but all are rather gloomy about things at the moment.
>
> Dec. 28. We had our first big air-raid last night, and tried out the air shelter. All right, but they are useless every time it rains (which is every day!) as they tend to flood and get washed out. Also the Chinese amahs push their way into the middle of the shelter, and do more to upset the children than help! Malacca had an air-raid, it seems ridiculous for sleepy Malacca to have anything so up to date.
>
> Dec. 29. From up-country the good news of very heavy losses to the Japs, near Sungei Siput, 15 miles from Ipoh. The Japs have very stupidly hit the great mosque in K.L. and killed people at prayers; now the Malays and Indians are against them. Jap planes have dropped leaflets on Singapore, the jolly text of which reads: "Burn all the White Devils in the sacred White Flame of Victory"!
>
> Dec. 29. A good trap was laid for the Japs in the north, by ambush in which we killed 400–500, and the rest fled. We are getting rather full of refugees, but two big loads of women and children have left for Australia; we can't keep too many here and want to get the children away quickly. Only four casualties last night in the air-raid, and those were really the people's own fault, they won't take precautions and stand about like stuck pigs when the bombs are falling.

The fighting spirit of the diarist shines through brightly. At the turn of the year there was no thought of defeat in Singapore. This was the line taken by Daisy Shenton Thomas when she broadcast to the women of Malaya on 28 December. She extolled the virtues of courage and the need to set an example:

> Stick to your job, whatever it is, and whatever happens. Courage is very catching and even though we may be frightened inside, if we do not show it others will take heart. There is work for everyone, hospitals to be

manned and equipped are but one example, and when we are working hard we shall have no time for worry. The men need any rest they can get, and we can help by not bothering them with our own worries.

Clearly Shenton Thomas felt let down by H.M.G. when official news reached Singapore of the surrender of Hong Kong to the Japanese on 25 December. He wrote about it in his War Diary, but made no mention of Christmas Day.

December 26
News of Hong Kong's capitulation. What a waste of men and money! It must have been obvious that the place could not hold out with no defence against the air, no ships, and only a few troops; the latter might have made just the difference if sent here as reinforcement. Instead we push in two battalions of Canadians, to Hong Kong, at the last minute. How much did our resistance retard the Japanese war effort there? Very little. There seems a lack of clear thinking and honest speaking at home.

Looking back, it is easy to appreciate the Governor's feelings of frustration when he compared the Hong Kong surrender with his own plight. The two Canadian battalions, however, had an unfortunate resemblance to those nine battalions of the British 18th Division that were yet to reach Singapore. The Canadians also disembarked *minus* their lorries or carriers and arrived in Hong Kong straight from peacetime garrison duty in the West Indies and Newfoundland, totally unfit for active service.

The entries in the Governor's diary for the last few days of 1941 mirrored his increasing problems with Duff Cooper. The two men seem to have been totally irreconcilable in their respective ideas and aims in every way. For Shenton Thomas it was unthinkable that he, the Governor and personal representative of the King, should be harassed in Council and subjected to personal attack and discourtesy by a Minister of the Crown – particularly one who had no formal authority of official power of any kind. Phrases like these appear in his diary:

Listened to a rather offensive harangue by D.C. on the law's delays over martial law; quite irrelevant as Percival refused his consent until December 24th.

Very difficult to deal with a man who is determined to find the civil government in the wrong on all matters.

Finally Shenton decided that he ought to visit Kuala Lumpur and Selangor, to see for himself the political, economic and administrative conditions, and do what he could to help his senior M.C.S. officers. Again it was typical of the man that he should try to get as close as possible, within the limits of his gubernatorial position, to the fighting and see how "his people" were getting on. He left for Kuala Lumpur by road early on 29 December, having entered in his diary:

> I knew I must be in Singapore if a big air raid, or attack came on, but I felt I must take the risk of being away, and the C-in-C [General Pownall] agreed.

Shenton wrote a five page story, attached to his diary, of his trip to K.L. There is no official account elsewhere of this journey which took him as far as Slim River, 60 miles north of Kuala Lumpur. He met many people, military and civil, including General Heath, the corps commander, and his own senior civil officers who were still running the administration as best they could. Though he made no mention of it, Shenton had taken Daisy with him – she had refused to stay behind – and she merely appears, in the account of his various visits, as "D came round with me and cheered up the girls". Otherwise Shenton's account reflected his determination to keep the government machine working, unless and until the military operations superseded all else. This shows clearly in the following extracts:

> Arrived in Malacca during air raid alert. Had long talk with Bryant [Resident Commissioner] who seemed rather at sea, and had let all his European women leave though much too soon. Generally he seemed to be guided by some nondescript junior military officer! Told him he must not act save on definite advice from III Corps, and in any doubt refer to me.
>
> In K.L. found Fraser [Federal Secretary] in King's House (our residence) working with Evans [Legal Adviser] and Treasury clerks – all very makeshift as indeed it has to be. Visited Post and Telegraph girls, Police, A.R.P., Food, Municipal, P.W.D. officers; all functioning quietly and well. Stayed with Jarrett [M.C.S.]; he and his wife very well and in hand. Next morning left early for Tanjong Malim where found Neave [District Officer], Baeza [Senior M.O.], Anderson [Health Officer] with Harrison Jones [Cadet]. All in one bungalow, with one so-called cook but otherwise no help; do own sanitation, etc., as no sweepers. I gave Neave a letter that, in the circumstances, if Military have to leave the State [Selangor] they should come away too, with any Asiatic staff who wished.
>
> Returning to K.L. went to Railway H.Q. where met Smart the General Manager. Trains running but only during night and guards and engine drivers now get free rice, having sent families away. Train control

working well with Asiatic staff carrying on. Met General Heath who agrees with my letter to Neave. He does not want martial law as existing legislation gives him all he wanted. To our great joy the little luxuries (beer, cigarettes, whisky, etc.) which Neave & Co at Tanjong Malim so badly needed have reached them.

On his return to Singapore late on 31 December Shenton Thomas found that Duff Cooper, during his absence, had authorised two new senior appointments under the civil government, and had promulgated each in a War Council Minute under his own authority. Copy of this Minute, dated 31 December, is below:

The present system of civil defence is unsound. A certain lack of. confidence exists in the civil population. A surer way of restoring public confidence was to take a new line, or some drastic step, *so that the public feel that at last something has been done* (author's italics). The time has now come when one man should be appointed who would have supreme control, unhampered by petty restrictions and applications to Committee. This man should have experience of air raids, and similar difficulties in this war. It was unanimously decided that Brigadier Simson should be appointed Controller of Civil Defence, with plenary powers under the War Council, through H.E. It was decided that the Colonial Secretary would report this to H.E. on his arrival this afternoon.

Shenton's reaction to this development is best shown by his diary.

December 31
There is serious political trouble. Duff Cooper, being led by the nose by Bisseker and Seabridge, demands a kind of Dictator for Civil Defence in Brig. Simson, who does know a lot about it and is in every sense welcome; and Bisseker is to be Director of Road Transport or something of the sort. Duff Cooper has officially appointed Bisseker, and War Council has officially appointed Simson, all in my absence and without my knowledge, though neither has authority to make any appointments under the civil government. I cannot agree to Bisseker; everyone would think I had gone mad, or had surrendered to D.C. Then Seabridge has written an article in the *Straits Times* in which he says that either I must give way to D.C., or D.C. to me. I don't care, but it is fearfully bad for morale, just at the most critical time. I must see D.C. and try to make him see light.

This is the first mention of Bisseker in Shenton's diary. Mr F. D. Bisseker had been General Manager of the Eastern Smelting (Tin) Co.

Ltd at Penang and was now, according to Duff Cooper, to be Deputy-General Civil Defence (under Brigadier Simson) and Director of Labour and Transport, all from 1 January, 1942; he was already an elected unofficial member of the Malayan Legislative Council. From 1939 onwards Bisseker had been a strong and persistent critic of the Governor, who in turn regarded Bisseker as highly unreliable and untrustworthy, and foremost in that "European scuttle" from Penang which Shenton Thomas had so vehemently condemned. Brigadier Simson was the Chief Engineer at Percival's Headquarters and had arrived in Malaya in August, 1941.*

A look at that Minute of Duff Cooper's clearly shows how he waited until the Governor had left Singapore in order, without mentioning the latter by name, to denounce him categorically and then try virtually to strip him of all responsibility for civil defence, even though martial law had been declared on 30 December. It shows the critical position, at the turn of the year, of the relationship between the two men – the near detestation of the one for the other.

The next day Shenton, typically, went to Duff Cooper and tackled him openly about his conduct during Shenton's absence; he wrote in his diary:

> *January 1, 1942*
> I questioned Duff Cooper at War Council Meeting. Surprisingly he was quite meek and agreed that I (not the War Council) should formally appoint and issue any communique about Simson who is to be responsible to me. We then went through the *Straits Times* leader and he agreed with all I said, including that I should repeat our conversation to Seabridge and say that he (D.C.) agreed. I did this later, pointing out to Seabridge that his article was written "on inside information" which must have come via D.C. who might, and probably did, talk to Bisseker who passed it on to Seabridge. All very lofty and helpful! It struck me that D.C. was a bit frightened, and well he might be. Later I was told that D.C. had 'phoned Seabridge as soon as I had left him! I then received a telegram from Colonial Office about Seabridge's article in *Straits Times* on December 31st. "What did it mean?" I toned down my reply as far as I could, but I had to hint that D.C. is very much in with Seabridge!

Meanwhile the tactical situation facing the unfortunate 11th Infantry Division developed rapidly and very adversely during the first week of the New Year, culminating in disastrous defeat for virtually the whole

---

* In his book *Singapore, too little, too late* (Leo Cooper 1970) Simson strongly blames both the Army and the Civil Government for the lack of pre-planned defences in Malaya.

division at the Slim River action on 7 January. Most writers on the campaign have agreed that the result of this battle as good as sealed the fate of Malaya and Singapore. After a brief pause, following their successful crossing of the Perak River, the Japanese staged a further relentless and very bold thrust down that vital main road and railway line, using tanks and light armoured fighting vehicles in strength. 11th Divison had no tanks and its anti-tank troops were weak and quickly overpowered, with the result that the enemy were able to capture the Slim River bridge intact. The British communications were poor, which added to their difficulties and increased their casualties. One infantry unit (the 5/2 Punjab Regiment) fought most gallantly, until at the end the effective strength of the battalion was reduced to one officer and eighty men. These figures speak for themselves and show the stamina and determination of Indian troops, and their British officers, to fight on until almost literally the last man.

Certainly the strategic result of the action at Slim River was a major disaster for General Percival's planning. He now knew that central Malaya must shortly be abandoned; by 7 January all British forces had withdrawn south of Slim River, and in Pahang the Japanese had occupied Kuantan. By 12 January the enemy had taken Kuala Lumpur and Port Swettenham. All this prejudiced his ability to hold Northern Johore long enough to enable his expected reinforcements to acclimatize, train, and re-equip for jungle warfare, before facing the enemy in battle.

By now important political and military changes, arising out of America's entry into the war, were beginning to effect the whole system of Allied High Command. General Sir Archibald Wavell had been appointed Commander-in-Chief of all armed forces in South East Asia (abbreviated to ABDACOM, Commander of American, British, Dutch, Australian Forces). His appointment was to have far-reaching results, particularly in Malaya, where Wavell's influence was apparent from the moment he arrived at Singapore:

January 7
General Wavell arrived late today from Chungking via Rangoon. He had a very lucky journey as the pilot lost his way and very nearly came down at Bangkok in mistake for Rangoon; then his pilot erred again and landed at Moulmein (Burma), eventually arriving at Rangoon 10 minutes before Japanese bombers raided the airfield – what time Wavell watched from a slit trench that was almost in the centre of the bomb bracket!
January 8
Wavell seemed as sturdy as ever after his air journey. Mrs Boxer and

Miss Murray (of my cypher staff) are to join Wavell. Quite right; he has a good picker on his staff! Discussed Johore with Wavell, Pownall and Dickinson (Inspector General, Police). Position on Slim River very bad as enemy have cut off our troops. Before the War Council Meeting Percival told me that we had taken a knock, and we should probably have to withdraw to somewhere about Segamat in Johore.

Clearly Wavell had arrived at a moment of grave crisis.

VII

DEFEAT AND SURRENDER

January 9

In War Council Duff Cooper announced that Wavell's appointment had made his own unnecessary and that he is leaving. Valediction to War Council. I said I thought his presence had been very useful as it had enabled us all to get a conspectus of the situation. Actually Duff Cooper's departure will be hailed with shouts of joy! He is suspect by most people; partly for his broadcast reference to the evacuation of the "majority" of the population from Penang (well knowing it could only refer to Europeans) and partly for the Simson-Bisseker-Seabridge racket. I shall see him out with a sigh of relief. A rotten judge of men, arrogant, obstinate, vain; how he could have crept into (Cabinet) Office is beyond me, and indeed beyond us all. Lady Diana has not appeared since the war began, and we gather has complete jitters! Their God is publicity. Wavell has said the Jap's breakthrough at Slim River should not have happened if proper dispositions had been made. It was Paris's* 11th Division. Poor wretched troops.

Thus Shenton Thomas in his war diary on the day he heard that the Duff Coopers were leaving Singapore and would not return.

Wavell had flown to Kuala Lumpur the previous day to see General Heath, and then on to the battle area to meet the 11th Division Commander and see for himself the parlous condition of the Division, after its disastrous defeat at Slim River. On his return to Singapore Wavell told Percival and the Governor that 11th Division had ceased to be an effective fighting force. He had therefore decided there was literally no alternative but to accept a complete withdrawal and concentration of all British forces, including 9th Division from Pahang, behind a new defence line on the Muar River in North Johore. This fateful decision would allow the Japanese to advance, with virtually no opposition, through the Malay States of Selangor, Negri Sembilan and the Malacca Settlement. Factually this would not be withdrawal; it would be a forced retreat by rail and road for 120 miles, through the most populous and busy States of Malaya with their considerable road

---

* Brigadier A. C. M. Paris, Acting Commander 11th Infantry Division.

systems and beaches suitable for landings by amphibious troops intent on cutting the communication lines of the forces retreating on Johore.

Above all, this long move would have to be made in great haste; there had been withdrawals before from North Malaya, but not on such a large scale, nor with a need to move immediately. For instance, Percival was now in no doubt that all European officials and residents, and the whole apparatus of civil government, must leave Kuala Lumpur not later than Friday 10 January. The army, too, must move south at speed, as the Japanese were closing in on K.L.

It has to be said that Wavell's decision, made suddenly on 8 January, to withdraw the entire III Corps into North Johore, without any attempt at delaying action, led to an immense loss of reserve stores at K.L. and elsewhere. Only the previous day Shenton had written in his diary, *à propos* denial of oil stocks to the enemy, that "Percival had agreed that one month's supply for civil use should be retained in the Negri Sembilan fuel tanks at Port Dickson". It followed that, for lack of time, bulky equipment and stores which could not be moved had to be destroyed; large petrol and oil stocks at Kuala Lumpur and Port Swettenham were run to waste or fired; buildings and store sheds, food stocks and military installations were demolished, and airfield runways cratered. Inevitably, however, much equipment and military stores of value fell into enemy hands, including many vehicles in working order.

Later Wavell admitted that his plan doubtless invited certain dangers; it involved taking a calculated risk by weakening the defences of the east coast to strengthen the immediately threatened west, which was in danger of being completely overrun. It was, he said, a question of timing, between the rate of Japanese advance and the arrival of British reinforcements. In the event the Japanese entered and took possession of Kuala Lumpur on 12 January; a large ship convoy, including several big American liners, reached Singapore on the 13th (one British Infantry Brigade, two artillery regiments, one Anti-Tank Regiment and fifty-one Hurricane aircraft in crates), while the retreat of III Corps continued, fortunately almost undisturbed by the enemy, to their new positions in North Johore. By 15 January the military withdrawal had been satisfactorily completed.

Still looking at this picture of military crisis, I well remember Shenton talking about the poor relations between III Corps and G.H.Q., stemming of course from the disparate professional careers and personalities of the two commanders – Heath and Percival; then I found the message* sent by General Percival to his corps commander

* Quoted in *Eastern Epic*, p. 321, by Sir Compton Mackenzie, Chatto & Windus, 1951.

about the time of the withdrawal from Penang (19 December). The text of this message is so extraordinary that it is worth quoting in full. Percival is giving his views on the future conduct of operations and the handling of troops by III Corps:

> Our young and inexperienced troops are now getting their second wind. While our policy for the moment is to keep our Forces in being as fighting formations, this does not mean that casualties must always be avoided. Provided greater losses are inflicted on the enemy, casualties can and should be expected within reasonable limits. Our Forces are now becoming more concentrated than hitherto, and therefore in a better position to hit back. I feel that the time has now come when we should accept casualties within reasonable limits if by doing so we can damage and impose greater delay on the enemy.

All soldiers know that casualties are inevitable, but they trust their commander as long as they know that he will do everything in his power to protect their lives; so it is not difficult to appreciate General Heath's feelings when he received Percival's message. The casualty rate in III Corps had always been very high; at Slim River it was excessive – seven British commanding officers were killed on 7 and 8 January, and the 11th Division lost virtually all its artillery and transport in the battle.

To date there has been very little criticism of the army in the Governor's War Diary. But now he comments on Japanese mobility and events were to show how right he was:

> *January 6*
> The Jap tactics are to get into the country, live on it, and harass our communications. They have the advantage of being rice eaters, and are much less dependent than we are on man-made communications. They enter the villages and live there, fed by the villagers (who can't refuse with a tommy gun at their stomachs). They then go out on guerrilla warfare. We on the other hand have gone in for mechanized transport to the nth degree; it is a fearfully cumbersome method and we have pinned our faith to the few roads. But the enemy uses the tracks and paths and cuts in behind us very much as he likes, particularly on bicycles – which require no petrol and present no administrative problem. He can ride his bicycle on the excellent roads that we made! and replace them easily from the villagers.

Now the vital task for Thomas was to oversee the evacuation, and the withdrawal of the civil government, from those 120 miles of country through which the army was to retreat and leave in enemy hands. The speed of the army's move made effective action by the civil authorities extremely difficult; nevertheless, what was achieved in the time was quite remarkable. Briefly, on 8 January (the day on which Wavell decided to move III Corps back to North Johore) the civil administration south of Kuala Lumpur was functioning normally; now it had four days in which to withdraw, leaving behind the minimum possible material which the enemy might find useful.

The fate of civilian refugees in war is always harrowing and this evacuation was no exception. Cecil Lee saw it all:

> Down through the countryside went the melancholy procession. The white civilians and civil defence workers, male and female; the planters after paying off, and distributing rice to, their bewildered labourers; all leaving pleasant homes and clubs on the green padangs beside the road, with bungalows which had been centres of social life, happiness and hospitality – all of which the troops that followed on found deserted and sometimes ransacked. Here were all the signs of a society in dissolution; all the confusion and paraphernalia of an army in retreat and a population in flight; with sometimes looted shops, clubs and offices. Smoke rising from rubber stocks denied to the enemy, and machinery in tin mines demolished. The Tamil and Chinese population streaming along the roads with such pathetic belongings, sometimes incongruous, as they could bring along with them.
>
> Of course the Malays from the Northern States, of Perlis, Kedah and Perak, had already seen their "tuans" depart. Now it was the turn of those in their wayside kampongs further south, in Selangor, Negri Sembilan and Malacca, to witness the same sad spectacle. What must have been their thoughts when even the oldest could remember only the benevolent protection of British rule?

Those days after the sudden withdrawal of the boundaries of civil administration back to Johore were naturally trying for the Governor. He had sent Jones to Kuala Lumpur to do everything possible, in cooperation with the army, in the three main fields of evacuation, denial schemes and food distribution. In spite of all the anxieties of the withdrawal to Johore, Shenton had to continue his formal gubernatorial functions. In his diary for those days much is clearly left unsaid for lack of time. For instance:

January 11
All civilians were to be out of Negri Sembilan by 11 a.m., and Bryant telephoned he expects Malacca to follow suit tomorrow or next day. K.L. seems to have been fairly well "denied", but it must have been dreadful there in the last days.

It was probably fortunate that he was not then able to read a report of the evacuation of the British Residency at Kuala Lumpur by Ian Morrison, the correspondent of *The Times* in Malaya:*

> We went up to the Residency to see if the Resident was still there. It was a large spacious white house set on a hill in park-like grounds filled with flowering trees, surrounded at a distance by other official residences. The place was deserted. The flag was down. There seemed to be no one within miles. The big house was empty. It reminded me somehow of the *Mary Celeste*, that ship which was found in the South Atlantic under full sail but with no one on board, and nothing to show what had happened. In the Residency a half-finished whisky and soda stood on the small table by the sofa in the drawing room. Upstairs a woman's dress, half-ironed, lay on the ironing board in one of the bedrooms. Two dispatches addressed to the Governor, typed but unsigned, lay on the desk upstairs. In the offices on the ground floor the files were intact. The staff appeared to have downed pens in the middle of whatever they were doing and made off. A lorry, still in good order, was parked at the side of the building. Cases of beautiful silver ornaments, daggers of superb native workmanship, the presentations, doubtless, of Malay Princes, lay in glass cases in the hall. The official portraits of the King and Queen smiled down from the walls.

The great retreat ordered by Wavell lasted for a week and fortunately the Japanese did not actively pursue III Corps into their new positions on the Muar River line. It was during this time that Shenton Thomas saw the last of the Duff Coopers, and entered in his diary:

January 12
The Duff Coopers dined with us preparatory to leaving.

However, the Governor soon found that he was wrong in thinking that "D.C. was out of my way and that it left me free to take over as Chairman of the War Council". He certainly took the appointment but it was by no means the last he heard of Duff Cooper. He did not know that on 3 January the latter had sent a most secret cypher telegram personally to the Secretary of State for the Colonies, Shenton's superior officer in London. In this cable** he repeated the views expressed in his letter to the Prime Minister of 18 December, and he now added that in his opinion the civil authorities had failed lamentably

---

* Later included in his book *Malayan Postscript*, Faber & Faber, 1942.
** Official History p. 295.

to make adequate preparations for war. On 11 January, the day before he and Lady Diana dined at Government House, Duff Cooper again cabled the Secretary of State, saying that there existed a widespread and profound lack of confidence in the administration; he added that, as a breakdown might well paralyse the fighting services, changes were desirable, and he suggested that the simplest solution would be to declare a state of seige and appoint a Military Governor for the duration of the emergency.

Before we see the result of these three secret and personal attacks on the conduct and ability of the Governor, it is worth searching for the motives underlying Duff Cooper's actions. After the war, on 7 November, 1952, Sir Shenton wrote:

> All the troubles which arose during Duff Cooper's time as President of the local War Council in my opinion stemmed from his endeavours to magnify the responsibilities entrusted to him by the Prime Minister. The P.M.'s instructions to him were published on page 543 of Volume III of Churchill's *War Memoirs*, and had been repeated to Duff Cooper in Singapore in Foreign Office telegram (Lanca 43) of December 12th 1941.

That may be, but there must have been more to it than that. Clearly the two men never got on well together, and Shenton later said that he rarely saw Duff Cooper except at War Council meetings. Furthermore the latter only once asked the Governor to see official files and made no effort to keep in touch with Christopher Dawson, the civil Secretary for Defence. For the rest Duff Cooper attempted to gain popularity by regaling dinner parties with imitations of the Governor, the Commander-in-Chief and the G.O.C. Worse still he canvassed the opinions of the Governor's subordinates, including Brigadier Simson, after the latter had been made Director General for Civil Defences, about the desirability of replacing Sir Shenton. Unfortunately D.C. took a dislike, or so it seemed, to most people in authority in Singapore, maybe because he found it irksome and frustrating to be sitting around with no special powers to do anything, and being simply a nuisance, a fifth wheel.*

This last point may be relevant because Professor Callahan has attributed much of the trouble to the actual existance of the War Council. "The War Council might have been useful earlier, but by the time it was put together it was too late to become more than

---

* *The Worst Disaster*, The Fall of Singapore, by Raymond Callahan, University of Delaware Press, 1977.

another cog in an already clumsy machine. It consumed the time of terribly busy men and produced additional friction in an already bad situation."

We shall see the hand of Duff Cooper at work again in a later chapter, but it looks as if his last attempt to discredit Shenton Thomas was probably made after his return to the U.K. In his admirable autobiography *Old Men Forget* Duff Cooper, on page 310, recorded his concern at being politically damaged by his association with the disaster at Singapore. He wanted to offset possible harm to his reputation and wrote a speech which he proposed to make in the House of Commons, but first sent a draft of it to Churchill who advised him not to make it. Duff Cooper wrote that he kept no copy of the draft speech, which would seem unlike a man of his literary experience. Presumably the Prime Minister had regarded the draft speech as too hot; but it would have been interesting to see which of the personalities at Singapore Duff Cooper had selected for character assassination in order to avoid possible repercussions on himself!

Wavell's plan involved bringing the 8th Australian Division, less one brigade*, to the front line for the first time, to form the main defence across Northern Johore on a general line Segamat – Mount Ophir – mouth of the Muar River. The Division was to be joined by 9th Indian Division from Pahang and the 45th Indian Infantry Brigade from Malacca. This seemingly large force was to be called "Westforce" and be under command of the Australian commander, Major-General Bennett. III Corps, or what was left of it, was to take command of the 22nd Australian Infantry Brigade and be responsible for Southern Johore, from coast to coast, on the line of the road Mersing-Kluang-Batu Pahat on the Malacca coast. The 11th Indian Division was to rest and reorganize in Southern Johore.

This large-scale redeployment appeared simple, but there were doubts about its likely effect. First it meant that troops of the Australian Division, splendid men, tough and very well trained, instead of fighting as one division under their Australian commander, would be split in half and have to work alongside Indian formations of which they knew little. Then, 45th Indian Brigade had only arrived in Singapore on 3 January and had been without its transport until the 6th. Finally, 9th Indian Division could not concentrate in Johore until relieved by the 53rd British Infantry Brigade, which was not due to reach Singapore until 13 January; this brigade was an early arrival from the 18th Division and was quite untrained for war. The overall effect of

---

* This Australian Division never had more than two brigades.

these moves gave "Westforce" an appearance of unbalance, without the time needed to settle into new defence positions.

We have seen how the enemy occupied Kuala Lumpur and Port Swettenham on 12 January. We should look next at the Japanese appreciation of the British withdrawal – how they themselves viewed the situation, having regard to their command of the sea and also, virtually, of the air.

The first intimation of Japanese intentions came during the second week in January when daylight air raids on Singapore Island were intensified and increased, in an obvious attempt to destroy the air defences. Yamashita also appreciated that the retreating British forces would seek to defend Northern Johore on the general line of the Muar River since this was, in his opinion, the last natural defence position on the mainland. This view, naturally enough, coincided with General Wavell's dispositions, though Yamashita had never thought the British would withdraw so far without offering any opposition except by demolitions.

In the front line in central Malaya Yamashita had under his command two divisions of the Japanese 25th Army – the 5th Division, which had been marching and fighting continuously since the war began, and the Imperial Guards Division. The latter was the crack formation of the Japanese Army and eventually led the final assault on Singapore Island. Yamashita now planned that the 5th Division should advance along that main trunk road towards Segamat, then on to Kluang, while the Imperial Guards Division moved down the western coast road to force a crossing of the Muar River and then turn inland to cut the communications of "Westforce" opposing the 5th Division – the classic Japanese assault on an enemy's rear. On the east coast the 18th Japanese Division, still under Southern Army, would advance south to capture Endau and Mersing.

Yamashita made the first move as early as 14 January when he sent forward a mobile detachment to contact and probe British forces astride the trunk road near Gemas. This Japanese detachment, consisting of a battalion of infantry mounted on bicycles, supported by a tank regiment with artillery and engineer units, came up against troops of the 27th Australian Brigade. It was about 4 p.m. when the advance guard of the Japanese, bicycling along the main road, ran into a defensive position carefully prepared by the Australians; it was their first action in the Malaya campaign and we shall see later what happened. Meanwhile, on the previous day, 13 January, General Wavell had arrived to pay his second visit to Singapore.

Wavell immediately became involved in the reaction, in Whitehall, to

Duff Cooper's* latest attacks on Shenton Thomas, particularly D.C.'s proposal to appoint a military governor. The Secretary of State for the Colonies had telegraphed to Wavell in Singapore, asking for his views. Wavell's reaction is shown by the following extract from the *Official History*:

> Having consulted General Pownall and Admiral Layton, and learnt from Brigadier Simson of the difficulties which he was experiencing in carrying out his task, General Wavell replied that he considered it advisable that there should be certain changes in the senior personnel in the administration, rather than the appointment of a military governor.

The results were sudden and drastic, and caused a considerable stir both in London and Malaya. The Governor wrote at length about the matter:

> On January 16th I received a telegram from the Colonial Office with the request that I should decypher it myself. It told me that Duff Cooper had reported a lack of confidence on the part of senior Service officers in the civil Government, and that the Prime Minister had ordered that Mr S. W. Jones, the Colonial Secretary, was to be compulsorily retired at once. This meant that I was deprived of the services of my chief executive officer at a very critical time. Unfortunately, Duff Cooper had left Singapore three days earlier, on January 13th, and I was unable to question him. . . . I told no one but Jones and Percival. But I summoned the members of the Executive Council on the 20th to inform them, and was very surprised to hear from them that not only Jones's departure, but also the appointment of his successor, had been talked about in the Singapore Club on the 13th January, three days before I received the instruction!
>
> It is natural that those who read what I have written should ask themselves how it all happened. I am afraid Duff Cooper allowed himself to listen to unworthy advisers. I know who they were and I shall not say more. Duff Cooper is dead. But I can say that the European unofficial community knew perfectly well that if they had any complaint they had only to come to me, or the Colonial Secretary, to get a fair hearing. Few, indeed, would have gone behind my back.**

Thus Sir Shenton Thomas, giving his account of the sacking of his Colonial Secretary, on the orders of Winston Churchill, just four

---

* Duff Cooper's telegram of 11 January refers.
** Extract from comments by Sir Shenton Thomas on the draft of *History of the War Against Japan*, Vol I, Rhodes House Library, 1954.

weeks before the fall of Singapore. Shenton asked, "How did it all happen?" Now, thanks to Professor Callahan's book, we have conclusive evidence of that, in the form of the following extract from the original letter that Duff Cooper wrote to the Prime Minister on 18 December, 1941:

> Sir Robert Brooke-Popham is a very much older man than his years warrant and sometimes seems on the verge of nervous collapse. I fear also that knowledge of his own failing powers renders him jealous of any encroachment on his sphere of influence. . . . The Governor, Sir Shenton Thomas, is one of those people who find it impossible to adjust their minds to war conditions. He is also the mouthpiece of the last person he speaks to, and much influenced by his Colonial Secretary, a sinister figure called Stanley Jones, who is universally detested in the Colony, where he is accused of having been defeatist since the beginning of the war. . . . General Percival is a nice, good man who began life as a schoolmaster. I am sometimes tempted to wish he had remained one. He is a good soldier too – calm, clear-headed and even clever. But he is not a leader, he cannot take a large view; it is all a field day at Aldershot to him.*

It seems extraordinary that Duff Cooper should not have checked the facts before writing that letter. General Percival had never been a schoolmaster. After leaving Rugby he went into business in London with a firm of iron-ore merchants, with whom he remained for seven years until the 1914 war began; he then enlisted in the army and was very soon commissioned. It was Shenton Thomas who had been a schoolmaster! However, it was the evidence of duplicity in Duff Cooper's letter that disturbed the Governor more than anything else, for he wrote this about it:

> On 15 December Duff Cooper had obtained the consent of the War Council to set up an Advisory Committee, with himself as chairman, to oversee all questions of civil defence. The Committee had no fault to find and on 19th December, after interviewing the Director of the Passive Defence Services in Singapore, Duff Cooper signed the Committee's minute that: "the general position appeared to be satisfactory".

One day earlier (18th) Duff Cooper had condemned the whole concern, lock, stock and barrel, in his letter to the Prime Minister.

Sir Shenton Thomas cabled the Prime Minister and the Secretary of

---

* Duff Cooper sent his letter to the P.M. by hand of a survivor from H.M.S. *Repulse* (Captain Tennant, R.N.) who addressed it to Winston Churchill in London on 6 January, 1942.

State for the Colonies, saying that the decision to sack his Colonial Secretary was regarded in Singapore and Malaya generally as a gross injustice to Stanley Jones, and that the P.M. and the Colonial Office had been misled. Sir Roland Braddell, probably the most distinguished lawyer in all Malaya, wrote strongly in the *Straits Times* in favour of Jones. The latter was highly thought of the M.C.S. as one of their foremost professional officers who, inter alia, was a first-class Malay scholar and popular with the Chinese. The affair did much harm locally to British popularity and reputation. But the war continued and physical dangers pre-occupied men's minds. Stanley Jones returned to England where he wrote a brilliant and scholarly work on Malayan administration; paradoxically he was often consulted by the Colonial Office on various matters. He died in 1962.

To return to the military picture, we are now approaching the final phase of the fighting on the mainland of Malaya, the last attempt to contain the Japanese advance long enough for reinforcements to reach Singapore and "retrieve the situation". For there still remained a hope, albeit slender, of stemming the tide and keeping Singapore Island under British control. Much of this hope centred round the Australians who were now joining the battle, fresh and full of courage, under their dynamic commander, Major-General Bennett. The latter's attitude to the campaign so far was most important. For Bennett had already reported to his superiors in Australia in terms that clearly mirrored his tactical doctrine, and in some important respects had unfortunate effects: He had written to Australia that Heath's men were tired and most units lacked determination, and that their former "purely defensive attitude should be replaced by strong counter-attack methods".* Fixed defensive positions were dangerous and fluid defence with as many men as possible for counterattack was sounder.

On the face of it such an offensive outlook seemed very desirable, particularly if all the troops were as fresh and as fit as the Australians; but they were not. Equally important and equally unwise was the feeling held by some Australian battalion commanders that, "in the jungle anti-tank guns hindered mobility and were an encumbrance."

When the Japanese advance guard bicycled down the trunk road west of Gemas on that sunny afternoon of 14 January, they were ambushed by a company of the 2/30th Australian Infantry, concealed in thick jungle and covering a bridge over a small river. After a considerable number of Japanese had crossed the river the bridge was blown and fire was opened, with very satisfactory results; a great

* *Singapore 1941–1942*, Chapter IX, Louis Allen, Davis Poynter, 1977.

number of the enemy were killed or wounded. This successful first action by troops of the 27th Australian Brigade was important because it led them to think that they were masters of the Japanese. The following day was also most encouraging, for the 2/30th Battalion again successfully counterattacked the Japanese who had advanced against the brigade position covering Gemas. However, it was clear that the enemy was being steadily reinforced and that evening, the 15th, 2/30th Battalion had to withdraw.

Meanwhile an altogether different, and dangerous, situation was developing on the western coast road where the defence of the Muar River line had been entrusted to 45th Infantry Brigade, recently arrived from India with a few pre-war British and Indian officers or sepoys, and certainly no knowledge or experience of jungle warfare. General Bennett had correctly assumed that the Japanese would make their main thrust down the trunk road and deployed the Australians to meet that attack. But did he appreciate that the crack Japanese Imperial Guards Division would then advance down the coast road? The 45th Brigade was composed of three historic regiments of the Indian Army – Rajputana Rifles, Jats and Garhwal Rifles – but they were children in experience and skill compared with the Imperial Guards. Worse still, because of the shortage of troops, the Rajputana Rifles were allotted a frontage of *nine miles*, from the mouth of the Muar to Jorak, while the Jats attempted to hold a further *fifteen miles* of river line; each battalion had two companies north of the river and the Garhwalis were in reserve near Bakri.

What then happened to the unfortunate 45th Brigade was surely predictable, in view of previous experience of Japanese tactics in northern Malaya. On the night of 15/16 January the 1/14th Guards Regiment left Malacca in boats and landed thirty miles *behind* the Muar River where they lay up in a rubber estate four miles from Batu Pahat. At the same time the 5th Guards Regiment, having surprised and completely overrun the Indian infantry companies north of the river, crossed the Muar in strength and advanced south to attack the main body of the brigade. In the confused fighting that followed, the commanding officers of both the Garhwalis and the Rajputana Rifles were killed, as well as the second-in-command of the latter. It was another classic example of Japanese encirclement tactics behind the British lines, which in this case set the scene for the eventual and almost total elimination of the 45th Indian Brigade. I have set out these military details because of the interest that Shenton Thomas evidently took in this action, possibly because of some evidence that the sad result might have been avoided but for a misunderstanding of instructions.

After the war General Percival wrote his detailed Despatch covering the whole Malaya Campaign, a copy of which was given to the Governor. Shenton Thomas annotated or side-lined any paragraph of the Despatch in which he had an interest. On paragraph 300, sidelined by Shenton, Percival explained his orders for deployment of "Westforce" in Johore, as required by Wavell. This included the positioning of 45th Brigade in the southern (Muar River) sector. Percival then added:

> The Supreme Commander had stated that he directed that the 9th Indian Division should be deployed on the southern (i.e. Muar River) sector of the position to be occupied. I have no recollection of this instruction.

If the 9th Division, still a fighting formation, fit and with recent experience of jungle warfare against the Japanese, had been sent to occupy the Muar River line, the rapid encirclement of the 45th Brigade position might perhaps have been avoided.

For the next eight days the battles again developed into an almost continuous retreat, despite the most gallant and courageous resistance by all ranks in every unit of the British Command. The unfortunate fact was that, under Wavell's strategy, a decisive battle had to be fought in Northern Johore, though Percival's army had no trained reserves. Equally important, as General Yamashita knew, the only natural obstacle left to hinder the Japanese advance was the Johore Strait separating mainland Malaya from Singapore Island. The *British Official History* summarized the plight of the army in Johore in these stark terms:

> During the period of eight days, from the 16th to 24th January, the Japanese out-generalled, out-manoeuvered and decisively defeated the British forces in the Muar–Yong Peng–Batu Pahat triangle and won the battle for Johore.

Though nearly all writers on the campaign have agreed with this strong condemnation of British arms, there are important factors which should be borne in mind. If General Bennett had been allowed to command his complete Australian division and fight with it in battle, as Wavell intended; if Percival had not broken the normal chain of command and communications by forming temporary *ad hoc* formations such as "Westforce", which merely complicated the command structure and increased his own burden; if, later in the battle, he had not compounded this mistake by forming a similar "Eastforce" – much-needed time might have been gained and maybe those eight days would have become sixteen. For, as so often, timing was the key to success, and Percival himself lost time by trying to command "Westforce" and "Eastforce", as well as all his other commitments, including III Corps, Singapore Garrison, etc. He had to motor long distances daily between Singapore and the combat areas, with little sleep and constant anxiety, working eighteeen hours a day; he tried to fill the roles of G.O.C. Malaya and an army corps commander in the field. It was too much.*

I have written the foregoing about General Percival because it underlines his increasing lack of *rapport* with Shenton Thomas, which we have seen before and which will become increasingly evident. It is also relevant to the inaccuracy of the charge in the *Official History* "that the Japanese out-generalled" the British. With rare exceptions British general officers, indeed all commanding officers at battalion level, were competent, experienced, and highly professional soldiers. Far too many of them were killed, wounded or taken prisoner in battle while leading their own men into action. Their troops, for reasons beyond their control, were largely untrained and inexperienced, and thus it was that senior officers, sometimes at the high level of divisional commander, were seen actually leading troops into battle, well knowing that inexperienced soldiers lacked effective leadership otherwise. Senior officers like General Barstow (killed), Generals Key and Paris, Brigadier Duncan (killed leading the ill-fated 45th Indian Brigade) and Brigadier Duke, (Commander of 53rd Brigade) were not out-generalled; too often the tasks they were given were beyond the capabilities of the untrained young soldiers they commanded.

Another factor in the Johore battle, indeed throughout the campaign, was the insistence of the military authorities that the British Officers of the Local (Volunteer) territorial forces, in both the Straits Settlements and the Malay States, should remain with their units for regimental duty once they had been called up for service. All these local forces were embodied during 1940; their British officers were mainly resident in Malaya on a long-service basis, either as planters, miners, forest officers, civil engineers or agents of mercantile houses and the like. Their knowledge of the country and its peoples was very great; they knew all the man-made paths and tracks in the jungles of the central mountain range, and the course and diversity of the many rivers and streams. Their ideal role in the regular armed forces would have

---

* *Singapore: Chain of Disaster,* Woodburn Kirby.

been as liaison officers with every unit in the Malaya command, particularly when the need for maps became an urgent priority after Kuala Lumpur fell to the Japanese in January; the map storage depot, containing thousands of maps of every scale and size, was not destroyed in the haste of the withdrawal.

This misemployment of expertise was eventually corrected, but far too late to be of real military value, and not before some astonishing anomalies were found. Sir William Goode, who later became Governor of Aden and of Singapore, was a District Officer when war broke out in 1939. In November, 1941, he was mobilized and called up for service in the ranks with B Company of the 1st Battalion the Straits Settlements Volunteer Force. He became a Lance-Corporal and spent most of the remaining weeks either on 24-hour guard duty, or digging holes in the ground, and filling them up again because they were in the wrong place. Later it was recognized something was wrong and he was appointed Assistant Commissioner for Civil Defence.* Vyvyan Frampton, the highly qualified civil engineer who constructed the R.A.F. station and airfield installations at Kuantan, had been enlisted as a private soldier in the Federated Malay States Volunteer Force. After completing the task at Kuantan, he was posted for duty with a local territorial unit on the west coast. But he failed to qualify for the lowest grade in rifle shooting and was thereupon "discharged" from the army! In the event this was a wise decision for he was able to revert to vital employment where he was urgently needed.

Meanwhile, as the fighting drew near to the Johore Strait, the realization that Singapore itself might be invaded did not seem to have got through to the civilian community in the city. Mrs Savage-Bailey was writing in her diary in terms which still seemed to envisage the possibility of defeat for the Japanese and relief for Singapore:

> Sunday Jan. 25th. More and more troops and equipment are pouring into the island, and soon with any luck, we shall have enough men, planes and tanks, to turn the Japs out. We are not out of the woods yet and must not relax for a second, but it is a wonderful comfort to us all to know that all these necessary fighting forces are on the way. Spent the day as usual at the [Tanglin] Club where I was able to entertain some up-country people – if it were not for the unhappy cause of their being in Singapore, it would be all the more delightful.
>
> Monday Jan. 26th. It was extraordinary how many more work people were moving about today; they had been frightened by the Jap broad-

---

* Sir William Goode to the author, November, 1982.

casts about flattening out the city on Sunday. The clerks were all smiling when I got down and their reaction to the whole thing is better.

At working level in the civil administration, particularly at Government House, the reality of the military situation was clearly giving great concern before mid-January. Yet, studying those War Council files and the mass of papers Shenton kept, and managed to send home, it is clear that strict departmental bureaucracy continued in spite of the bombing and war conditions. As a result the Governor had to issue his personal edict to all departments of government:

> Government House
> 15th January 1942
>
> The day of minute papers is gone. There must be no more passing of files between departments. It is the duty of every officer to act, and if the decision is beyond him he must go and get it. . . . The essential thing is speed in action. Nothing matters which is not directly concerned with defence . . .
>
> T S W T
> Governor

The extracts from Shenton's diary show his personal frustration at the outcome of the campaign:

> *January 21*
> Two nasty bomb raids, all along Beach Road to the Cricket Club, which was set on fire, but put out. Hit on Volunteer's H.Q., and P.W.D. got direct hit, as well as other streets off Beach Road. Went down immediately but police and Passive Defence working admirably. Went again at 5 p.m. and helped dig out woman who was still alive. After War Council today Spooner (Rear Admiral) blazed out and said "we had just walked out of Malaya". And yet they have the nerve to criticize my officers. The behaviour "of the military" ever since the retreat began has been disgraceful. . . . If Singapore falls it will be the army's fault; they have been incredibly inefficient.
> *January 22*
> "We had 1000 casualties yesterday, 304 killed.

The Governor's outburst against the army coincided with Wavell's third visit to Singapore on 20 January, when the latter clearly took the view that British forces could no longer remain in defence of Johore and must therefore withdraw to Singapore Island. Wavell also doubted whether the Island alone could be defended, and then sent his now famous cable to Churchill in London: "I warn you that I doubt whether island can be held for long once Johore is lost." Events were to show how right he was.

Against that background the next, inevitable phase of the campaign took place between 24 January and the end of the month. During those seven days there was much hard fighting and severe casualties on both sides, but on the 26th Percival issued orders for a withdrawal over the Causeway to the Island on the night of 31 January.

Accounts of this campaign probably contain too many "if's". But one *if* is surely justified now. General Dobbie had recommended, and begun construction of, defence works in Southern Johore, though these were discontinued by General Bond. If, however, such works had been completed, covering the approaches to Johore Bahru, then, once again, much time might have been gained. Southern Johore was much easier ground to defend than the north coast of the island. However, without such defences there remained no alternative but a coordinated withdrawal to Singapore Island.

Those last seven days of January were a particularly difficult time for Shenton Thomas and appear accordingly in his diary entries:

January 29
Raids in the morning. Visited Tan Tock Seng hospital to see today's and yesterday's injured. Percival at 3 p.m. He says the army is crossing into Singapore tomorrow, also that Barstow is missing, believed killed. A very harassing day with hardly a moment free from some problem or other. During dinner we had an alert, and suddenly the whistle of a bomb put us all (about 10) under the table together. Two more alerts before getting to bed, one with several bombs very close. Another during the night, but I slept right through it.

Early in January, after the Japanese Air Force began raiding Singapore indiscriminately, dropping bombs on the city as well as on military targets, life at Government House changed drastically. Although Shenton and Daisy were always treated with the proper deference and respect due to the Governor and his wife, there was no longer any official ceremony or entertainment. The house was generally full of guests, officials and officers from up-country, or friends whose homes had been destroyed in air raids. But there were no formalities in dress or procedure; nobody dressed for dinner and most men wore uniform. The golf course and tennis courts were unattended and nobody had time for leisure. The stories that have been published of luxury and formalities continuing at G.H. until the very end, with H.E. changing into a dinner jacket every night and the like, are totally untrue.* The Governor's diary continues on a sombre note:

January 30
Discovered in War Council that when the Johore Causeway goes up, after our troops are across, the water mains supply to the Island will go too. I confess I did not realize the latter, and, as a number of taps have to be fitted to standpipes which will have to come into use when house supplies are cut off, there is need for great haste. Curfew is being imposed from tonight from 9 p.m. to 5 a.m. More raids this morning and damage to godowns in harbour area and in coolie lines. Probably aimed at ships, such as *Empress of Japan*, which are taking away a lot of women, including Mollie Puckridge and her friend. Wavell for ½ hour at 2 p.m.

It is fair to wonder why the Governor was not aware that the Causeway carried the mains water supply as well as the road and railway line! And did Wavell also not know? Actually Singapore Island had, and still has, additional water supply from two large reservoirs, in a catchment area bordered by the hills in the centre of the Island.

January 31
Causeway blown up at 8 a.m. Shook G.H. but Percival not sure it has been successful! Our troops withdrawn from mainland. Alerts all morning but few bombs. Yesterday's raid on the harbour pretty bad. 3 godowns destroyed, main offices untenable, one dry dock damaged; about 70 casualties. Labour situation: very few at work. Visited M.A.S. [Medical Auxiliary Service] posts with Daisy, and then broadcast to the people of Malaya. Two bomb alerts during dinner, but no bombs.

Many accounts have been written of the withdrawal of the Imperial Army from the mainland to Singapore Island and the subsequent blowing up of the Causeway. Fortunately the Japanese Air Force made no attempt to interrupt this final departure from Johore. The last moments have been well told by Lt-Colonel Angus Rose, commanding the Argyll and Sutherland Highlanders.

I sent our pipes down to the Causeway to play through the Australian battalions and the Gordon Highlanders who formed the left rear-guard. . . . It was a well executed movement and, from my vantage point, I might have been watching a turn at the Aldershot Tattoo.
Down at the lock gates the pipers had struck up and the troops swung

---

* Leslie Davis to the author November, 1982. Davis went back to G.H. and stayed there from 31 January until the surrender.

across the Causeway, still in open tactical formation, but to the accompaniment of "Blue Bonnets over the Border".*

So, in the space of under two months, the British had been evicted from mainland Malaya. Now there only remain fourteen more days of British rule on the Island of Singapore. We had better look closer at this island, for its topography, population and infrastructure had a considerable influence on the short battle to come.

The land is generally undulating, with two hills, Bukit Timah and Bukit Mandai, each about 600 feet high, in the centre of the island, and the Lower Pasir Panjang ridge in the south near to the city and the port area; the main population of about one million lived in this southern part of the settlement. Distances are short, about 27 miles from east to west, and 13 miles from north to south. The north-east and north-west coasts, facing the Johore Strait and divided by the Causeway, are indented by rivers, creeks, and dense mangrove swamps. The great Naval Base was east of the Causeway abutting on a region of low hills and cliffs. The island was well provided with good roads and bisected by the main road and railway line, which ran from the Causeway into Singapore town and harbour. There were airfields at Tengah in the north-west, Sembawang and Seletar in the north-east, and Kallang in the south, close to Singapore town; Kallang was the last airfield we held on to, from which the final flight out was made.

On 1 February, 1942, the million or so people on this small island were joined by some 80,000 troops of all arms of the Imperial Army. The great majority of this army had already experienced defeat and retreat and had suffered casualties, hardship and fatigue; but the 18th British Division, less its 53rd Brigade, had only arrived two days before the Causeway was blown. Unfortunately, as we have seen, the troops of this Division had been trained for mobile warfare against Germans and Italians; they had just spent weeks in their troopships and were not physically fit for active service. All in all, then, this force from the mainland could not be described as a confident army with faith in its leadership; they had seen too much defeat already. There were six general officers in this army – Percival, Heath, Bennett, Key and Simmons (in command of the so-called Singapore Fortress), and the newly-arrived Major-General Beckwith-Smith, commanding the 18th Division.

On the mainland in Southern Johore, facing south across the Johore Strait, was General Yamashita with his Japanese 25th Army, which had

---

* From *The Bitter End*, Richard Holmes & Anthony Kemp, Anthony Bird, 1982.

just won the battle for Johore, and now also the 18th Division. Significantly, each of these three Japanese formations included engineer units specially detailed "for crossing the Johore Straits". These special units included "River Crossing Material Companies" and "Bridge Building Material Companies". The Imperial Guards Division had a specially designated "Assault Group", consisting of Guards infantry with anti-tank battalions, and an Engineer regiment. Thus there was little doubt of the Japanese intention to attempt an early assault and capture of Singapore Island. The thoroughness of the enemy's preparations for the next battle is shown in their order of battle which included companies entitled "Water Purification Units".

In Johore Bahru General Yamashita installed his advance headquarters in the Palace of the Sultan of Johore. From the Palace tower, a prominent landmark visible from Singapore, Yamashita had a bird's eye view of the Island. He is said to have made his tactical headquarters in the tower, from where, with a large-scale map of the island, he could control the assault. Presumably British artillery would have found no difficulty in destroying Yamashita's 5-storey observation post, but, for some reason never properly explained, Percival's Headquarters would not allow it to be bombarded. Possibly political reasons prompted this prohibition, and if so Sir Shenton would surely have been on record as making the order; but there is no mention of it in his diary or in War Council records.

In his dispositions for the defence of Singapore General Percival had the choice of extending his forces along the coastline to prevent landings anywhere, or to hold the coast thinly while retaining his reserves ready for immediate and strong counterattack at the point of landing. Unfortunately he chose the former; as a result each formation had to find its own reserve, amounting to little more than a battalion in strength, which inevitably left very little for a central command reserve. In short Percival made the fatal mistake of trying to defend too much territory with two few men. This was the cardinal error which made certain he would lose the battle for Singapore.

Wavell always thought the north-west coast of the island would be the main objective of the Japanese attack and he was proved right. But Percival took a different view, maintaining that the attack would come east of the Causeway. Once again Percival wasted, or lost, valuable time in making up his mind on dispositions, and his final plan ignored Wavell's sound advice to create mobile reserves, able to deliver rapid counterattacks at the right time and place. Finally Percival gave orders for three defence areas. The "Northern Area", from Changi to the Causeway, was allotted to III Corps, consisting of the 11th and 18th

Divisions. The "Western Area", from the Causeway westward to the mouth of the Jurong River, was given to the Australian Division with one Indian Infantry Brigade. The "Southern Area", from the Jurong River to Changi, constituted the old Singapore Fortress Command under General Simmons. Tragically, no defence positions had been prepared in any of the three areas, and this hastened the ending.

This was the setting when the Japanese began shelling and bombing the Island soon after 1 February. Daily there were air raids and by 5 February the bombing and shelling was general and increasingly heavy. Surprisingly, almost unbelievably at this stage, Percival still thought he could hold out for a three-month siege.

Let us now return to Government House, where extracts from Shenton's diary show how he and his wife fared during those last fourteen days of his rule as Governor and High Commissioner.

February 1
A midnight raid. All my cypher ladies except Mrs Nelson wish to leave! A lot of Service ballyhoo at the Golf Club and Rex Hotel (Australians, British Navy and Army). Told Admiral Spooner and the Provost Marshal this must be stopped at once. We cannot allow our own men to riot, and refuse it to Asiatics.

February 2
7–8 raids on Naval Base oil tanks; godowns and mineral water factory destroyed. Railway offices out of action and oil barges burning all day. Went to bombed area a.m. and again in evening with Daisy. Leslie Davis [Private Secretary] turned up, having got through Johore with troops who were cut off, and then rescued by the navy. He said the Australian Air Force at Kuantan were dreadful. Panicked out at first bombing. I have heard the R.A.F. panicked in exactly the same way at Alor Star.

February 3
More raids on the harbour. Went down with Percival to see. Summoned Chinese Mobilisation Council and told them plainly that unless they could prevent labour from running away they might find themselves doing coolie work for Japs at point of bayonet.

February 4
Dutch Consul General and staff pushed off without a word. Many European women in essential jobs are also pushing off without notice. Their places are filled by Chinese and Eurasians. Col. Bretherton* rang to ask did we know that if you want anything out of the Naval Base you have only got to go and get it. Apparently since Navy evacuated it a few days ago it has been at the mercy of anyone in uniform. Blankets, clothes, food, wireless sets – things that are desperately needed here.

---

* Jack Bretherton, who raised the Malay Regiment in the 1930s.

February 5
Brought up Naval Base evacuation at War Council with Percival and
Spooner. Spooner said the military told him they wanted no navy
personnel in operational area, so he took them all away. Percival said he
had never been consulted in the matter at all. I said I could not
understand how a great Base could be handed over by the Navy at the
request of anyone but the G.O.C. Bretherton says the whole place looks
as if the staff had left for lunch and never returned. Maps and plans left
on office tables and so on. A dreadful thing.
February 6
In the afternoon met deputation of Chinese communists, most of whom
have been in gaol. Tremlett [Singapore Police] was there and told me
that he thought the interview very satisfactory. Splendid day for evacuees being embarked – 2,000. Near miss on G.H. swimming pool,
probably fired on from mainland. Survivors from S.S. *Empress of Asia*
nearly 90%,* but military indiscipline disquietening. Percival is doing
all he can but unless offenders can be caught it's impossible to do
anything but threaten. Daisy went down with a sharp chill yesterday and
about the same today. These noises are not good for a headache. Very
heavy bombardment at Sembawang airfield and Base area.

That first sentence on 6 February is important as it is the only
reference to clandestine operations in Shenton's diary. As far back as
January, 1941, he had been told by Whitehall that the S.O.E. (Special
Operations Executive) would be operating in Malaya, under cover as
the "Oriental Mission" from the Ministry of Economic Warfare; but
otherwise he was not personally involved in the later Operations of
Force 136. When the campaign began it became essential to enlist the
support of the Chinese community as a whole in the fight against Japan,
notwithstanding that the majority of Malaya's Chinese belonged to the
Communist Party. A meeting had been held in Singapore on Christmas Day, 1941, which brought together both Chinese political parties,
the Kuomintang and the Communists, and made possible the formation of a loyal and very successful Chinese military force, DALFORCE,
operating under military command. Shenton's meeting with those
Chinese Communists from the gaol shows the determination of the
Malayan Chinese to resist the Japanese invader. After all, the Chinese
had been fighting the Japanese since 1930, and the success of Chinese
stay-behind parties on the mainland after the surrender is now well
known.

* She was the last troopship, bringing elements of 18th Division, to reach Singapore on 5
February. When entering the harbour she was heavily attacked by Japanese aircraft and set ablaze
from stern to stem. Ironically she was carrying the guns of 125 Anti-Tank Regiment.

February 8

Percival telephoned at midnight to say that enemy had landed to the west of the Causeway. Could not say how many. I warned Police and Simson for civil defence. Disturbed by shelling in my bath! Same 4-inch gun as before. Also shelling during War Council. Daisy not at all well with temp. 103.

February 9

Brig. Torrance (Command H.Q.) attended War Council vice Percival. Enemy have landed in force near Jurong road and pressing on Tengah aerodrome, possibly 2 brigades. But Australians are not fighting well. They had been heavily shelled and many had been found wandering about the roads. Not easy to proceed with denial schemes when we are given no progress reports. Absence of personality in the High Command most unfortunate. Percival doubtless good on paper but not a leader and his staff are all small men. Simmons is excellent and Bennett and Key are staunch fighters, but there is no one to whom the troops as a whole can look to. R.A.F. much worse – Pulford nice but no more. Air Marshal Maltby is easily the best. I asked Percival yesterday if it would be possible for either Simmons or Bennett to be G.O.C. Fortress, and himself G.O.C.-in-C. He replied Fortress is the only area we have! Then I asked whether one or the other could be made Deputy G.O.C. He pointed out this would mean Heath's supercession. I said Heath is a tired man who has retreated 400 miles in a few weeks and no one has confidence in him. We need someone really big here.

February 10

Percival rang at 7 a.m. Japs have progressed more quickly than he expected. 300 R.A.F. ground staff ran away from Tengah aerodrome last night. Am meeting the heads of essential Depts now and am arranging to send all cyphers, save one, to British Consul General in Batavia. A very heavy day and noisy with shelling, explosions and air raids. Australians half-hearted.

Wavell called in the evening, very distressed. He sat in our sitting room, thumping his knees with his fists and saying, "It shouldn't have happened" over and over again. I suggested we had no leaders and he admitted this, and that most of our troops seemed to have an inferiority complex; there had been faulty dispositions at Slim River and at Muar. After his last visit he had considered whether to relieve Percival, "but," he said, "it's not easy to get leaders nowadays." He had thought Heath was good and I replied that he had a heavy job in Eritrea, and that Key had done well too. He agreed. The troops should not be blamed. He had seen a good deal of fighting and Malaya was a very difficult country. Before leaving he went to say goodbye to Daisy who (so she told me later) said to him: "*You* ought to be here!" which seemed to please him. Waiting in the hall I found Air Marshal Sir Richard Peirse (R.A.F.,

India) whom I had not seen for years, and Pulford, and we all said goodbye. Wavell is leaving at dead of night.

To cap it all, my little D has dysentery; where from and how no one can say. Dr Wallace is attending her.

11 February (1942)

Very heavy night of shelling, and many raids and shelling during the day. Practically no labour left. Enemy just beyond the racecourse. Full house here all the same. Daisy's dysentery bad. I tried to persuade her to go to Java with Wavell, but she would have none of it. She is perfectly right of course but I could wish she was out of it. Still, I must admit to being glad she is here to see things through, and fear I didn't try very hard. Her calmness is amazing and many have borne tribute to the help she has given by her example. Yet she feels she is being a nuisance breaking down at such a time. Dreadfully pathetic to see her laid low amid all this noise.

February 12

Many air raids. Battery of guns in the garden quite close to the House, which was shelled very badly, with appalling noise. One shell landed on the back verandahs under which many of our boys were sheltering. Twelve killed, including my own boy, three Gurkha soldiers and one amah. During a lull I crawled under the House with Dawson and Simson and found several bodies. The Gurkhas kneeling with rifles in their hands, the amah resting against the wall. No sign of wounds, and death must have been instantaneous from blast – all covered with yellow dust and almost unrecognisable. After that there was a panic-stricken rush into the House and the Malays asked for the lorry to take them to the Mosque. The Chinese I parked under the billiard table which seems as safe as anywhere! Terribly sad about my boy. He was such a faithful soul. We brought Daisy downstairs. A bed has been put in the verandah at the back of the Reception Room where she will be near to us all. We all slept downstairs also.

The last day on which Sir Shenton Thomas wrote his diary while still in residence at Government House was 13 February, 1942:

February 13

Rest of G.H. Staff left, except Ah Ling, Daisy's Chinese boy. I urged him to go but he burst into tears and said: "I can't leave Lady". What faithfulness. I found my boy's widow in the kitchen and sat down on the floor by her side and tried to comfort her. Gave her all the money I had. Then we were deliberately bombed. One bomb fell in the parking place at the back while I was in the pantry getting a drink for a dispatch rider. He got under the table and I behind the refrigerator – bits flying about everywhere. The small saluting guns on the front steps were demolished. Then more shelling. Told members of the Air Observation

Unit (Roof top) they could make a get-away if they wished as no work for them now. G.H. no longer really habitable as such. On advice of all in the House we left in the evening for Singapore Club where McKerron*, unbeknown to me, had got two rooms for us. Garden in a dreadful state, 15 great craters on the tennis courts. Daisy quite prepared to stay put in G.H., but I explained that by now we were out of touch with affairs; no telephones and motoring dangerous.

Lady Thomas wrote as follows of the last few moments in Government House on the evening of Friday 13 February, 1942:

> We then decided to move to the Club. The Union Jack was still flying over Government House, so we had it taken down and took it with us, rather than let the Japs have it. It was hidden during our 3½ years in prison, and eventually flew again over G.H.

On 13 February when G.H. became uninhabitable, due to artillery bombardment, Shenton and his wife moved to the Singapore Club.

February 14 (The last entry before the Surrender)
Much quieter night in the cool and comfortable rooms at Singapore Club. More air raids and very noisy most of the day with heavy shelling all the afternoon, and counter-barrage by our artillery close by. Daisy now has two of our hospital matrons to nurse her, Miss Smith and Miss Harness, who are splendid. Miss Smith was blown out of her bed, in the spare wing at G.H., yesterday afternoon, by a direct hit on the building, but said nothing at the time. Percival came in and said position no worse. Therefore we would carry on.

After these lengthy quotations from Shenton's diaries, which have been an indispensible source in the compilation of this work, it is appropriate to pause for a moment to see how they came to be preserved. The story is told in the following two letters, both written in ink, to Sir Charles Parkinson at the Colonial Office in London. The first was written on the day that the retreating army moved back across the Causeway to Singapore Island:

Government House
Singapore
Jan. 30, 1942

My dear Parkinson
    I am sending home addressed to you my diary for the local war period and also files in regard to the work of the War Council. They aren't of

---

* The Singapore Club was in the Fullerton Building. Sir Patrick McKerron, K.B.E., C.M.G., Malayan Civil Service, Acting Governor of Singapore 1947.

any value but I don't want to have to burn them here. You may read them if you like.

The rest of our troops cross over from the mainland tonight, so in just under 8 weeks the Japs have walked us out of Malaya. 50 miles a week. It has been a very inglorious show with bad and timid leadership. There are many who think that we ought still to have been in Kedah. Murray Lyon lost us that, and since then we seem all the time to have been looking over our shoulder for the next step back. Then we had the breakthrough in Perak, which Wavell himself told me should never have happened if proper dispositions had been made. And so it has gone on. I fear the Army has become a byword throughout Malaya for incompetence and muddle, and its indiscipline has scared the people out of their wits.

Here there is the same sort of defeatist talk, how that we must be sure to destroy this or that, and get this or that away, so that the Japs shan't get it. I refuse to accept that sort of thing. It ought to be the assumption that we shall hold Singapore, not lose it. What we want here are some first rate fighting commanders and we haven't got them. The only one with that spirit is Spooner.

I had better stop or I shall be indiscreet. I think you had better read my diary. Best wishes to you all.

> Yours sincerely,
> Shenton Thomas

The second was written only five days before the end and enclosed the diaries up to 9 February inclusive.

> Government House
> Singapore
> Feb: 9th 1942

Dear Parkinson,

I send the latter pages of my diary to add to the others. I believe I sent those to you: if not it was to Sir Edward Gent.

Things look grim. Percival tells me the Australians are very half-hearted. Still, we hope for the best.

> Yours ever,
> Shenton Thomas

To return now to the military picture, on that first night of the assault on the Island the Japanese had successfully landed sixteen infantry battalions, with four more in reserve, on a front of four miles; altogether 13,000 Japanese troops landed during the night and another 10,000 before dawn on 9 February. They were opposed by one Australian infantry brigade around Tengah Airfield, so the result was inevitable. If there had been prepared defence works on the north coast the result might have been different, but there were none. This pattern of immense superiority of numbers against an army already tired and conscious of its previous defeats produced the same dismal pattern of withdrawal, this time on to and around Singapore City. The end was clearly in sight when the enemy gained control of the high ground at Bukit Timah and Bukit Mandai and of the large reservoirs in the catchment area, thus cutting off the Island's essential water supply. By now a million people had crowded into the city area. Prisoners had been released from the gaols, stragglers from the armed forces appeared in the town and parties were formed to round them up. There was an air of dissolution in the once gay, imperial city.

On the morning of Sunday, 15 February, at his Headquarters at Fort Canning, General Percival reviewed the position of his army in the beleaguered city. He had come to the end of his supplies of food, ammunition and petrol; the hospitals and hotels were overcrowded with the wounded and sick; above all the water situation for the entire city, let alone the army, was highly critical as the Japanese controlled the outlets from the reservoirs. Unless the water supply could be restored an outbreak of disease would be inevitable. But Wavell had already telegraphed to Percival on the previous day (14th):

> Where water supply exists for troops they must repeat must go on fighting. Your gallant stand is serving its purpose and must be continued to the limit of endurance.

On that afternoon (14th) Percival had reported this situation to the Governor, then at the Singapore Club.

The street scene in Singapore, as described by an eye witness at that time, well shows the disastrous conditions that prevailed in the city. Dr Cecily Williams, who was working in the Tan Tock Seng Hospital, wrote as follows:

> During the last week everything became more and more harassing and disintegrated. When I drove about, the town was full of evacuating and deserting soldiers, most of them Australians looking utterly disorganised and defeated. They had mostly thrown off their equipment, they were looting the shops or sitting in rows with their boots off down near the quays; they were pushing women and children out of the way to get behind buildings when bombs were falling nearby; they were crowding females and children off the boats that were getting away. Many of them must have been killed by the Japanese on the islands off Singapore. It was a terrible show.

About the hospital, where so many non-British children were patients, Dr Williams added:

> By 5 a.m. the shelling was so intense that I cannot imagine why we were not hit – bits of metal seemed to be flying about everywhere. So I picked up the babies in armfuls and put them under beds with three or four mattresses. In the early dawn British soldiers came round for dressings. . . . I had just lain down (under my bed) for a rest when Margaret Smallwood arrived to say we had orders to evacuate the hospital in twelve minutes. The Bishop of Singapore had come with some Medical Auxiliary Service people to get us out, and between us we shifted 100 children, sick, wounded, idiots, and in plaster frames.

Very early on the 15th the following telegram from Wavell reached Percival:

> So long as you are in a position to inflict losses and damage to the enemy and your troops are physically capable of doing so, you must fight on. When you are fully satisfied that is no longer possible I give you discretion to cease resistance.

Now, in conference with his senior commanders at Fort Canning at 9.30 a.m. on that Sunday morning, General Percival had to make a decision. He wrote:

> As I viewed the situation the alternatives were either (a) to counter-attack immediately to regain control of the reservoirs and military food depots, or (b) to capitulate immediately. Formation commanders were all unanimously of opinion that in the existing circumstances a counter-attack was impracticable. I could see no immediate solution for the critical water situation and decided to capitulate. . . . At 11.45 hrs I reported to the Governor at the Singapore Club.

What followed has often been described – how a preliminary delegation went first to see the Japanese, under flag of truce, to arrange a meeting for the surrender proceedings. Here it should be said, and the official historian has stated, "that Percival was quite right to have surrendered, for the disaster to the million Asians in the city, and to the troops, would have been very great had the surrender been delayed by even a few hours." Earlier Percival had been to the Communion Service at Singapore Cathedral, conducted by Bishop Wilson and attended by a very large congregation; the Nave was in use as a casualty station and its floor was blood-stained.

That afternoon, accompanied by Brigadier Torrance (General Staff), Brigadier Newbigging (Chief Administrator) and Major Wild of the 43rd Light Infantry (the interpreter), Lieutenant-General Percival drove to the Bukit Timah crossroads; there they were met by Colonel Sugita, from the staff of General Yamashita. Then came the short walk, with one brigadier carrying the Union Jack and the other a large white flag, to the large but damaged Ford Motor Company premises at Milestone 9 on the Bukit Timah Road. This was the site selected by General Yamashita for the surrender ceremony. Few British officers can have had to undergo such a traumatic experience. The sense of defeat and humiliation that marked, not only military defeat, but the end of British rule in the Far East must have predominated. Meanwhile their leader was to sign his capitulation. Apparently Yamashita kept the four men waiting for some time before he arrived, but the two Generals shook hands before sitting down for the signing ceremony. One wonders if the four British officers were buoyed up by the knowledge that this was but a transient scene, and that one day revenge, retribution and victory for British arms would come? Certainly this knowledge was in Churchill's mind, but he was 10,000 miles away and he did not have to sign an agreement to surrender!

The terms demanded by Yamashita were short but decisive. Surrender was to be *unconditional* and the British Army was to cease hostilities at 8.30 p.m. The Japanese undertook to protect *British* civilians – men, women and children.

Looking again at General Percival's own account of these events, in his formal despatch to H.M.G., written after the war, it is noticeable that he wrote:

> As far as my recollection goes, only one copy [of the surrender document] was produced by the Japanese and this was retained by them. Certainly no copy was handed to me.

What a tragedy for historical records. We shall see later how far this undertaking to protect British lives was implemented. But why only British and not *all* civilians? Shenton Thomas would surely have insisted on the latter.

In connection with the surrender one should note that whenever General Percival spoke to the Governor about important military developments, the latter had invariably telegraphed the information to the Colonial Office. Now he could no longer do so, as all communications with London had ceased. It is significant to look at Shenton's constitutional position, as Governor and High Commissioner and personal representative of the King, vis à vis the act of surrender signed by the G.O.C.-in-C. Malaya. Percival had signed the document as a *military* surrender between his armed forces and the commander of the Japanese – nothing more. In *Singapore 1941–1942* Louis Allen quoted a record* of the conversation between General Yamashita and General Percival immediately before the latter signed his surrender; neither General made any mention of surrendering the Crown Colony to Japanese rule.

Sir Shenton had always refused to meet the Japanese or treat with them on any matter, particularly a surrender by British armed forces. In short he never personally surrendered his office. Looking back, however, at that traumatic sequence of defeats – Pearl Harbour, the invasion of Thailand, Malaya, Hong Kong, Singapore, Borneo and the Netherlands East Indies – its real significance was the disappearance of three colonial empires; but each one under very varied circumstances. The Americans were driven out of the Philippines and from the Pacific. The Dutch lost all their possessions in the East Indies.

In the British colonies three widely different procedures were followed. At Hong Kong on Christmas Day, 1941, in the Peninsula Hotel, Kowloon, Sir Mark Young, the Governor, unconditionally surrendered the Crown Colony, including the British armed forces, to Lieutenant-General Sakai, Commander 23rd Japanese Army. In Burma the Governor, Sir Reginald Dorman-Smith, did not remain in the Colony while another Imperial Army, under General Slim, was withdrawing to India; instead he went to Calcutta by air, and there was no surrender of Burma to Japanese armed forces. In Malaya Sir Shenton Thomas chose to remain in the Colony, with his wife, after the military surrender to the Japanese, and was imprisoned by his enemy until the final British victory.

In these circumstances it seems appropriate to look at the procedure that British Colonial Governors have followed, when their territory has been conquered by a foreign aggressor, or indeed what should happen if such an occasion arises in the future. In the Falklands Islands, to the best of my knowledge, Sir Rex Hunt ordered his small garrison of Royal Marines to cease all resistance in the face of a massive onslaught by heavily armed Argentine military forces. He certainly did not surrender the Crown Colony to the Argentine commander, and was evacuated by the latter to a neutral country. Sir Rex had been given authority by the Foreign and Commonwealth Office to use his discretion in any act he might take, or not take, in the event of invasion.

* From Vol. I of the Japanese *Official History*.

There are still a few British colonial possessions where invasion could happen again.

I end this chapter with a letter from Sir Charles Parkinson to Sir Archibald Weigall, K.C.M.G. The letter is undated but was presumably written not later than 8 February, 1942, when the Japanese landed on Singapore Island. It shows that certainly at that date, probably earlier, H.M.G. had no doubt the military surrender of Singapore was inevitable. Yet the 18th Division was allowed to disembark at Singapore on 29 January.

Private & Personal   Colonial Office
S.W.

My dear Weigall,
    I am sending you this note to let you know that, so far as we can judge, the end is near in Singapore. This, of course, is in strict confidence. What is worrying me is the question of giving Mrs Lotinga some kind of warning. But it may be that she is really expecting it and you may judge it best to say nothing to her – or at any rate nothing more than that things look very grave now.
    Sir Shenton Thomas will undoubtedly stay to the very end, and we must assume that he will be interned – and if Lady Thomas is still with him, she will, I suppose, be interned too. Where or in what conditions we do not know; but, as I told you when you called, we heard from what we believe to be a reliable source, that in the case of Hong Kong Sir Mark Young and the Colonial Secretary and the Secretary for Chinese Affairs were in the Y.M.C.A. at Kowloon and were being treated by the Japanese in a reasonable sort of way, and we should hope that Sir Shenton Thomas (and Lady Thomas if she is with him still) would have similar treatment.

Yours sincerely,
A. C. C. Parkinson

Bridget Lotinga was Shenton's daughter. After the surrender it was generally concluded, unofficially, that her mother, Lady Thomas, must be dead, though Bridget herself never believed this rumour, and happily, as we have seen, she was proved right. She was then living at Englemere in Berkshire, close to Sir Archibald Weigall, who was a friend of the family.

VIII

CAPTIVITY

COMMUNIQUE

The Japanese High Command has issued the following instructions:

1. (i) The existing administrative and economic systems continue to exist, all personnel retaining their present positions for the time being.
   (ii) Public utility services should be restored as quickly as possible, and all employees should continue in their normal duties for the time being.
   (iii) Wireless communication and broadcasting is prohibited.
   (iv) The air defence regulations are to be strictly enforced with special reference to the control of lighting during the hours of darkness. The "brown-out" and "black-out" will therefore continue.
   (v) No communication with the outside world is permitted.
   (vi) No person may leave Singapore Island without permission of the Japanese High Command.
   (vii) All institutions and services relating to the public health and the care of the sick must be carefully supervised and any deficiencies made good as quickly as is practicable. The staff should carry on with their normal duties, tending the sick and wounded and prisoners.
   (viii) The Japanese Army will afford protection to the civilian population. Civilians should remain in their normal places of residence, unless they have received special permission from the Japanese Army to move.
   (ix) There is to be no spying or espionage against the Japanese.
2. The Civil Government is assisting in the restoration of normal conditions in Singapore.
   Committees will be set up to deal with (a) questions of administration, (b) public health, (c) economics and finance, (d) prisoners of war, (e) military affairs including the public peace, communications, war material and supplies, (f) naval affairs, (g) air affairs. There will also be a Liaison Committee, one of whose duties will be to arrange for the eventual transfer of administration to the Japanese High Command.

3. It is the duty of every man and woman in Singapore to co-operate in the task of restoring order and cleanliness in the town. We owe this to the wounded, for whom the existing facilities are inadequate; we must not allow the appearance of disease to reduce these facilities. We owe it also to all the women and children in the town, to all those who have been bereaved, or have lost all they possess. I am confident that everyone will help.

4. I thank all those who have rendered such devoted service during the past days. I thank the civil population for the way in which they have remained quiet.

T. S. W. THOMAS

Feb. 16, 1942

The above is a copy of the last message of Sir Shenton Thomas to the people of Singapore, broadcast by him in English from the Singapore (Radio) Broadcasting Station on the day *after* the British Army's surrender to General Yamashita, the Japanese Army Commander.

The original script of this document, which the Governor himself drafted in pencil on an ordinary office scribbling block, first came into the possession of an Englishman, Mr Thomas Hope, an employee of the *Straits Times* press, when it was published in the Japanese newspaper *Syonan Shimbun* on 21 February, 1942. Mr Hope kept the script folded in an envelope in his wallet until after the war. The draft of the broadcast had been endorsed by Shenton in laconic style: "Note for printer. Do not put Governor under my name. TSWT." He did this because he was certain that if he still described himself as Governor the Japanese would not broadcast the communique. As we saw in the previous chapter, Shenton Thomas did not surrender to the Japanese and always insisted on maintaining his formal position as Head and representative of the Malayan peoples, albeit in practice he could no longer be active as Governor and High Commissioner.

The significance of this document stems from the fact that it was written and broadcast by order of the Japanese, who fully appreciated the immensity of their task in restoring "order and cleanliness" in a city of a million inhabitants. As a result of the bombardment public works and services were virtually non-existent. The Governor well knew that unless these were quickly restored contagious disease and sickness would flourish unchecked. Hence the need for the message as the only means of getting the Asian population back to work. The Japanese also appreciated that they had an obligation to guard and maintain some 80,000 prisoners of war of all ranks and several nationalities, and many thousands more civilian internees.

In this uneasy climate, with no established police force at work, the

Governor was allowed to remain at the Singapore Club premises in the Fullerton Building. This was fortunate as Daisy was still very ill with dysentery and the building had become an improvised hospital, where hundreds of seriously wounded servicemen were installed, and makeshift operating theatres set up. The conditions were indescribable; patients slept on mattresses or rugs laid on the floor, while the landings and corridors were stacked with the bodies of those who had died, awaiting "improvised" burial. *Improvisation* was a feature of day-to-day life and other large buildings, such as the Cricket Club, also became temporary hospitals.

It was in the Fullerton Building that Freddy Bloom began the famous series of letters to her husband, published under the title *Dear Philip**, which she continued to write from Changi Gaol for the next 3½ years. Her husband was in the military wing at Changi and her letters to him reveal the conditions and atmosphere of prison life under the Japanese.

This period, before all prisoners, civil and military, were incarcerated in Changi Gaol, must have been an agonizing time for Shenton. Apart from the sheer physical contrast of his translation from the status of Governor to that of prisoner, he knew how much now depended on his relations with the Japanese. The very sight of Singapore reminded him of the surrender, the failure of the British and the denial schemes which there had not been time to complete. But there had been some luck there too, of which the following is an example. By 11 February the Fighter Aircraft Operations Rooms at Kallang airfield had been disbanded, but fortunately the Senior Radio Officer then in Singapore, Flight-Lieutenant Carter**, was still there and has described what he found:

> On Feb. 12 I felt a little uneasy about the speed with which the Operations Room had been disbanded, and went to make sure no secret material had been left there. It had. In a desk drawer there was a complete plot, on tracing paper, of that first air raid on Singapore on December 8th. I burnt it. We, who faced capture, did not wish to be interrogated by the Japanese about the performance of British radar.

During his long captivity Shenton Thomas still kept his daily diary, but now he could only write in that small leather-bound volume with five days to a page; nor could he write daily, and there are some

---

* Bodley Head, 1980.
** Dr T. C. Carter, op. cit.

1. The Reverend Thomas William Thomas and Mrs. Hugh Thomas (nee Susanne Whilelegge) Shenton Thomas' parents.

2. Shenton Thomas in 1912, the year of his marriage.

3. Daisy in 1912.

4. Colonel James
Alexander Lawrence
Montgomery ("Uncle
Jimmie")

5. Home in Nairobi –
Uncle Jimmie's House,
where Daisy lived.

6. On safari – from left to right: Daisy, Harold Montgomery (her cousin) and Uncle Jimmie.

7. Christiansborg Castle, Accra, residence of the Governor of the Gold Coast.

8. A view of Singapore from the roof of Government House, 1932.

9. Government House, Singapore 1934.

10. The Presidential Palace, Singapore 1984.

11. His Excellency The Governor, 1936.

12. The Governor's Lady.

13. "S.S. Sea Belle II".

14. The Promenade Deck.

15. Malay Sultans: Front row from left to right: Yang-di-Pertuan, Negri Sembilan; The Sultan of Perak; H.E. The Governor; Lady Thomas; The Sultan of Selangor; The Sultan of Pahang. Back row; Left and Centre two A.D.C.s. Far right: Noel Ross, Private Secretary.

6. Professor (Emeritus)
. J. H. Corner, C.B.E.,
.R.S., F.L.S.

17. R.A.F. "Passing Out" Parade at Singapore. Sir Shenton Thomas inspects the cadets on parade.

18. In the course of his adventurous journey from Moscow to Washington to take up his duties as the new Soviet Ambassador there, M. Litvinov called at Singapore.

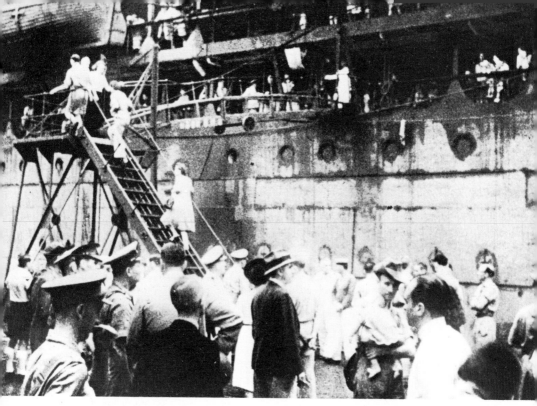

19. A scene on the quayside at Singapore as women and children were evacuated from the city shortly before the Japanese onslaught on the Island.

20. A ship raked by enemy bombs, settled alongside a ruined pier. Smoke rises behind from British stores burned to prevent their falling into Japanese hands.

21. Japanese Infantry advancing on bicycles.

22. Japanese troops parading near Raffles Place, Singapore.

日本衛兵諸君に告ぐ

日本の陸、海、空軍は全部聯合國に投降せり。

この投降條件に日本天皇陛下が親しく御

署名せられたので、太平洋戦争はこれを以て

終了した。

聯合國の航空機は二、三数日中に英語、オ

ランダ語及び印度語で書いた傳單を日本軍

の抑留下にある聯合國の兵士と人民に指令を

与へて落す。聯合國の兵士と人民は須く沈着冷

静を保ち現位置に止まるべし。

日本の衛兵は二の傳單を手に入れた時、直ちに聯

合國の捕虜、人民に渡し、彼等を丁寧に取扱ふべ

し。衛兵諸君が二の傳單を渡した後、夫々各自

宿営地に帰るべし。

日本軍游兵は聯合國の捕虜が人民に対し、より食

物を与へ出来得べくの優遇を惜まざるやう夫々

責任を負ふべし。一名または数名の聯合軍游兵が近日

中に無電機を携行して日本側の聯合國兵士収容所に

来迎すべきとなって居り、其の任務は主として聯合軍兵士

と連絡を保ち、彼等と聯合軍最高指揮官に通

達するにあり。よって日本衛兵はこれら聯合軍、游兵の行動

を手助し又は妨害せぬ進んで彼等に協力を与へ善を保渡す

べし。

23. Japanese orders to surrender.

25. *Above:* Marshal Terauchi. He lived in Government House, with Major General Kawamura, Commander of Syonan (Singapore) Defence Force.

24. *Left:* General Yamashita, victor of Singapore.

26. Captivity. Lady Thomas sweeping out her cell.

27. P.O.W. Camp, Taihoku. 9 September 1943. Sir Shenton Thomas at nine stone.

28. Release at last for Sir
Shenton Thomas.

29. Lady Thomas attends
the ceremony of rehoisting
the Union Flag in
Singapore.

30. Bridget. Daughter of Sir Shenton and Lady Thomas.

31. Scroll presented to Lady Thomas by her fellow inmates in Changi Jail on the occasion of her birthday.

significant gaps, for reasons beyond his control which will appear later. Extracts covering his stay in the Fullerton Building show how he negotiated with the Japanese.

> *February 15, 1942*
> Very heavy shelling by both sides. Fraser (Colonial Secretary) and Brigadier Newbigging went to contact Japanese for armistice. Percival sent for. Air raids close to the Club. Cease Fire 8.30 p.m. General Heath gave orders for parade 4 p.m. and I had to harangue the troops. Water, food, ammunition all finished so Percival told me in the evening. Executive Council p.m.

The fact that the Governor "harangued the troops" at the request of General Sir Lewis Heath is not on record elsewhere to the best of my knowledge; equally, there is no record of the Government's last executive meeting, presumably to take note officially of the military surrender to the Japanese armed forces.

> *February 16*
> Met the Japanese at Fort Canning. Various Committees set up. Back to G.H. for stores, etc. Place very badly knocked about. My office especially with a hole right through my own desk!

In those early days of the occupation the Japanese allowed the Governor to use one of the Government House cars, without which he could not usefully negotiate with them; generally he was driven by Leslie Davis.

> *February 17*
> This day all British troops marched to Changi. Some women to Sultan of Trengganu's House and the Roxy Cinema, some civilian men to Karikal and Hoo Chiat Police Station, and Indians to Farrer Park. Saw Col. Suzuki about all this. Arranged for passes with Toyoda, ex-Consul General, who was most helpful. To G.H. again, brought away some wool and more stores. Visited Dickinson in General Hospital, now taken over by Japanese.

From the beginning of the occupation sometimes quite large numbers of military prisoners and civil internees were brought out of gaol for essential construction work and rebuilding. Indian sepoys were used extensively, as well as professional British engineers, to restore water supplies, power and light, rebuild bridges, repair communication lines, etc. The "helpful" Toyoda had to cope with the issue of the many passes involved. With limited space in his diary Shenton could not mention his interview with Mr Corner of the Malay Civil Service.

E. J. H. Corner had joined the M. C. S. in 1929 as Assistant Director of the Gardens Department of the Straits Settlements. He became a highly qualified botanist and it was he who advised Shenton Thomas on the upkeep and maintenance of the Government House gardens; he had also accompanied the Governor on his tour of Malaya with the Game Warden of Kenya in connection with game preservation laws. When surrender came, Mr Corner, with many other officials, sought refuge in the Fullerton Building. Uppermost in his mind was the absolute need to safeguard and preserve the "scientific treasure houses of knowledge" which existed in Malaya, yet had no military significance. Their loss would be a cultural disaster. He therefore considered it his job to remain in Singapore, contact the Japanese, explain his problem and try to solve it with their co-operation. With this in mind, he went into action at about 6.30 a.m. on 17 February. He has recently published an account of his experiences:*

> I dressed quickly and went to find the Governor, Sir Shenton Thomas, to seek his approval for my mission. As I opened the door to go downstairs up came the Private Secretary, to order me to Sir Shenton who had the same idea. Sir Shenton quickly wrote a pencilled note in which he requested the Japanese authorities to preserve the scientific collections, libraries, and matters of historic interest, particularly at the Museum and Botanical Gardens. He handed me the note, and with a twinkle in his eye, charged me to deliver it. That note, so precious to me, was taken by Professor Tanakadate to Tokyo in 1943, where it was consumed in a fire that raged after an air raid in 1945. I then returned to my companions at Fullerton, who included several foresters and agriculturalists, showed them the note and asked if they would follow my example; but clearly there was a determination to stand together, shoulder to shoulder in custody and humility, *which I would not*, and I saw at heart they were not scientists.
>
> Later that morning I went to the Municipal Building where I found Mr Rayman, President of the Municipality, arranging for various British persons to stay out from internment in order to repair and maintain essential services until Japanese replacements arrived. In all about a hundred were so delegated. I explained my problem to Mr Rayman, showed him my note from Sir Shenton and asked for priority in interview with the Japanese because of the danger of looting. He took my point at once, giving me precedence in spite of protests and dissent from

---

* *The Marquis* by Professor E. J. H. Corner, C.B.E., Professor Emeritus of Tropical Botany, Cambridge University, Heinemann Asia, 1981.

those waiting before me. But I was undeterred and ruthless in the insane circumstances, and cast off all hesitation; the plague of my stammer left me *for ever*. In a few minutes I found myself in the presence of Mr Toyoda. This cultured and clever man was in the process of taking over from Rayman. He took the note of Sir Shenton, read it carefully and surveyed me as if my future were in the balance. He told me a professor (Tanakadate) was arriving from Saigon to take charge of scientific affairs and that I should return tomorrow at 10 a.m.; in the meantime I must remain at Fullerton Building. He provided me with an official pass and armband; and I saw the vision happening.

I wish I had space in this work to review the whole fascinating story of Professor Corner in Singapore for the next three and a half years. The actual offer he received from the Japanese is important and is again best told in his own words:

> I cannot recall the exact words of Sir Shenton's note; it was in my hands for only half a day. It was not addressed to me but to the Japanese Authority and was signed simply "T. Shenton Thomas". It instructed E. J. H. Corner, of the Botanical Gardens (Singapore): "To hand over to the Japanese Authority the historical, scientific and cultural records and libraries in Singapore, especially at Raffles Museum and Library, the Botanical Gardens, Raffles College and the King Edward VII College of Medicine." I could not know to what it would lead, but the intention of the note is clear in my mind and Sir Shenton's twinkle implied "Do what you can!" Later on Professor Tanakadate, Professor Kariba and the Marquis Tokugawa (the latter is the subject of my book, and was appointed Supreme Adviser to the Japanese Military Administration and Civil Governor of Malaya) jointly asked me to stay with them and "help" in the purpose of Sir Shenton's note, rather than be interned. The only Englishman, other than myself, who foresaw to preserve records and libraries, cultural and scientific archives and specimens, was Sir Shenton Thomas, and this marks him out as far above the other administrators then in Singapore.*

Professor Corner's book *The Marquis* reveals him, all too belatedly, as a great man, possessing courage and determination not often seen; above all, he had the moral courage to stand his ground and put up with much unfair criticism and comment. For, not surprisingly, he was often the subject of jealousy and accusation by some British prisoners of war, who saw him apparently free and untrammelled while they lived as prisoners in hardship and privation. He wrote in his book:

* From a letter to the author.

Many times in those early days I searched my soul. Was I working cryptically for the return of the British or, as Japanese propaganda swelled and filled the newspapers and was our only fount of world events, openly for this Southern Empire? Invariably the middle course burst through, to save for posterity the records of the Malay Peninsula. The Japanese accused the Professor [Tanakadate] of being pro-British and anti-Japanese. The British internees accused me of being anti-British and pro-Japanese.

Readers of *The Marquis* will find a series of highly interesting vignettes of the people who lived and worked in Singapore during the years of occupation; they are all there – the Japanese conquerors whose attitude changes as they fear the collapse of their country; the indigenous population who have to work for the conquerors but long for their departure; the prisoners in their thousands, some of whom never leave gaol and others who are taken out only for interrogation and torture by the infamous Kempetai in the Y.M.C.A. building. Others leave Changi Gaol under temporary parole for reconstruction work. Lady Heath was allowed out to have her baby delivered by a British doctor in the Miyako hospital in Singapore city.* Of course, conditions for prisoners working outside Changi under temporary license were far better than inside the gaol. But they all had to return to Changi, to the cells or to the prison hospital.

Corner frequently saw the prisoners who were sent out of Changi. He often risked torture, and probably death, when he passed close to a captive and surreptitiously slipped bank notes into his hands. After the war official recognition came to him in the shape of a C.B.E., as well as Fellowship of the Royal Society and the Linnaean Society.

Notwithstanding his many worries at this time, Shenton's mind must often have turned to the fate of the Straits Settlements, of which he was constitutionally the ruler. The smallest of these was Labuan, a tiny island six miles off the coast of Borneo and 700 miles from Singapore. What happened there has been described by the Resident of the Settlement, Hugh Humphrey,** who had been Sir Shenton's Private Secretary from 1936 to 1938:

> The first positive indication that war was very close was a cable from Singapore telling me that Admiral Sir Tom Phillips, with 3 staff officers, was arriving by sea 'plane on December 5th and would leave the following day. Labuan commanded the approaches to Brunei Bay in

---

* The Miyako had been the hospital for the M.C.S.
** H. Humphrey, C.M.G., O.B.E., P.M.N., to the author November 1982.

which there was safe anchorage for almost all the fleets of the world. At dinner that night I asked the Admiral if he thought Japan would go to war. He replied "I don't think so".

Some 8,000 people (5,000 Chinese, 3,000 Malays and 6 British) lived on Labuan. The latter, in addition to myself, consisted of the Manager of the Cable and Wireless Station with his Assistant, the Customs Officer, the Harbour Master, and the Agent for Harrison and Crosfield who owned the commercial wharves and godowns. I had no soldiers, but there was an unarmed force of 30 constables of the Malay police under an Asian Inspector.

Of course I had prepared our denial scheme, designed in particular for destruction of the cable and W/T installation and the stocks of oil fuel, with everything else likely to be of use to the enemy. On 27th December a Japanese aircraft flew low over the island and machine-gunned Government House, the Harbour area, the Hospital and the Convent, as well as dropping leaflets showing John Bull standing over down-trodden Asians! I thereupon put into effect our denial scheme, destroying harbour works, oil and food stocks, and confidential papers, with all secret codes, except one of the latter. I also moved my Headquarters to join Graham Lawrie, the Manager at the Cable and Wireless Station. He and I were to man the cable terminal till the last possible moment, but I had ordered the other four British to leave by fast motor launch for the mainland before that "last moment" arrived.

At 7.30 p.m. on January 1st 1942, it was pitch dark and raining hard, when a police constable, wet and breathless, rushed in to report that Japanese troops were disembarking at the Government jetty and seizing the harbour installations and official buildings. I told the other four British to leave at once for the mainland, taking with them all the reserve currency from the safe, which they did. They were captured weeks later, hundreds of miles away in Sarawak.

This left myself, Graham Lawrie and one Chinese operator, at the cable station from where I sent a MOST IMMEDIATE cable to Singapore. "1st Jan. Japs have landed. Am destroying codes." A few minutes later, another cable: "W/T destroyed. Cable soon will be." Finally the last communication from Labuan. "Code destroyed."

It was a stark and eerie atmosphere at the Cable Station that night with just shaded lights and the now useless electrical equipment. I recall when Graham Lawrie had thrown a switch, and wisps of smoke with an acrid smell arose, to prove the cable link was destroyed. He then told his Chinese operator, who had been calmly doing his job, to leave by a back window to avoid the road.

Left alone, we two sat on chairs at a work table. At 8.10 p.m. there were noises of people outside under the porch where my car was. I wondered if the Japs might fire through the wooden walls, or fling in a grenade. They did neither. They smashed in doors and windows with their rifle butts, and we were surrounded by short wet soldiers, jabbering

and pointing their rifles at us. We held up our hands, and were then
quickly taken outside and I was shoved into my car and told to "drive to
town", with soldiers inside and on the running boards. We stopped at
the Government Rest House, and when I got out a soldier swung his
right fist with all his strength and hit me on the jaw. I fell flat on the
ground but was kicked up again, and told to lie on the floor with Lawrie.
There I saw the Harbour Master, who had delayed too long at his post,
was captured and given similar treatment. Then an officer in field boots
and wearing a sword arrived. We were taken to the Court House where
the wooden (Prisoner's) dock was brought out and we three were forced
to sit inside on its floor. By now it was 11 p.m. and the officer returned,
poked his sword scabbard between the bars of the dock and hit me with it
repeatedly on the face and head, shouting: "Bad prisoner, burn oil". We
spent all night there, wet, cold and unable to stretch a limb, until at dawn
we were told to get up and local people (Malays) began to arrive. When
we indicated we needed the lavatory we were forced to urinate in front of
the crowd. It seems public humiliation was the policy, for we were
kicked back into the dock, where we remained until 4 p.m. while various
people were encouraged to come and view us. Then we were put into
separate cells in the police station.

Thus ended British rule in one lone outpost in the South China Sea.
Hugh Humphrey and his British colleagues were imprisoned in
Sarawak until the Allied victory in 1945, when Humphrey returned to
Labuan. He was received there by the entire population with joy and
affection.

Meanwhile Shenton's diary for the time he was in Fullerton Building
shows the degree to which the Japanese responded to his efforts to
improve the lot of the prisoners. Clearly they were making use of their
captives' skills to put Singapore back on a working basis as quickly as
possible: then they would put them all under prison control, which was
much cheaper and easier, in Changi Gaol. Before that, however, at the
end of February, the civil internees were moved temporarily to the
coast at Katong. After the war Daisy wrote of this pre-Changi time and
of her own arrival at the prison:

> After the surrender our first reaction was that we should all be killed by
> the Japs. But everyone was summoned to the padang where a General
> made a long speech saying that by the kindness of the Emperor we
> should not be killed, but imprisoned. After some time we were trans-
> ferred to derelict houses on the waterfront [at Katong] where my
> husband and I, with others, were put in an old, very filthy Japanese
> restaurant; it had some iron bedsteads, a few tables and some crockery,
> but all the water was cut off and there were no sanitary arrangements. I

was still pretty ill but the nurses and Dr Wallace were allowed to stay with us, and Shenton and another man made an excellent commode for the ladies. Next door there was a smaller house for women only and I was dreading being moved, but one day the Japs insisted that we, the two nurses and Jill Dawson (we said she was my lady-in-waiting as her husband had been Shenton's Secretary for Defence!) must all go. However, we told the Japs I was much too ill to be moved, and they agreed to send their own doctor to see me. Before he arrived the nurses covered my face with powder till I looked ghastly, much worse than I really was, and they did not even tell Dr Wallace. When the latter came with the Jap doctor I saw his face of horror, and the nurse standing by me holding my hand. The Jap doctor said I need not move!

A few days later all the civil internees were ordered to parade for the march to Changi Gaol, to be led by my husband – the distance was over 8 miles, in the hottest part of the day. Shenton duly led that march to prison, and the Japanese hoped the local population would turn out to jeer at their Governor; but the marchers passed through streets of people with sad and silent faces, who proferred glasses of water when the captives were allowed to stop for the rest.

In *Dear Philip* Freddy Bloom gives this vivid account of the way the women internees made their journey to Changi:

> We formed up in lines of five. If only you could have seen us – the very old or ill were loaded in transport but the rest covered a great span of years, types and temperament. We had all dressed with only one idea – comfort and the greatest care for our feet. . . . I looked splendid in my khaki trousers and a looted white evening blouse which was the only thing I owned with long sleeves. . . . Can you imagine several hundred females dressed in similar haphazard fashion marching forth under a strong, armed guard! . . .
>
> A number of women fell out and had to be picked up, but the majority struggled on and as we came in sight of the prison we all got into step, and, singing *There'll Always Be an England* at the top of our voices, we marched through the high walls. The men, already there at the other side, cheered themselves hoarse.

Instead of going to Changi Gaol Daisy was sent first to a so-called "hospital" which was formerly the lunatic asylum; Dr Wallace and the two nurses were allowed to accompany her.

> When we arrived it was the most awful shock. The poor lunatics were still there, starving, and a few cells were vacant for us. There was a long room where patients from other hospitals had been taken, lying on the floor without mattresses, and the doctors who were there were allowed

to go out for a few things. Luckily I had some money (our Colonial currency was still in use) so we managed to get mattresses and pillows for 2 men who were lying alone on the cement floor; they each had terrible burns from an oil tank that had blown up. I had heard nothing from my husband and was feeling very ill, finding it hard to cope with things at first. Then the Roman Catholic Bishop came to see me. He was doing wonderful work, collecting all the young Chinese girls he could find and placing them with the Little Sisters of the Poor who were still in their Convent; he had found a dear old Chinese amah from Government House and took her to the Convent, but she died.

It was very gruesome in that asylum as I heard people shuffling along outside my cell, and found it was people who had died being carried out on stretchers.

In April I recovered and was sent into Changi Gaol where I had a cell to myself on the 4th floor. It was a native prison and the loo was a cement-bordered hole in the floor with a chain to flush the water. There was no basin, but we managed to stand on the cement and pour cans of water over ourselves. The one window was very high in the wall, and the bed was a cement slab in the middle. However I did have a mattress and I had brought a pillow with me; later on both these were cut in half to make do also for women who had not brought such things; the Japs provided nothing in that way. Gradually we all settled down and things were not too bad. Food was extremely scanty and boring. For breakfast a plate of rice boiled in water and left stodgy, a mug of tea without milk, though with a small ration of raw sugar which helped. Lunch was a kind of soup, made of spinach and dried rice which we called "Duck Pond Soup" because it was always covered with a green slime! The men cooked it on their side and brought it over in tubs, and we all lined up with plates for our ration. In the afternoon more rice, and generally the men managed to make small rice buns, so we were able to keep something for later on. We did all the cleaning of our cells. But I was not allowed to see or hear from my husband.

By the end of this first week in March, 1942, all the Singapore captives, the prisoners of war and the civilian internees, were incarcerated behind the grim walls of Changi Gaol. They numbered some 2,000 men, mainly British of over military age who had remained behind, with 400 or so women and children in the separate female wing; the prison had been built to house 700 convicted criminals. In the women's camp the population was more mixed, but fell into three broad categories. There were nurses, doctors and professional women who had remained to look after the sick and distressed; there were the wives of the men who had stayed behind, civil and military; lastly there were the non-European wives, mostly with children, of men in Changi, including a large number of Jewish families who had been rounded up by the Japanese. One of the progressively difficult problems was the overcrowding, made worse by the number of internees sent in later on by the Japanese. After two years the men in Changi numbered some 3,000, with 650 women and children; at the end of three and a half years the total numbers were 4,000 men and 1,350 women and children. During the whole period there were about 200 deaths, mostly among the elderly, and some 20 births in prison*.

Once all the captives were behind bars the true attitude of the Japanese began to show itself. Without exception every captive in Changi for the next three and a half years suffered from hunger and hardship, loneliness and depression, as well as humiliation and insults from camp guards and sentries. Shenton Thomas wrote that when the Japanese found any prisoner with a shirt or coat button undone he was ordered to stand while a guard administered a painful "flick" on the tip of the nose for each unfastened button. He himself was once flicked five times for five loosened buttons. Men or women who did not bow deeply enough to a sentry were kicked or beaten, or were locked up for 48 hours without food or water. Cecily Williams wrote: "This bowing business was a perfect farce. I never felt it was worth worrying about and used to bow to the Nipponese front, back or side! But some people never seemed to get used to it."

All this was in addition to the physical illness that became a commonplace of daily life; aches and pains, festering sores that spread and would not heal, were such frequent ailments that only very serious cases were referred to the prison hospital. But I must also record the dreadful ordeals which befell those unfortunate captives who were sent for interrogation by the Kempetai in the Y.M.C.A. building.

On the Double Tenth (10 October, 1943) the Kempetai descended on the Civilian Internee Camp at Changi convinced that they would find an organized spy ring transmitting messages and organizing sabotage on Singapore Island. On 27 September, 1943, there had been a daring raid by frogmen of the Royal Australian Navy, led by a British officer (Major Lyon of the Highland Light Infantry), on warships and merchant vessels in Keppel Harbour. Seven Japanese ships had been sunk and several more extensively damaged, and the Japanese were determined on revenge. The fact that the accusations were false did not prevent the imprisonment and torture (sometimes death) of a number of men (including the Bishop of Singapore) and three women. After the war an official commission at Singapore took evidence from the 57

---

* For these and other descriptions of life in Changi Gaol I am greatly indebted to Dr Cecily Williams, C.M.G., D.M., F.R.C.P., and Freddy Bloom.

internees who had been removed from Changi Prison on or after that 10 October, and were interrogated in the Y.M.C.A. Building or at other Japanese Military Police Centres. Below are some extracts from the Commission's report.

Usually interrogation started quietly and would continue thus as long as the inquisitors got the required answers. If, for any reason, such answers were not forthcoming then physical violence followed immediately. The methods used were:

(a) Beating with metal bars, sticks, bamboos, wet knotted ropes, belts with buckles, or revolver butts, all over the body. While these beatings were being inflicted, the victims were sometimes suspended by their wrists from a rope passed over a beam. Sometimes their hands were tied behind their backs and they were forced to kneel while sharp-edged pieces of wood or metal were placed behind their knees so as to cut into the flesh as they knelt. A guard would then jump on their thighs or on the projecting ends of the bar behind their knees; sometimes, to increase the pressure on this bar, a Japanese would perch on the shoulders of the victim, or the victim would be compelled to hold heavy weights above his head. They were often forced to remain in this position without intermission for 9/10 hours, during which period interrogation would go on remorselessly. At times the victim would be tied to a table and flogged until he lost consciousness. In one case, the man thus flogged counted over 200 blows before losing consciousness. This treatment was, in some cases, carried on daily for 4/5 days consecutively. Once a European, who died later, was interrogated, with the usual beatings, for 55 hours at a stretch and another European, since dead, underwent 44 hours of beatings in all, according to the estimates of his cell-mates.

(b) *Water torture.* There were two forms of water torture. In the first, the victim was tied or held down on his back and a cloth placed over his nose and mouth. Water was then poured on the cloth. Interrogation proceeded and the victim was beaten if he did not reply. As he opened his mouth to breathe or to answer questions, water went down his throat until he could hold no more. Sometimes he was then beaten over his distended stomach, or a Japanese jumped or stood on it.

Alternatively the victim was tied lengthways on a ladder, face upwards, with a rung of the steps across his throat and his head beneath the ladder. In this position he was slid head first into a tub of water and kept there until almost drowned. After being revived, interrogation continued and he would be re-immersed.

(c) *Electric torture.* There were two forms of this. In the first an induction coil was used, one electrode being attached to the hand or foot; alternatively a bare wire was applied to various parts of the body. One victim reports that he was thrown across the room by the violence of the shock, with an effect that produced physical and mental disintegration.

(d) During interrogation the inquisitor, in many cases, burnt the victim with cigarette and cheroot ends, even on the most sensitive parts of the body, e.g. the arm-pits, between the toes, on the scrotum and penis. Several Asiatics had petrol poured on their bellies and ignited, and another Asiatic had his hands tied together and immersed in a bowl of methylated spirit which was then ignited.

(e) In addition to these forms of torture, the inquisitors often employed other methods such as twisting of limbs, bending back of fingers, punching, repeated blows on the same spot, and so on. These methods in many cases resulted in dislocations and permanent damage to limbs and joints. In one case the inquisitor punctuated his questions by flicking off, with the frayed end of a bamboo, the flesh bruised in a previous beating. This left a permanent scar, six inches by three inches, on the victim's thigh.

(f) In several cases victims were led to believe that their execution, either by beheading or shooting, was imminent. They were advised to write a letter of farewell. Preparations for execution were carried out, up to the penultimate stage, with such realism that in two cases the victims fainted.

(g) *Threats to families.* Threats were also made to take action against the family of the victim (the wives of some internees were believed to be in Japanese custody in other parts of Asia). Torture was carried to the limit of human endurance. One internee attempted to commit suicide by jumping over the verandah. In his fall he fractured his pelvis but, despite his condition, his interrogation under torture continued until just before he died. In another case, the internee asked his inquisitors for the means to commit suicide. A pistol was produced and was snatched away only when the man was about to carry out his declared intention.

Of the 57 internees detained as a result of the Japanese investigation on 10/10/43, 12 died of sickness directly attributable to the appalling conditions under which they were detained; one died as described in the preceding paragraph and one was executed. The survivors, who returned after lengthy custody by the Military Police, required prolonged treatment in the Camp Hospital for extreme emaciation, including chronic dysentery, neuritis, sores, ulcers, scabies, beri-beri, weak hearts, or injuries to joints and limbs.

The three women taken from Changi Prison were detained in exactly the same conditions as the men and shared cells with male prisoners of all races. They were afforded no privacy, even for their most intimate requirements, and any attempt on the part of European men to screen them was broken down by the guards. They were subjected to insults and obscene gestures by Japanese prisoners in the same cell, who, with the assent of the guards, tried to compel them to perform the most sordid tasks.

The buildings occupied by the Japanese Military Police resounded day and night with blows, the bellowings of the inquisitors and the shrieks of the tortured. From time to time victims from the torture chambers would stagger back or, if unconscious, would be dragged back to their cells with the marks of ill-treatment on their bodies. In one such case an unconscious victim died during the night, without receiving any medical attention, and his body was not removed until the afternoon. In these conditions and this atmosphere of terror men and women waited their summons to interrogation, which might come at any hour of the day or night.

After the war Lady Thomas published significant details of these atrocities in a letter to *The Spectator* dated 25 October, 1946, in which, inter alia, she said:

> That so few, in comparison with our numbers, died is solely due to the magnificent work carried out in shocking conditions by our own doctors and nursing sisters, for whom no praise can be too high.

She herself was questioned in Changi Gaol on 1 April, 1943, by a senior Japanese officer (identity unknown), accompanied by Lieutenant Suzuki and a Mr Tomigaura. Dr Cecily Williams was allowed to be present and recorded the long proceedings, from which the following extract is pertinent, in view of its bearing on the surrender issue:

Nipponese Officer (N.O.)	You, Mrs Thomas.
Lady T.	Yes.
N.O.	I come here special to see you.
Lady T.	That is very kind of you.
N.O.	You told them to hang out the white flag at

	Government House so Singapore had to surrender.
Lady T.	No, certainly not. I did not want to surrender.
N.O. (insisting)	But you told them to hang out the flag at Government House.
Lady T.	Certainly not. Nothing of the sort. You have been misinformed.
N.O.	Then who surrendered? Your husband?
Lady T.	The Military were in command. We had to do what they advised.
N.O.	Oh, so you did not surrender but Percival surrendered Singapore. Singapore – you know what that name means? Lion's city. . . .
Lady T.	Yes, the British lion, it means.
N.O.	Now you have lost it. It is no more British. It is now Syonan. The "shining" in the South, and after a little time it will become the "brilliance" in the South. Now it is no longer British – it is Nipponese.
Lady T.	Yes, temporarily.
N.O.	Temporarily?
Lady T.	Yes; only temporarily.

Shining through all personal stories of the captives at Changi who were tortured or interrogated by the Kempetai is one common factor: compassion for each other and the unbreakable bonds of mutual help, no matter what penalty from their captors might follow. Freddy Bloom's account makes this very clear:

When I was taken from Changi for interrogation I was transported into town in an elegant car, with a cultured interpreter sitting next to me. In the office my shoulder bag was taken from me, so were my hairpins, glasses and rings. The elastic in my knickers was removed. I was led through a passage, which had thick wooden bars along its whole length with cells about 10′ by 17′ on either side, each holding some 15 people. I was pushed into a cell where two rows of men, Europeans, Chinese, Indians, sat upright facing the bars. Their legs were crossed, their hands folded in their laps. . . . The cell was quite bare with one large electric light bulb in the ceiling; in the corner was a lavatory, European but with no seat, and an ordinary tap from which the flow of water could be controlled. We sat for several hours when my back began to hurt and I leaned against the wall. But the sentry would not allow that, and prodded me with his gun to sit upright.

Once the door was opened and two Japanese, bare from the waist up, dragged in an unconscious figure. Two men rose and lifted the body, laying it carefully in a corner. The Japanese stayed a minute to make certain nobody had ideas of tending the wounded man.

Then they left and the sentry continued marching up and down. . . . During all this time men rose and used the toilet in the corner . . . I continued to sit but eventually became aware not only of my own discomfort but of that of all the men as well. It was extraordinary, but as I got up and walked to the corner I could feel each man retire within himself in his effort to give me a privacy that was not there. . . .

When steaming hot tea, no milk or sugar, arrived we had to drink through rusty tins with holes which had to be plugged with fingers. My fingers blistered until a short, broad, bearded Chinese took my mug from me and covered the holes with his rough, strong, filthy hands and held it for me to drink, gently like a mother feeding a child. For the next five months he did this for me every day.

It would be wrong to give the impression that all the men, European and Asiatic, behaved heroically at all times. A few broke and behaved very badly. The light never went out and after dark we were ordered to lie down, body stretched out next to body, sixteen in all. Three times a day we had rice and a bucket of tea. The only events that followed no set pattern were the dreaded visits of the interrogators. They would stop in front of our cells and shout out the names of those wanted for questioning. The victims would get up, put on their shoes and then disappear. . . . There was no way of knowing how they would come back, or never come back at all. . . .

I had a particular Indian friend, Makinder Singh, a tall, young, well-built Sikh. At night the guard insisted that he sleep next to me, probably with the idea of degrading both of us. Once I woke when something moved inside my blouse. I sat up with a start which woke the Sikh who was only an inch away. I had instinctively grasped the moving object, which jumped out and ran away; it was a mouse and I was horrified. The bearded, ferocious-looking Sikh smiled reassuringly and patted my arm: "*Tid apa* (never mind) *memsahib. Is only leedle mize.*"

Certain people one never forgets. Norman Coulson was accused of being a ringleader in the sabotage plot. They tried to make him confess that he had worked a transmitter, and make him implicate another man. For several weeks he was taken out every single day and then flung back into the cell, bleeding and green with pain. They never broke him. Then he died. . . .

The Japanese never used any instruments of torture on me. Once, when I was taken out, a guard socked me on the jaw and sent me clear across the room. . . . One of the Japanese sentries, typical, short-legged, bespectacled, who patrolled the corridor during the worst times, always stopped and stared at me, and I tried not to think what was in his mind. One day he suddenly put down his gun, stuck his hand in his pocket and shoved a piece of chocolate through the bars at me. The expression on his face never changed. . . .

When I got beri-beri it did not hit me suddenly. Gradually one takes on a certain puffiness, noticeably in the feet, until your whole body swells, and you blow up like an oddly-shaped balloon, and become enormous. We had all by then developed scabies, and our bug bites became septic; the wounds of the tortured men stank and so did everything else. When I collapsed completely it was fortunate for me that Cecily Williams had been transferred to my cell, for she is a brilliant, dedicated doctor. . . .

We had been five months as prisoners of the Kempetai when Cecily and I were put in an open lorry and driven back to Changi.

Dr Cecily Williams has already figured largely in this story, if only because there was no captive in Changi Prison who did not know her, or of her, and so many owed their lives to her. She was guide and counsellor to Daisy, as well as her doctor in captivity. Furthermore, not only was Dr Williams a prisoner of the dreaded Kempetai for those five months with Freddy Bloom, but her life otherwise, and her experience during those 3½ years, was so varied as to be of immeasurable help to the captives. When she was first taken by the Japanese into the Women's Camp at Changi she had dysentery very badly, but from the outset the Japanese made constant use of her medical knowledge and skill. Then in July, 1942, she needed a major operation herself and was sent out, for a hysterectomy, to the Myako Hospital; there she met many of her old friends among the nurses and doctors, retained there by the Japanese as essential for the peoples' health. Because of those contacts, her time during her operation in the Myako was, she said, "Quite a pleasant interlude, as my friends were always bringing me bits of food and fruit."

When she returned to Changi Gaol in August Mr Asahi, the new Japanese Custodian of Enemy Aliens, approached her with a proposition which she wrote about after the war:

Asahi was a very decent man who had lived in England, and he now wanted six men to leave prison and go to work in his office, with one male and one female doctor to write and report on the food situation in Changi. I think it was pure decency on his part to give some of us the opportunity of a change. The six men included Harry Miller, a journalist on the *Straits Times*, Duncan Mackintosh (a police officer I knew well; I think he took a great risk in joining us) and Dr Eric Byron. We were driven to Singapore in a lorry and taken to a house in Maxwell Road, where all the Europeans lived who were still looking after the essential services in the town; except for Bishop Wilson and two other padres who had a house to themselves.

I was given a small flat to myself in Maxwell Road and later Katherine de Mowbray joined me there. Our office was in the Chartered Bank Building in Raffles Place, and we walked there daily from our flat. We generally had lunch in one of the little Indian or Chinese restaurants close by, and we did all our own marketing, cooking and housework; so life was really very pleasant and a wonderful change from Changi Prison. Every Sunday we lunched with the Bishop and spent the afternoon at his house; he was always very good to us. I know some of the men in our party, to whom we owed so much, thought it most unwise for us to be on parole at all because we went about freely and were therefore in danger. But I thought it an unparalleled opportunity of seeing Singapore under Japanese rule and of keeping in contact, though always slight and risky, with many of our friends; also by seeing something of the Japanese we had a chance of getting privileges for the internees in Changi.

Altogether we had an extraordinary, yet "strangely pleasant" four months, but I had lost all my medical notes and was very anxious to resume medical reading. All the libraries, with their invaluable cultural records (public and private), had been swept up by the Nipponese into Raffles Museum. There two Englishmen, John Corner and Birtwhistle, the former Director of Fisheries, assisted by Quan Ah Gun (Chief Clerk of the Botanical Gardens) were trying to rescue from destruction, or from removal to Japan, everything that they could. Birtwhistle had been ordered by Sir Shenton Thomas to remain at his post in Singapore because of his unrivalled knowledge of the fishermen, who provided so much food for the city's population. However, I found it impossible to gain access to the Museum without personal permission from the Japanese Professor Tanakadate, to whom I tried to get an introduction. The only answer I got was an invitation to lunch with him, and John Corner and Birtwhistle, at Tanakadate's house. We had naturally been unwilling to "fraternise" with the enemy, so we refused. Then the invitation was repeated "in a way that he hoped would be unobjectionable to us," i.e. Mr Corner and Mr Birthwhistle were asking us to lunch, but the meal would be at Professor Tanakadate's house.

After some qualms Katherine and I accepted this invitation, first because I badly needed access to books, and secondly we did not see the wisdom of being implacably unfriendly to a man whom we knew was trying to help us. So we went to lunch. Personally I did not like Tanakadate; he was a nasty old man, but he was prepared to do quite a lot for us. He took us for a drive in the Botanical Gardens where we all sat and drank orange pop in a kiosk. At any rate from that lunch substantial advantages flowed; we were able to work in Raffles Museum and Library, sorting the looted books and reading on our own account; we persuaded the Professor to send a large number of books to the civilian and military prison camps; we urged the importance for *all* prisoners of walks *outside* prison walls, and the need for relatives to meet each other – both these facilities were granted. Finally, I was allowed to keep books for a medical library at the women's camp.

We never regretted anything we did during our "time outside" and I do not believe the way in which we behaved did any harm to our prestige in the eyes of Asiatics. Then suddenly in January 1943 we were sent back to Changi.

Dr Cecily Williams had been taken for interrogation by the Kempe-tai at the same time as Freddy Bloom and suffered similar treatment. But she never forgot that first and foremost she was a doctor and her notes are redolent of the care she took to relieve the suffering and pain of others in like predicament. When she returned to Changi she weighed 7 stone. In one paragraph she described the feelings and impressions of the prisoners immediately following their release:

> Now it is all over I realize how little one imagines of these things until one has the personal experience. I had no idea that fear could create such severe reactions. I had no idea that people could be so courageous. And I had no idea of how much one could enjoy the security of bacon and eggs.

From the outset Sir Shenton Thomas was left in no doubt that, though the Japanese were prepared to use him as a negotiator with their captives, they also intended to exploit his status and endeavour to humiliate him publicly, for their own propaganda purposes. He was put in a cell by himself in the worst part of the gaol over the kitchens where parties of tourists and other visitors were deliberately brought to view him. At one stage, because he refused to provide some information the Japanese demanded, he had to endure long periods of solitary confine-ment in the now customary surroundings of a small concrete cell, with a cement bed and cement pillow, with a hole-in-the-floor lavatory and one iron-barred slit window 10 feet up in the concrete wall. On another occasion he was locked alone in a separate lavatory for twenty-four hours for saying something that annoyed his captors*.

When I saw those references, with details of the hardship and privation inflicted on Shenton, I was sure they provided the reason, hitherto not apparent, why, on forty days at Changi between 21 March and 28 May, he made no entry in his daily diary. It was so unlike him that the evidence strongly suggests that his will to write during those forty days was eroded. There were two consecutive periods (every day from 21 March to 10 April and again from 12 April to 20 April) when he

---

* Royal Commonwealth Society Papers.

wrote nothing; otherwise the gaps were haphazard, and there were a few other days with entries like "As usual" or just "At Changi". On 5 and 6 May he wrote nothing, but the following day he entered, presumably on a last day of punishment:

> *May 7*
> Solitary confinement in a room by the entrance porch. Rather grisly to be locked up alone – yet poor little D.

This emphasizes his reticence about himself; it was not in his character to enlarge on his own sufferings or adversity; his thoughts turned automatically to his wife, who he was not allowed to see. However, three weeks later he did meet her, for he made this entry in his diary:

> *May 27*
> Lovely day and able to get a few words with D in the camp office. First since we parted on Feb. 15th."

Later, on 8 July, comes another surprising entry:

> *July 8*
> Very warm day. Lt General Yamashita sent me 150 bottles of beer, 30 tins of butter, 30 cheese, 2 sherry (actually Crabbie's Ginger Wine!).

This gift to a British prisoner by a Japanese General was surely unique. Shenton replied to the General the same day, and left a type-written copy of his letter, which he initialled.

> Changi
> July 8th 1942
>
> Your Excellency,
> I write to thank you very sincerely for the very generous gift which you have been so good as to make to me in token of your interest in my personal welfare. I appreciate your courtesy most highly.
> Please accept this assurance of my high consideration.
> Yours sincerely,
> T.S.W.T.
>
> His Excellency
> Lieutenant General Yamashita
> Singapore

After the war Yamashita was convicted by the Americans as a war criminal. In 1945 he had been Commander-in-Chief of the Japanese forces in the Philippines when General Douglas MacArthur returned there, at the head of a vast Allied armada, intent on reconquest of the islands. But MacArthur also wanted retribution for the atrocities perpetrated on the Philippino population as the Japanese Army was driven back into the mountains. According to United States evidence some 60,000 Philippino civilians, of both sexes and all ages, *and* the few remaining Americans still alive in Japanese hands, were butchered before Yamashita surrendered on 2 September, 1945. At his trial Yamashita protested that he had neither ordered nor known of these atrocities; he was altogether preoccupied with the burdens of his defeat which had so disrupted his chain of command that he had no idea what was going on. Although a strong appeal on Yamashita's behalf was lodged with the U.S. Supreme Court, it failed; he was found guilty by a military court of five American generals and sentenced to death. He was hanged in February, 1946.

Under British law Yamashita would presumably have been held officially responsible for the killing of British soldiers and subjects before and after the surrender on 15 February. Japanese soldiers under his command had burst into the Alexandra Military Hospital and there bayoneted many seriously wounded British servicemen as they lay helpless in bed. Equally frightful were the murders of thousands of Chinese citizens of Singapore, generally preceded by the rape of their women and young girls, whose male relatives or friends were then beheaded in the presence of their women by an executioner using a two-handed Samurai sword. In his book Mamoru Shinozaki had this to say about the "Chinese Massacre at Singapore":

> After the surrender 25th Army Headquarters issued an astounding decree; all male Chinese in Singapore between the ages of 18 and 50 years were ordered to concentrate at five assembly points at noon on 21 February 1942. The dreaded Kempetai went round searching for young men, and girls, and dragged them into the open. . . . Thousands of Chinese were huddled together, waiting for the execution that was their fate, particularly for any Chinese volunteers who had fought so tenaciously against the Japanese; 6,000 Chinese were thus murdered in what the Kempetai called their operation clean-up. Major-General Kawamura, commander of Syonan Defence Force, went to 25th Army Headquarters to question the wisdom of this action, but was told it had been approved by the commander-in-chief, General Yamashita.

Japanese killings were not confined only to soldiers and Chinese, as Shinozaki noted:

At this time looters were busy, breaking into the mainly European residential areas of Holland Road, Tanglin Road, and Bukit Timah Road. It seemed nothing could stop them until one day eight looters broke into a Japanese military store and were caught red-handed by soldiers. They were immediately beheaded and their heads stuck on pikes at eight different road junctions. The looting stopped.

In such circumstances British evidence inevitably built up against General Yamashita; according to American military law, he was the most senior officer in the Japanese High Command, and therefore inevitably must be held personally responsible for every action of men under his command. Will history judge the execution of Yamashita as altogether right and fair? Some will think not. On the other hand 135 Japanese officers and men were executed by the British, as war criminals, at Changi Prison and 79 more in Malaysia for similar reasons. But in the case of Yamashita might he have been saved from execution if, say, he had been tried in a European (a "Nuremburg") setting on grounds of "mitigating circumstances"? Finally, and para-doxically, Yamashita's policy in Singapore was not approved by his superiors in Japan and he was withdrawn from his appointment, with loss of face, as Shinozaki has written:

The Japanese love ceremonies, and in Syonan, where I was now Director of Education, I was always approached whenever some signifi-cant occasion was about to take place. The first time was the Emperor's birthday on 29 April, 1942. The Education Department was to organize a march of school children through the city, singing the patriotic song *Aikohu Koshin Kyoku* and carrying Japanese flags. When the C-in-C, General Yamashita, appeared on the balcony of the City Hall (the Municipal Building) everyone on the padang would sing the Japanese national anthem, and then shout *Banzai* ("Long Live the Emperor") three times. I had appointed Mr Herman de Souza, the ex-Principal of an English school, as an additional inspector of education but neither he nor I could find a single sheet of Japanese music let alone the patriotic song and national anthem. But I managed to find a soldier who had been a music teacher in Japan, who quickly wrote the score for the patriotic song and the national anthem. Once I had copies made I gathered all the music teachers who rushed back to their schools, where every day the schoolchildren rehearsed their songs. Precisely at 10 o'clock that morning General Yamashita stepped out on to the balcony. . . . At first he stood with his hands behind his back; his pot-belly protruded a bit, but he looked dignified. Gradually the sound of the police band became louder. Then we could hear the voices of the children singing, the tune was correct and the timing superb. Impressed, General Yamashita moved to the front of the balcony. . . .

Later, at the Adelphi Hotel, Yamashita spoke to hundreds of Singaporeans.

"Today we celebrate the Emperor's birthday with you. You have just become our new subjects. It is my great pleasure to be with you on this auspicious day. I want the people of Malaya and Sumatra to carry on with their affairs, for they are now our new subject people."

Japanese reporters cabled his remarks back to their newspapers but Tokyo's reaction was that General Yamashita had made a political blunder. Then Field-Marshal Terauchi came to stay at the Istana, formerly Government House, and conveyed to General Yamashita his orders from Prime Minister General Tojo. Yamashita was to proceed direct to Northern Manchuria from Syonan. This order deprived him of the opportunity of seeing his Emperor, an honour he would have valued highly. Tojo was known to dislike Yamashita and to be jealous of him, and Yamashita's speech had caused displeasure. He had no prior approval to talk about "our subject people", and he paid dearly for the mistake. Maybe if he had retained his Emperor's regard then Prime Minister Tojo would not have sent him to the Philippines early in 1945, where by then the Japanese were doomed to certain defeat.

I hope the entry in Shenton's diary for 29 April, 1942, stemmed equally from a magnanimous gesture by General Yamashita:

April 29
Birthday of Emperor of Japan. High Command sent us pineapples in honour of the occasion.

Late in July of that first year at Changi, presumably because of overcrowding, the Japanese decided to move large numbers of captives by sea to Japan, including Shenton Thomas, but not his wife in spite of his plea that she should accompany him. On 21 July all the "Changi Prisoners" gave a farewell party for Shenton and those leaving with him a few days later. This party also marked the only occasion when Shenton received a formal typewritten letter, *inside* Changi Prison, addressed to him as "H. E. Sir Shenton Thomas, G.C.M.G, O.B.E., Governor and Commander-in-Chief, Straits Settlements"; it was given him by the camp cooks, who were mainly British members of the Malay Police Force, and expressed their high appreciation of Shenton's conduct "as His Majesty's representative under circumstances which must be unique in the annals of the British Empire, but which serve to show more than ever how closely knit are the bonds of our great democracy".

In the event Shenton could not leave for Japan; two days before sailing he became seriously ill with bacillary dysentery and was sent to the prison hospital. He was not discharged until 14 August when he was warned to stand by for embarkation with another large party of prisoners. On the morning of the 16th he was allowed to see Daisy from 9.45 to 12.15 to say goodbye. He did not see her again for over three years. Then events moved quickly for the worse, as his diary shows:

August 16
Went through disinfection ship. No lunch. Embarked about 4 p.m.: 400 officers and 1,000 men, all crammed in the holds. Our hold has 540 officers and men, allowed 6′ × 1′6″ each. Bit of cheese and turned in. No food from the Nips, very crowded and warm night.

The Japanese "disinfection" process included fumigation of all baggage by formalin at 60° temperature, and spraying all packs and hand luggage with carbolic acid.

Next morning 400 men, with Shenton, were transferred to another vessel apparently already loaded, with everyone in the same hold, in which there were plenty of rats. There was very little deck space with the galleys on the port side and the latrines to starboard. Lorries were loaded on top of the hatches, leaving only a quarter of the hatch covers open. What happened in these dreadful conditions has been well described by one of the officer prisoners:

We were ordered on to the filthiest little boat (less than 3,000 tons) lying at Collyer Quay; there must have been 1,500–2,000 of us. Once aboard pandemonium reigned, for the Japs had no idea what to do. The forward hatches had been loaded with bauxite, and there was a flimsy wooden ladder leading down to the bottom of our (rear) hatch, with just three tiers of bare boards – our beds! – stretching from each side of the vessel to a narrow centre gangway. There was hardly room to stand up and yet still more were embarked. Then we heard that Sir Shenton Thomas and his party had come on board too, and I recall standing near the Governor who was remonstrating with the Jap officer and saying that he was not going on the ship; and that several hundred soldiers should be taken off. The situation became very, very ugly indeed, and there was a dire threat by the Jap officer when he drew his revolver and intimated that he was going to get rid of Sir Shenton and some surplus soldiers. However, the Governor stood his ground, and we had a pretty awful two or three hours before I think they took some men off. I shudder to think how much worse it would have been had Sir Shenton not bravely stuck out against

the Japanese. . . . It was a courageous act on his part and he was still
upholding the dignity of his former position, and earned the respect of
many hundreds of us.*

The *S.S. Fukkai Maru* remained alongside Collyer Quay for another
twenty-four hours, during which time all the prisoners were disembarked to stand on the wharf all the afternoon – "very exhausting"
Shenton wrote. It must have been strange indeed to see again, under
very different circumstances, the well remembered Singapore water-
front, where Shenton and Daisy had so often disembarked with all the
splendour and ceremony befitting their status. She finally sailed from
Singapore on 20 August, to reach Takao, a port on the south-west coast
of Formosa, on 29 August. Shenton gives a description of conditions
during th .t nine-day voyage:

> Generally a time of heavy rainstorms and much suffering with hatches of
> the hold closed most of the day. Luckily sea calm as impossible to find
> dry spot on deck, and floor of the hold very unpleasant for men sleeping
> on it, and the hatch roof leaks; in bad weather the hold would have been
> a shambles. Estimate 100 cases of diarrhoea with some really bad; floor
> space per man was one square metre! Our speed is 7 knots and we have
> one small armed merchantman as escort.

In spite of the overcrowding, the prisoners in the *Fukkai Maru*
managed to make deck space, "to go to church on Sunday", and
Shenton wrote in his diary: "August 23. Early church."

Throughout the whole three and a half years of captivity at Changi
daily prayers were always said by Canon Jack Bennett, or one of the
other clergy. There was always a weekly communion service which
Daisy (and Shenton when he was with her) never missed. Canon A. J.
Bennett M.A. worked for many years as a Missionary for the church in
China, including five years in Hong Kong. He spoke Cantonese and
was well known in Singapore where he was a Chaplain, responsible
directly to Bishop Wilson. He was one of several clergy in captivity who
gave devoted service to members of all the racial communities.

Cannon Bennett recalls of Shenton Thomas:

> I always felt he was a man of deep humility who attended service as an
> ordinary member of the congregation, and always wanted the special
> position he held outside to be completely forgotten in the circumstances

---

* Colonel Ivor Thomas to the author January, 1982.

of the prison camp. Of course the Japs did realize who he was and took him away to be given special treatment.

In this connection General Percival wrote, "A body of men who had a great opportunity were the padres, as our men turned to religion for moral support. . . . Many a man who had never entered a church in his own homeland attended their services." In particular those men who suffered such barbarous brutalities from the Kempetai turned naturally to their faith for help and stamina, during their hours of brutal interrogation.

The clearest evidence of religious influence at this time comes to us in a remarkable book by the Rev. J. N. Lewis Bryan* who had been a chaplain in III Indian Corps during the campaign and was made a prisoner of war:

> The Japanese made it quite clear following the surrender that the penalty for any attempt at escape by a prisoner was immediate execution. I and five senior British Officers were ordered, on 2nd September 1942, to witness the execution of four soldiers – Corporal Bravington and Private Page of the Australian Division, Private Walters of the East Surrey Regiment and Private Fletcher of the R.A.O.C. These four men had been captured after attempting to escape in the first few weeks. The padre gave them absolution and shook them by the hand. Corporal Bravington's last words were: "I have my New Testament here, sir, and I am going to read it while they shoot me." And he did. They all four refused to be blindfolded, and met their deaths like heroes.

Before the voyage to Formosa was over Shenton was again in trouble with the Japanese guards on the ship. A fellow prisoner on board wrote this about it:**

> Some days after we had been at sea was the only time I ever really met Sir Shenton Thomas. He was of course in civilian clothes and crouched in a fairly dark corner between decks, which, I suppose, was his for the trip. I was near at hand when I heard a commotion and the usual bad-tempered shouting of a Japanese soldier. Obviously Shenton Thomas had caused annoyance (perhaps failure to show due respect for a soldier of the Imperial Nippon Army). The soldier leapt at him, seized his trilby hat, drew his bayonet, fixed it to his rifle and then, after threatening Sir Shenton, who took not the slightest notice of him, threw the hat on the deck and bayoneted it four or five times. Shenton Thomas merely

---

* *The Churches of the Captivity in Malaya* by Lewis Bryan, S.P.C.K, 1946.
** Lt-Colonel H. T. Heard to the author, January, 1982.

laughed aloud at him, which took all the steam out of the soldier who looked a bit of an ass. I found this incident an interesting sidelight on someone I had not met before.

When Sir Shenton Thomas and his fellow prisoners landed at Takao they still had three years of captivity ahead of them. I found it difficult to obtain the exact dates of their time in the various prison camps to which they were sent. But from the available evidence their movements appear to have been as follows: on 29 August, 1942, they went to a camp at Haito, close to Takao, where they stayed a month before being transferred by train on 27 September to No. 4 P.O.W. camp at Karenko on the east coast of the island. They remaind at Karenko, a large camp, for nearly fifteen months until they were moved to the north-east corner of the island at Taihoku, where they certainly spent Christmas, 1943. Then, ten months later, they were moved to the mainland and went by train through Korea, over the Yalu River to a camp at Hsian in Manchuria. There they stayed until the Japanese surrender.

From the evidence of Shenton's diary it seems clear that captives generally in those prison camps in occupied China were not treated with the same degree of physical cruelty that prevailed at Changi. Their chief troubles were privation, malnutrition, boredom, climatic extremes (great heat or extreme cold, for neither of which were they properly equipped with clothing) and particularly lack of mail or any news of their wives, families and friends. In their own letters they had to paint a false gloss of comfort and beneficial treatment by their captors; otherwise their mail was censored and sent back to them for correction. The communications they did receive from outside were sparse indeed, and the Red Cross parcels that reached them had always been partially looted en route and held back a long time before delivery.

Food, its quantity and quality, was almost always their main problem. So often in the diary I found entries of this kind:

A few bananas today
Bread instead of rice for breakfast.
Bread with sugar is a grand dish!
A good piece of fish for supper.

Shenton often recorded his weight, a good indication of diet effect; e.g. on 3 June, 1943, "Official weighing Kg. 57.5 (about 8½ stone)". But it was the general boredom of life in captivity that was clearly so hard to bear, only alleviated by the tasks Shenton and his colleagues were sometimes set, such as herding goats and pigs. Fortunately the captives were generally able to make gardens and grow tomatoes, beans, lettuce and other vegetables. In that way, and with the aid of bridge, they succeeded in making a way of life. In one respect Shenton was fortunate in that after November, 1942, he was given a soldier servant who remained with him until they were released. This was John Drew who had been orderly to Major-General Beckwith-Smith, commander of the ill-fated 18th Division. The General had died in captivity at Karenko and Drew was then appointed to Shenton Thomas. John Drew is very important to this story, for after the Japanese surrender he brought home Shenton's personal effects, including his 5-year diary, and restored them to their owner. Drew kept in touch with Shenton and Daisy, of whom he wrote: "Sir Shenton was a very great gentleman, truly of the old school, and his wife too suffered very much."*

At one stage in Formosa the Japanese placed a number of very senior officers in one camp, including Sir Shenton Thomas, Sir Mark Young (Governor of Hong Kong), Mr Charles Smith (Governor of British North Borneo), Lieutenant-General Percival, Lieutenant-General Sir Lewis Heath, Sir Percy McElwaine (Chief Justice, Straits Settlements), Sir Harry Trusted (Chief Justice, Federated Malay States) and Brigadier Ivan Simson, whom Duff Cooper had appointed Director General of Civil Defence.

This concentration of senior and distinguished officers, all well known to each other, was useful, for it gave them an opportunity to ponder and discuss their past, present, and likely future experiences. One topic of discussion, naturally enough in their current circumstances, was the problem of evacuation of civilians from Singapore, particularly at the end of the siege when defeat was close and certain. How well had the plans been carried out? What mistakes or failures had occurred? Where did blame lie? Shenton Thomas, as head of the Civil Government, had been much concerned with these problems, particularly the events of 13 February. While in the prison camp Shenton wrote a five page note, in manuscript, on the subject, which he discussed with and showed to Brigadier Simson, with interesting results. For Simson did not publish his own version of the civilian evacuation, particularly the events of 13 February, until 1970, in his well-presented book *Singapore: Too Little, Too Late.***

I have summarised below the main points in Sir Shenton's Note on

---

* John Drew to the author, December, 1981.
** Leo Cooper, 1970.

Evacuation and Ivan Simson's chapter on the same subject. Both are about the same length, but each flatly contradicts the other, and it therefore seems important to present each in juxtaposition for easy comparison.

Sir Shenton Thomas on Civilian Evacuation

(a) When a man from home goes out to a colony to live and work among backward people, he takes on himself, whether he likes it or not, his share of the responsibility for the good name of Great Britain.

(b) That being so, in the context of evacuation policy, the Secretary of State decreed, and I issued orders, that able-bodied men could not be compelled to leave and equally could not be given special assistance to get away at a time when the people of Malaya were in the greatest need. Of course the old and the sick, and particularly women and children, should be, and always were, given assistance to leave.

(c) Brigadier Simson tells me he attended a conference at Malaya Command early on 13 February, attended also by Admiral Spooner and Air Vice-Marshal Pulford, to discuss the best means of evacuating, by a ship sailing that day, technicians (preferably young men) who would be useful for the war effort in other areas. Simson says that he informed me of this conference, and that he had been given space for 300 civilians.

(d) Simson did not report this conference to me, at Government House, nor to Mr Fraser (Colonial Secretary), nor Mr Dawson (Defence Secretary), though we four lunched together that day. He added he had requested my agreement that Mr Bisseker (Director of Labour and Transport) should be allowed to leave, and that I had so agreed. This is not correct and I would certainly not have accepted that Mr Bisseker should go; in view of his responsibilities it was his vital duty to remain, and I did not give him permission to get away before capitulation.

(e) Equally I would never have agreed that Major Nunn (Head of the P.W.D.) should leave on the 13th. However, Simson added that Major Nunn had included his own name on the list of engineer evacuees for departure on the 13th because he (Nunn) claimed he was a Group Captain, R.A.F., and therefore a serviceman. Apparently Simson accepted this. I had already told Major Nunn twice that his place was at his departmental Headquarters in the event of capitulation. It has been said that

Major Nunn stated he was carrying official despatches from myself, in order to claim priority in evacuation. I deny this absolutely.

(f) The overall authority for civilian evacuation was in the hands of Mr Justice Aitken, who was well known to have that authority and should have been consulted. Major Nunn was aware of the official instruction that officers who left Malaya, or did not attend office, without permission, would be regarded as having vacated their appointments.

Brigadier Ivan Simson on Civilian Evacuation

On 13 February there was the last official civilian evacuation of Singapore. I was allotted 300 places in 13 small vessels due to sail that day. The intention was to allot the 300 places to young British technicians, including professional civil engineers, who would be needed to continue the war effort elsewhere. . . . I ordered Mr Bisseker to leave this day with the Governor's agreement. . . . I stress it was by my order (agreed by the Governor) that Mr Bisseker left, and with reluctance on his part, so as to refute rumours which spread later that he had "bolted". . . . In my opinion it should never be left to the civilian population to decide for themselves whether they should go or stay.

Of course Simson had great faith in Bisseker's ability and had always countered frequent suggestions that he should be sacked. In Karenko Sir Shenton endorsed his own account: "I have shown this note to Brigadier Simson, who does not wish to comment." In London the late Ivan Simson published his own version 28 years later. Ironically the final tragedy was that almost all those 13 small vessels were sunk by Japanese naval craft after sailing from Singapore; the heavy death toll included Mr Bisseker and Major Nunn. But for Shenton Thomas a sequence to this unhappy affair appeared five years later, as we shall see in the next chapter.

Meanwhile in Changi, early in May, 1944, a considerable change took place for all the prisoners, civil and military, and generally for the better. The Japanese decided that the whole of Changi Gaol was now required for their own military needs, and therefore all prisoners, male and female, were evacuated to a new camp in the Sime Road area. There they were housed in old army huts generally with wooden or earthen floors, not the perpetual concrete, and there were the enormous advantages of open spaces, trees, scope for gardens and open skies. The horrors of prison noise, sound of women's voices, of children crying, of domestic clutter, of wooden clogs on iron staircases and strident echoes from prison walls, were things of the past. There was still over-crowding and lack of food, but on the whole Sime Road was a vast improvement on Changi Gaol.*

* Extract from Personal Notes by Dr Cicely Williams, 1941–45.

IX

AFTERMATH

Orders to All Japanese Guard Troops

All Japanese land, sea and air forces have surrendered. His Imperial Majesty The Emperor has been graciously pleased to sign the surrender document and with this the Pacific War is ended.

During the next few days Allied Aircraft will drop leaflets written in English, Dutch and Indian languages where Allied soldiers and civilians are held by Japanese guards telling them to remain calm and composed, and to stay in their present positions.

Where such leaflets come into the possession of Japanese guards they are immediately to pass them politely to Allied soldiers or civilians. After handing over the leaflets all guards are to return to their own billets.

Japanese guard troops are responsible for providing Allied prisoners and internees with food and for their correct treatment. In the next few days Allied officers carrying wireless sets will come to places where Allied soldiers are held by the Japanese. Their principal task will be to make contact with Allied soldiers and to communicate their requirements to the Allied Supreme Command. Japanese guard troops are not to obstruct them and are to assist them when possible.

The above orders, issued by the Japanese High Command, did not reach the troops guarding Allied captives until some days after 15 August, 1945, and often very much later. However, at Singapore all the prisoners at Sime Road were alerted in the late evening of 15 August by a young Eurasian boy who twice rode his bicycle round the high barbed wire fence that encircled the camp, singing a song into which he introduced the news of the Japanese surrender.

That was how news first reached the captives that the Emperor of Japan had signed an Imperial Proclamation announcing the capitulation of his country and the unconditional surrender of all Japanese Armed Forces to the Western Allies. There had long been rumours in the goals that this was about to happen, but authentic information was slow in coming and Freddy Bloom described the initial effect of the longed-for event:

There was never any official notice to us that the war was over. Peace trickled in gradually. Some of our hosts faded away. Those who stayed rarely appeared and one or two actually tried to ingratiate themselves with us. Red Cross stores were released. Letters that had been held up were distributed. Then, one beautiful day, a small squad of supermen in red berets came to the Camp. They were some of Mountbatten's commandos. Each seemed ten feet tall, tanned, bursting with strength and unlike anything we had seen in years.

A similar sense of rumour and uncertainty seems to have prevailed in the camp at Hsian in Manchuria, where Shenton Thomas actually anticipated the surrender date when he wrote in his diary:

August 14
3 piglets killed, but we're eating largely potatoes these days. A good deal of pain over the small of my back and all down both legs. Doctor says nutritional deficiency aggravated by packing. Rumours we are to leave here on 16th, and pick up Major Generals and Brigadiers, en route to going north. *Japan capitulated.*

Only one who has actually experienced the conditions of life in Japanese prison camps in the Second World War can properly appreciate, let alone describe, the relief of the captives when they knew their ordeal was over and they were free. Shenton Thomas described his own feelings in a letter he wrote to his daughter from the British Embassy in Chungking on 29 August. He and the seven other senior officers who had been with him at Karenko were flown out to Chungking, in non-occupied China, where they arrived on 28 August. It was their first taste of normal living for three and a half years. This is what Shenton made of it:

> At British Embassy
> Chungking
> 29 Aug. 1945

My Darling Bridget,
    You can't imagine the joy with which I heard the B.B.C. last night for the first time for 3½ years, and knew that you and Mummy had been told that I was safe here. I know how fearfully bad the arrangements for letters have been, and the months and months you have had without news. Now my great anxiety is Mummy. . . . I have heard nothing from or of her since June 1944 (only 2 letters in 3 years from her). So the British Ambassador here has wired Mountbatten in Ceylon asking him to help me get to her, either at Singapore or elsewhere. . . . I must warn you that I have nothing with me but one old white suit, 1 pair khaki shorts and 2 shirts! No coat, so when you fix up our resting place on our arrival (Brown's Hotel would be good) please send there the baggage which I

left at Malaya House. I may arrive in a Red Cross overcoat and grey flannel bags which I shall buy!

As to Mummy, I plan to buy for her a collection of things like undies, pyjamas, powder, stockings, etc., and have them handy to meet her. . . . Do you think you could buy her a town dress, black or something of that sort, and a hat that will do for her to go out in? Also gloves. Have them put down.

It was surely typical of Shenton that his thoughts turned first to his family and their predicament in his absence. His concern for his wife's wardrobe on arrival no doubt reflected their joint gubernatorial responsibility always to appear well turned out. He had been a Governor and the King's representative since 1930. Later in the letter he wrote of himself:

I am organically quite fit so far as I know, but am not up to anything strenuous and am liable to get a bit shaky under stress. One can't endure semi-starvation for 3½ years without feeling it somehow – practically a vegetarian and teetotaller! I have a waist of 30 inches and a chest of 35! I weigh only 9½ stone, my pre-war being 12, and my p.o.w. minimum 8½ stone. . . . I so long to see you. I do hope Michael will approve of grandad. Anyhow I'll do my best. It will be lovely to be at home in the country and do nothing. . . .

All my love
Always your own Daddy

P.S. I want simple food! Eggs, milk, bread, cheese, beer, lettuces and sugar please!

Then Shenton was flown to Calcutta, where he was met by the Governor of Bengal, Sir Richard Casey* and his wife, who looked after him with care and understanding. Daisy joined him there on 11 September from Singapore, having been flown out in an aircraft provided by Mountbatten, together with Leslie Davis and Dr Wallace. Shenton and Daisy could not have had a more perfect reunion than in the setting and comfort of Government House. The large mansion, which had been the Viceroy's residence until 1912, reminded them much of their own G.H. at Singapore, and there the Caseys made certain they lacked for nothing that could ensure peace and rest for them both. Shenton wrote at length to Bridget from Calcutta, still in the same firm and elegant handwriting in his usual easy and flowing style, page upon page without one deletion or amendment to either text or

* The late Baron Casey, G.C.M.G, C.H., D.S.O., M.C., P.C., who became Governor-General of Australia in 1965.

punctuation; certainly his years of imprisonment had no effect whatever on his clarity of brain and mind, nor his ability to express his thoughts clearly and legibly. Extracts from the letters to his daughter breathe his deep love and affection for his family, and his complete admiration for Daisy during her captivity.

> Government House
> Calcutta
> Sept. 14, 1945
>
> My darling Bridget,
> Leslie Davis goes home by this plane and will get in touch with you. He will tell you all about us. My dear, your Ma is quite a miracle. I look and wonder how she could possibly have survived through such an ordeal. So do others. She looks younger every minute, and chatters away with a perpetual beaming smile. Not a grey hair in her head. Thin, of course, and she's got a completely Chinese figure which is the envy of everyone. . . . I got her really a rather nice sapphire ring to buck her up on arrival, and Lady Casey has given her a coat and skirt, and dresses and all sorts of other things.
> A man from Singapore has told me that when the Japs had surrendered all the prisoners and internees held a ceremony at the Camp. Your Ma was given the place of honour by the flagstaff. One of the internees made a short speech and then hoisted the flag for her. Then they all (4,000 of them) gave three cheers for the King, and then three cheers for Mummy. He said it was the grandest sight he ever saw; everyone was weeping for joy. My dear, they all worship her; she has been absolutely magnificent and when she appeared in Singapore they just cheered and cheered. She will never be forgotten there. I've had a lovely message from the King and Queen who want to see us both when we get home. Your Ma did a broadcast from Singapore before she left, but I didn't hear it! maddening.
>
> All my love
> Always your Daddy
>
> P.S. My dear, does no one wear any stockings at home in the winter? Do try and find a pair for Mummy.

There is a photograph of Daisy at that flag ceremony in the civil internees camp; the caption beneath it reads:

Sime Road Internment Camp 5th Sept. 1945
Lady Thomas and Mr E. C. Collinge, C.B.E.*, at the unfurling of the first Union Jack to be flown in Malaya after the Japanese occupation.

---

* Head of the Men's P.O.W. Camp at Sime Road, and a senior officer of the M.C.S.

It was the same Union Jack that had flown over Government House, Singapore, and which had been successfully concealed from the Japanese for 3½ years.

From Singapore Daisy brought with her a copy of the broadcast she made to the peoples of Malaya; it must have been well received.

Broadcast by Lady Thomas
from Singapore

Now that I am free again I want to say a few words to the people of Malaya. The long-awaited moment has now come when the flag of freedom flies once more over this country. I know that most of you have been undergoing miseries and hardships and I sympathize deeply with all who have endured suffering and loss under Japanese rule. I realize only too well what this has meant, because I, and those who have been interned all this time, have experienced something of it ourselves. Now that this miserable time is over, I am more than ever glad that I stayed here after Singapore fell to share with you all whatever might befall us until the British forces came across the seas and skies to relieve us. I wish very much that my husband were here to speak to you also. I expect you know that he and other senior officers were sent to Formosa after six months' internment at Changi. Later on I received a letter from him saying that he was in Manchuria and since then I have heard he is in Calcutta. Just before he left Changi he made a farewell speech in which he asked all those who remained in Changi Prison always to remember the people of Malaya and to do what they could for them when they were free again. So I know he will be thinking of you all now and hoping that everything possible will be done to restore this country to its former happiness and prosperity. I also hope that what we have experienced during these last three and a half years will be of some use in rebuilding for the future. Those of us who have been imprisoned have learned that when times are hard our misfortunes can be met with cheerfulness and without grumbling. The women who had to walk, with their baggage in their hands, the eight miles from Katong to Changi Prison did not despair but arrived at the Prison gates singing. In those early days most of the internees were Europeans, but, as time went on, many Malayans of other races joined us, and the members of the different communities showed the same friendship and tolerance towards each other as they used to do before the Japanese came here. We were all equal and we all had the time and opportunity to get to know each other better than before and to understand and sympathize with one another. So I have great hopes that in the future, Chinese, Eurasians, Malays, Europeans and Indians will work together and help each other even more than before.

I have received very many kindnesses from those who live in this country. I have shared your days of happiness and your days of sorrow, so I feel myself a true Malayan and when I go back to England to rejoin my family, I shall take the greatest interest in everything which happens here and shall be wishing you and your children prosperity and health and happiness and peace.

Lucy Marguerite Thomas

In his letters to Bridget and members of his family, Shenton Thomas concealed the truth of the treatment which had been the lot of many prisoners. The nearest he came to it was in a letter from Calcutta to his brother William Thomas, undated, in which he wrote:

> I am so thankful to know that you at home had so little idea of what was going on: it would have worried you frightfully. But it's all over now and Daisy and I intend to forget it as soon as we can.

After the war, in London, my wife and I asked Shenton and Daisy about their attitude to the Japanese. "Do you hate them for what they did to you and so many others?" They replied "No", but they did not enlarge on it. I have often asked the same question of former prisoners of the Japanese, and the answer has always been the same, "No." Freddy Bloom discusses this issue on the penultimate page of her book *Dear Philip*.

> Even today people still ask whether I hate the Japanese. The answer is and was, "No". I hate violence, greed, sadism, stupidity, arrogance, intolerance, ruthlessness. They are abhorrent no matter where they appear. The Japanese never had a monopoly of them.

Is it not difficult for anyone who fought in the war against the Japanese, who escaped capture and wounds, but knows *and saw* the evidence of their atrocities, and then their final humiliation and defeat, to appreciate the rationale of that "No". I believe the answer may lie in reflecting on the character and outlook of the Japanese people in the 1940s. Sir John Fletcher-Cooke described this in his book *The Emperor's Guest*:

(a) The Japanese had never lost a war in the whole of their history.
(b) It was an integral part of Japanese philosophy that nothing was more disgraceful than to surrender, either as an individual or as a group, or as a country.
(c) It was a religious duty, impressed upon every Japanese from birth, to die for Japan if necessary and never to surrender, once Japan was engaged in war.

(d) Every Japanese, whether in the Armed Forces or not, was firmly convinced that surrender would be followed by complete
slavery.

In this light it is perhaps well to remember, and not difficult to
understand, how, during the Second World War, the Japanese were
prone to kill their own wounded in battle rather than allow them to fall
alive into Allied hands. *Their* rationale was two-fold, to save their
comrades from disgrace and to safeguard their information.

It may not be generally known, and certainly Shenton and Daisy
were not aware when they were released, how near to "No Surrender"
the whole Japanese nation came in August, 1945. On Monday, 6
August the first atomic bomb was dropped on Hiroshima killing 64,000
people outright. On 9 August the second atomic bomb was dropped on
Nagasaki destroying the entire city. The following day the Supreme
War Council, presided over by His Imperial Majesty the Emperor,
decided to capitulate and preparations were made for a broadcast to the
nation by the Emperor.

However, notwithstanding the acquiescence of Amani, the War
Minister, in the Emperor's decision to surrender, a large number of
senior army officers determined to continue the war; they plotted to
assassinate the Prime Minister and the Foreign Minister and then to
occupy the Imperial Palace and take the Emperor into "protective
custody". Included in their plans were hundreds of Kamikaze suicide
pilots, with thousands of aircraft, who stood ready at a huge naval air
station near Yokohama. Events then moved quickly. Early on the
morning of the 15th, the fateful day, Amani committed ritual suicide by
cutting his carotid artery with a dagger. A number of the disaffected
officers, led by Major Hatanaka of the War Ministry, with some officers
from the Imperial Guard, went to the Palace, to the office of General
Mori, Commander of the Imperial Guard. There Hatanaka drew his
revolver and killed Mori, while another officer decapitated with his
sword Colonel Shiraish, Mori's brother-in-law. For a time the
mutineers controlled the Palace; and a detachment of the Imperial
Guard, led by Hatanaka, tried to capture the broadcasting station and
destroy the recordings of the Emperor's broadcast, the disc of which
had been made. But they failed.

Finally General Tanaka, Commander-in-Chief of the Eastern Army
in Tokyo, arrived at the Palace and the rebellion was crushed. It was
continuously announced from the Broadcasting Station that His Imperial Majesty would address the nation at noon. Hatanaka and a fellow
mutineer committed suicide on the lawns surrounding the Palace

walls; other officers also committed suicide, one of them by the side of General Mori.

One day in late September, 1945, Sir Shenton and Lady Thomas arrived at Poole Harbour in a flying boat from Calcutta. On disembarking they went on to London by train where their daughter Bridget met them, and took them both to Brown's Hotel in Dover Street. There they had their longed-for reunion with their family, including their first sight of their grandson Michael. It was a time of great rapture, as it were of life restored.

Shenton had chosen Brown's Hotel, which he knew well, as a suitable place for quiet relaxation and peace in highly comfortable surroundings, with good food and every attention. After their 3½ years in captivity they sorely needed this rehabilitation, together with the opportunity to renew their clothing, see their bankers, solicitors and the like, visit the Colonial Office, and generally resume normal life. But they stayed only a week or so in London before moving to Bridget's home, The Pound House at Brabourne in Kent. The two months they spent there with their family, in the peace and quiet of rural England in the autumn and early winter, did much to restore their equilibrium, particularly their ability to face life once more in the, to them, quite strange conditions of post-war England.

It says much for the resilience of Daisy and Shenton that they both wished to return to London and not continue their life in the country. Above all Shenton, although he was now 66, was anxious not to lose all contact with "Colonial" business and service, which had occupied his professional life for close on 40 years. It was late 1945 and the British Commonwealth and Empire now covered a larger area of the world than ever before, particularly in Africa where Shenton had served so long. De-colonization was still below the horizon, though men of Shenton's experience foresaw, within the Imperial ambit, a quickening of the pace towards political independence, but always under the umbrella of the British Commonwealth. Factually Shenton remained as Governor and High Commissioner from 1934 until, in 1946, he formally requested the Secretary of State for the Colonies to submit his resignation to the King. His total service as a Colonial Governor therefore amounted to 16 consecutive years, 3½ of which were spent in gaol – a most unusual, possibly unique, experience. Shenton was summoned to Buckingham Palace for an audience with King George VI.

After he had formally retired he and Daisy returned to London to live in a comfortable flat in Porchester Terrace. It was there that he was pleased to receive an invitation to become Chairman of the Council of the Royal Overseas League, with its Headquarters at Overseas House in Park Place, St James. The appointment suited him admirably, for it brought him into close contact with representatives of every country in the British Commonwealth and Empire, as well as with the senior ministers and officials of H.M. Government in London. When he had completed his four years of duty as Chairman he was made a Vice-President of the League and remained in that capacity for the rest of his life.

Later on Shenton was also invited to be Chairman of the British Empire Leprosy Relief Association and held that appointment for six years until 1955, during which time the annual income of the Association, from fund raising, increased from £40,000 to over £80,000. It was during this period that the Thomases moved to a larger flat at Oakwood Court in Holland Park, where they found it easier to receive their many friends from all the countries of the Empire.

The years they spent thus in London, with all the work and activities entailed in his various commitments, as well as visits from his family and friends, were, on the whole, a happy time for Shenton and Daisy. Nevertheless, after 1947 long shadows of past events in Malaya and Singapore gathered and caused much trouble for both of them.

Soon after his return to England Shenton began to think about writing his own version of the events that had influenced the civil government of Malaya before and during the campaign of 1941–42. He had expected that H.M.G. would require him to do this, but as time passed and he received no instructions or invitation to account for events, he wrote an appreciation for himself personally:

> I wanted to clarify and record the facts as I knew them. The capitulation of Singapore had given rise to very severe criticism, not only in this country but elsewhere. Singapore had been proclaimed to be an impregnable fortress: it fell in a few days: there must have been incompetence, apathy, and indecision; the whole affair was a disgrace. Our system of Colonial administration was called in question and a Royal Commission was demanded. I knew that many believed these criticisms to be justified and that many others were gravely uneasy. But few knew the truth of the matter. When, therefore, I arrived in England at the end of 1945, I expected to be asked by the Secretary of State for a statement. It may have been kindly forbearance in view of my condition at the time which caused this request to be waived, but the fact remains that never has even a suggestion been made to me that I should furnish a record of the campaign and of the preparatory work that was under-taken, so far as the civil government and the civil population were

concerned; and no account has ever been given to the public. I have never even been questioned as to what we did.

So, not long after the Thomases came to live at Porchester Terrace, he prepared a long and comprehensive review entitled *Malay's War Effort*. This document presented all the facts, and the planning preceding them, of the scope, range and performance of civil defence, *before and during the war*, in the Straits Settlements and the Malay States. In his Foreword Shenton wrote:

> I believe the review contains much that is not generally known, and it seems right that such information as is available should be placed on record, in common fairness to the civilian population who suffered so terribly through no fault of their own. I have told the story from official documents which completely disposes of any charges of official incapacity.

It is impossible to reproduce the whole review in this book and I have therefore tabulated its main subject headings. These show the great variety of actions which the civil government had to take in order to prosecute the war as its first priority, while simultaneously maintaining the administrative structure of the country, but always without prejudice to the plans and operations of the armed forces, their training, movement, and co-operation with the civil authorities.

Top Priority Production of Rubber and Tin
Logistic (materials) support for the armed forces
Financial aid and foreign exchange earnings
All A.R.P. (including Recruiting and Training Wardens
    and air raid shelters)
Air Field Construction and Protection
Medical Auxiliary Service
Auxiliary Fire Service (Fire Fighters)
Local Defence Corps (Home Guard)
Coast Watching
Boat Denial Schemes
Guarding Vulnerable Strategic Points
Internment Camps for Enemy Aliens
Censorship, Propaganda and Press Control
Denial Schemes
Man Power Control and Labour
Extra Hospital Accommodation
Public Health and Sanitation
Water Supplies

Expansion of Roads, Railways, Harbours
Export and Import Control
Recruiting of Ten Battalions of Volunteers for Local Malay
  Naval, Army and Air Force Units
Reception of Refugees (Shelter for Homeless)
Evacuation of Refugees of all Communities.

Of course the Governor could not, and was not expected to, control personally all the varied tasks on this formidable list, but he was the Head of the Government and therefore liable to be held ultimately responsible for any deterioration in standards in any matter covered by that very flexible term "Civil Defence". By and large he had to rely on existing local resources of manpower and material for this tremendous expansion of work, though some senior officers were brought in from outside Malaya, such as Sir George Sansom who was responsible for Propaganda and Press Control.

Clearly the main Civil Defence problem, once war came to Malaya, was the timing imposed on every task by the unexpected speed of the military withdrawal. Shenton was at pains to express this very forcibly in his telegram to the Colonial Office of 22 January, 1942:

> Civil Government had to reverse at short notice practically the whole of its defence machinery which had been built up on military advice that we might have to face blockade and also attempted invasion in Kelantan and East coast of Johore. We were never asked to provide against contingency of invasion from sea on the West coast, nor for the practically uninterrupted march of the enemy through Malaya. Port Swettenham was prepared as a suitable internment camp but we had to evacuate all internees hurriedly to Singapore and thence to India. . . . We have had to arrange for totally unexpected withdrawals from threatened areas, though, owing to urgent military needs, it has been very difficult, often impossible, to obtain any transport at all.

Shenton Thomas completed his review in July 1947. About the same time the official despatches of the three Service commanders, and of Air Chief Marshal Sir Robert Brooke-Popham, were being written, and draft copies of each were sent to Shenton in London. From that moment, one might say, the *"Battle for Civil Defence in Malaya"* began (indeed it is not yet at an end). The draft despatch of Lieutenant-General Percival in particular was strongly condemned by Shenton Thomas for inaccuracy and injustice in its comments on civil defence in Malaya; and for its timing, as the despatch was eventually published without even a mention of Shenton's review, *which the latter had sent to the Secretary of State for the Colonies asking for its publication at the same time as the Service despatches.*

Those adverse comments on the civil government by Percival were later mirrored in the draft of the Official History, written by the Cabinet Office. This equally aroused the ire of Shenton Thomas, particularly the following passage which, very briefly, set out the gravamen of the charges made in Percival's military despatch:

> The pre-war attitude of the civil authorities had been that an attack on Malaya was not in the realm of practical politics and that time and money spent on civil defence would be wasted. Thus, despite the fact that all the necessary data, based on the experience of the bombing in Britain in 1940, had been sent to Malaya, civil defence in the large towns, such as Kuala Lumpur and Singapore, did not exist in the sense that it did in Britain. A few blast walls for important buildings had been built, but the organisation of the Air Raid Precaution and Fire Fighting Services was on too small a scale and quite inadequate to deal with anything but sporadic raids.

Shenton Thomas annotated his copy of the above extract: "In Singapore at a military conference on 22 October, 1941, General Playfair, Brooke-Popham's Chief of Staff, read a paper the conclusion of which was that the *Japs could not make war on us!*"

In the light of all that he knew had been done before the war, and he had in mind his own interview before the Joint Planning Sub-Committee of the War Cabinet on 1 August, 1940, when he had appealed strongly for assistance for Malaya, Shenton Thomas was horrified by the unwarranted attacks on his administration. Unwarranted, if only because his own case had not been heard, or at any rate had not been considered. Of course he saw the hand of Duff Cooper in those despatches. But he made his own case personally in a long letter which he sent to the Under-Secretary of State at the Colonial Office late in 1947. He wrote it in reply to an official letter telling him that his Review could not be published. The following is an extract from his letter:

> When I read the draft despatches of the Service commanders, and especially that written by General Percival, it was clear to me that their publication would revive the previous agitation and that more mud would be thrown at those who cannot speak for themselves. It was

obvious that I must act on their behalf unless I was prepared to let their case go by default. I could not do that. So long as the past seemed likely to be forgotten, it was probably wise – or so I felt – not to run the risk of creating fresh controversy by publishing any account of what Malaya did; but now that past criticism is to be invigorated by statements made in officially sponsored Service despatches, it is my bounden duty to answer it on behalf of Malaya so far as I can. It is for this reason that I wrote my Review, and asked the Secretary of State to authorise its publication at the same time as the Service despatches are published.

You have stated that the reason why authority to publish my Review officially cannot be given is that other Colonial territories might feel aggrieved at the "special treatment" accorded to Malaya. I feel that this reason is based on a complete misconception of the question at issue. I did not write my Review to boost Malaya: what Malaya did before and during the campaign was nothing more than her plain duty. I wrote the Review because Malaya has been accused of not doing her duty, and this accusation will be brought up again when the Service despatches are published and the time will be ripe for a final judgment; and these similar accusations have never been answered and they must be answered if the judgment is to be fair, in the interests of Britain as trustee for all the peoples of the Empire.

Nothing of the sort can be argued on behalf of any other British territory. Those who, like Malaya, were overrun have suffered, so far as I am aware, none of the aspersions which have been cast upon Malaya. Her case is unique: it has no parallel within or without the Colonial Empire. There is thus a perfectly good answer to any complaint of special treatment, and to this answer it might well be added that, if any Colony is anxious for its achievements to be known to the world, it might have thought of it two years ago.

I fear it is unlikely that General Percival will modify the criticisms in his despatch to the extent desired. Even if he did, there will still be criticisms in his and the other Service despatches. It would be hardly reasonable to expect otherwise, but I feel sure that the appearance of these, and certain other features in the despatches which do not call for comment here, will not go unnoticed by the public and the Press. It is clear to me that my Review should be published whether or not General Percival accepts the modifications requested of him.

There is another point. I have recently ascertained that the private publication of my Review in this country would, owing to paper shortage and other difficulties, be probably a matter of months and, if the Service despatches are to be published in the autumn, it is hardly possible that my Review could be ready in time. Judgment would thus be given against Malaya by default and I submit that this would be unfair as it would be undeserved. And so, after consideration of all possibilities, I find myself forced to the conclusion that the Secretary of State is our only hope, and

I do sincerely trust that he will respond to my appeal and authorise the official publication in England of my Review.

I am, Sir,
Your obedient servant,
Shenton Thomas

The Under-Secretary of State
The Colonial Office,
London S.W.1.

In the event the Secretary of State refused to reconsider his decision not to publish *Malaya's War Effort*, thus adding, over the years, to Shenton's concern. Matters became even worse in 1957 when the *Official History of the War against Japan*, by Major-General S. Woodburn Kirby, appeared, in which were repeated grave accusations against the civil government of Malaya. Shenton Thomas's feelings when this large, well-publicized, official volume was published by Her Majesty's Stationery Office have never been made public. His reactions began during the preparation of the history, as the following letter to the Cabinet Office, and the reply to it, will show.

28 Oakwood Court
1st Nov. 1956

My dear Macpherson,
    Regarding publication of the Official History of the war in Malaya I feel obliged to point out that I was never consulted by the historians in the preparation of the original draft; nor, as far as I can trace, on any points arising out of my own commentary, nor in the preparation of the revised and final draft. Nor did they allow me to see any of the documents affecting the civil population on which the history is based, though some of them were written by officers serving under me during the campaign. I regard this as unfair to Malaya.

Yours sincerely,
Shenton Thomas

Sir John Macpherson, K.C.M.G.
Historical Section
The Cabinet Office
London, S.W.1.

Macpherson replied in the following terms.

Cabinet Office
6th November 1956

No decision has yet been taken on the date of the publication of the History. We feel that we cannot take this matter any further in view of the conditions governing the writing of these histories. The authors have a duty to ensure that the picture of events which they give is exact and truthful, but the responsibility for the work as a whole, and for the views expressed in it, is theirs and theirs alone; and it is important that they should not feel they are in any way discouraged from expressing the considered judgments which on assessment of all the evidence has led them to make. For this reason it is felt that it would not be proper, at this stage, to ask them to undertake renewed consultations with individuals, which might lead to their being pressed to make still further revisions on points on which conflicting views are known to be held. I am sure you will understand that in all these matters there is a point of "No Return", after which consultation with individual persons cannot be continued.

Yours sincerely,
John Macpherson

The glaring paradox between these two letters is painfully obvious. Shenton declares that he himself was never consulted and not allowed access to any of the evidence in the draft which affected the civil population. But Macpherson refers to the "considered judgment which an assessment of *all* the evidence has led them [the historians] to make"; he then adds that "a point of No Return" has been reached and *further* consultation is not allowed, although Shenton had never been consulted!

Naturally, he felt deeply hurt by this astonishing situation; grave accusations, "unfair to Malaya", had been made, but evidence in defence, in rebuttal of the charges, had been deliberately *withheld* and set aside. The case drawn up by himself had been received but not heard, and was therefore lost by default. He could not avoid feeling that there was an unexplained bias against publication of any evidence by himself, and therefore against the civil administration of Malaya.

He found particular grievance in two points made against his administration: the warning, or lack of it, of the first Japanese air raid on Singapore, and the improper use of his name by civilians attempting to escape from Singapore immediately before the surrender.

The *Official History* accused the civil defence authorities of laxity in not warning the population of Singapore of the approach of Japanese bombers early on 8 December, 1941, "because the A.R.P. Headquarters was not manned"; and also because there was no attempt at blackout and the street lights of the city were blazing. We have seen in an earlier chapter that the A.R.P. centre *was* manned, but the Alarm Sirens could not have been sounded as the Chief Warden was at the cinema and had the control key with him. As regards the lighting, Shenton had pointed out that: "A crash blackout was not possible in

Singapore as much of the lighting was by gas which had to be put out by men going round to extinguish each light with a pole!" But his main point was that everyone, including himself, was caught napping. On the information available nobody expected an air raid. For that matter, neither did the Americans at Pearl Harbor. Of course, with the benefit of hindsight, it is easy to assert that when Percival telephoned Shenton at 1.15 a.m. to report that the Japanese were bombarding Kota Bharu from the sea, then both men should have have seen the red light immediately and ordered maximum precautions everywhere. But they didn't: they could not envisage the possibility that Japanese aircraft had anything approaching sufficient range to bomb the city. As Shenton wrote: "Surely it was not conceivable that on the night in question any one of us should have neglected any precaution, if we had thought that a raid was even remotely possible."

The policy for the evacuation of all civilians had been laid down by H.M.G. during December, 1941, and was governed by two principles: (a) no racial discrimination and (b) women and children first. At the same time a committee to adjudicate on all applications had been set up, with Mr Justice Aitken as Chairman. Then, on 3 February, 1942, just after the withdrawal to Singapore Island, the War Council issued the following instruction:

> It is decided that compulsory evacuation of civilians is not possible owing to the policy of non-discrimination between races which must be adhered to. A communique is to be issued suggesting that all women who wish to leave the country, *apart from those doing war work*, should register their names. The communique will be drafted by the G.O.C. and His Excellency the Governor.

Shenton Thomas made this comment on what followed:

> General Percival's reference to this matter in his official despatch (para 239) is misleading where the civil government is concerned. It suggests that passages *were to be allotted* to families of Service Officers and civilians who wished to leave, *whether doing war work or not*. In consequence only 4 service women stayed behind to be interned, and some 300 civilian women were interned. All the services nursing sisters were sent away, whilst 80 civilian sisters were interned in Changi Prison, where they did such wonderful work for the 3½ years of captivity.

But then, from 1947 onwards, came renewed evidence of false use of the Governor's name in attempts to leave Singapore. Leslie Smart, General Manager of the Railways, wrote to Shenton about it:

                                                    Salisbury,
                                                    Southern Rhodesia
                                                    12th August 1947

Dear Sir Shenton,

On the afternoon of Friday, the 13th February, 1942, Mr Sanders (Transportation Manager) informed me that Brigadier Simson was in his (Sanders's) office at Singapore Station and wished to see me urgently. I went to that office and Brigadier Simson informed me that he had come from you with instructions that I should leave Singapore by ship that afternoon and take with me up to six officers. I protested against leaving Singapore, pointing out that it meant leaving behind practically all my European officers. We then went to an improvised air-raid shelter (where my wife was sitting) to continue the discussion, and, on hearing what was being said, my wife objected to our leaving. Brigadier Simson said "This is war: it is an order and must be obeyed." He asked me to give the names of the officers who could usefully accompany me, and made out exit permits for Mr (and Mrs) Smart, Mr Sanders, Mr Wegener, Mr Gordon Brown, Mr Sykes and Mr Davies. Mr Sanders and Mr Davies (my Office assistant) were present throughout the interview with Brigadier Simson.

I left Singapore solely because of what I was informed was an instruction from you, and the fact that Brigadier Simson came personally to the railway station and issued exit permits, without any approach from me, confirmed that belief.

                                                    Your sincere,
                                                    L. M. Sharp

Shenton endorsed this letter with the following footnote:

"Completely unauthorised by me."

When I had finished writing this chapter I felt obliged to ask myself the following question: Is it possible that Sir Shenton Thomas was made the scapegoat for much of the humiliation that Great Britain and the Commonwealth suffered at Singapore? His attempts to get a fair hearing, and publication of his own views, failed completely. Was there an attempt in London to shut him up?

X

BLAME?

In a speech made to the Central Council of the Conservative Party at Caxton Hall on 26 March, 1942, Churchill called the fall of Singapore "the greatest disaster to British arms which our history records". But, strategically, there was more to it than a historic and humiliating defeat in battle, albeit without precedent in scale; it was the focal point in a series of international military, political and economic disasters in the Far East that began in December, 1941.

The American fleet in the Pacific Ocean had been crippled at Pearl Harbor; the *Prince of Wales* and *Repulse* lay at the bottom of the South China Sea, and later the Dutch Navy in the East Indies was annihilated. Hong Kong surrendered on 25 December and, once Malaya and Singapore had fallen, the Japanese could raid at will into the Indian Ocean and very soon obtained complete control of the Bay of Bengal. Thus both India and Ceylon lay wide open to attack and their coasts were in fact bombarded by Japanese warships. In India, in particular, political agitation, inspired by Mahatma Gandhi, led to serious internal uprising. Japanese forces went on to conquer Burma, the Andaman Islands, Java and Sumatra, Timor, Borneo, Formosa and the Philippines.

Economically the stark fact emerged that the Japanese had obtained total access to those sinews of war without which they could not sustain their military advance in either China or South-East Asia. They needed British and Dutch oil, rubber, tin and rice, and now had all these commodities in abundance; they would continue to enjoy them so long as they controlled the sea lanes in the Pacific Ocean leading to their homeland.

Later on the Japanese occupied the Solomon Islands, thereby directly threatening United States' communications with Australia; they also gained a footing in New Guinea, so Australia and New Zealand could no longer feel safe from invasion. To complete a dark picture for the Western Allies, German armies were on the outskirts of Leningrad and only 20 miles from Moscow.

Of course it is easy to assert that we were unprepared, and no one had expected that retribution for our lack of preparation would be so swift or catastrophic. Is this then were all blame lies, and can we leave all reason for blame at that? I doubt it; for if we had succeeded in holding Singapore by adequate military means and foresight (which we might well have done), then afterwards people would surely have said that, had we lost Singapore, we should also have lost the war. In the event we did lose Singapore but we also won the war! Look also at what happened after the First World War; everybody maintained that, had the Germans taken the Channel ports, then we would have lost that war. Nevertheless in the Second World War our enemy certainly gained all the Channel ports, and the Biscay ports as well, yet we won again.* This is why I started this chapter with a reminder of the magnitude and significance of the fall of Singapore. Only in that light is it fair to reappraise the very complex reasons for blame, and to decide where, if at all, it should lie. Bearing this in mind, I have reached some conclusions, while still "trying always to look at yesterday with the eyes of yesterday".

Lieutenant-General A. E. Percival, the G.O.C. Malaya, arrived in Singapore in May, 1941. He knew the whole country and its problems very well, having been senior staff officer at Singapore Army Command during 1936–37 and he was probably also well known to Shenton Thomas. He had been on the staff at Military Headquarters in Nigeria when Shenton was Deputy Chief Secretary at Lagos. In defence matters Percival was steeped in the strategy and tactics advocated by General Dobbie, whose words he had quoted in his own book**.

> It is an attack from the northward that I regard as the greatest potential danger to the fortress (Singapore). Such an attack could be carried out during the period of the north-east monsoon. The jungle is not in most places impassable to infantry.

These were admirable sentiments, so what went wrong after Percival arrived? Virtually every writer on the campaign has blamed him in the strongest terms, and Professor Callahan made this telling point: that Percival knew of photographic evidence, taken from a British ship in 1938, showing "Japanese troops landing on the Chinese coast in rough seas during the height of the N.E. monsoon". He never made any attempt to deny the widely held, yet fallacious, belief that landings during the monsoon were impossible. The trouble was that Percival

---

* These thoughts came to me in 1977, following a discussion with Dr Noble Frankland, then Director of the Imperial War Museum.
** *The War in Malaya*, by A. E. Percival, Eyre & Spotiswoode, 1949.

was not a leader, and altogether lacked the strength of mind and character to command troops in battle. Ronald Lewin probably recorded the verdict of history against Percival when he wrote:*

> Nobody can carp with any justice at an officer who is posted to a position for which he is not suited; the responsibility lies with his superiors or the military secretariat. The man himself does what he can, within his limits; yet when things go wrong it is he who is condemned.

Yes, Percival was a military failure, but surely blame rests with the C.I.G.S., Field-Marshal Sir John Dill, who had personally appointed him.

After the war, when all the captives had come home, the post-mortems on the campaign really began and I have often wondered why some of the principal officers involved, who disagreed about major issues, apparently seldom, if ever, met again, in spite of the bonds of shared experiences during their captivity. So often in Shenton's diary at Karenko there are entries like: "Sunday. Percival took church." or "Sunday. I took church." Yet, to the best of my knowledge, Percival and Shenton Thomas never met again.

In an earlier chapter we saw how Air Chief Marshal Sir Robert Brooke-Popham, the Commander-in-Chief Far East from November, 1940, until 27 December, 1941, achieved virtually nothing in spite of the high hopes expected from his appointment. Yet his early letters from Singapore to General Sir Hastings Ismay (then Secretary of the Committee of Imperial Defence) show great vigour and a determination to co-ordinate and control an effective British war machine. At first he was also strongly critical of the civil government, and wrote accordingly:

> General Headquarters Far East Command
> Singapore
> 5th December 1940
>
> My dear Ismay,
> To my mind the main thing that stands out about Singapore is the lack of touch and indeed the latent hostility between the Central Government, the Services and the Civilian Community. The result is that the three do not mix as they should and don't understand each other's point of view. I feel quite certain that the great majority of civilians and some of the Government officials don't grasp the realities of the situation and, possibly deliberately, close their eyes to the fact that, say, a naval defeat in the Mediterranean might bring bombs to Singapore in a few days. . . .

* *The Chieftain*, Hutchinson & Co., 1980.

I feel that until one can break down the walls dividing the different sections progress will be slow and difficult. But I also feel convinced of this, that once we can break the walls down, get the Government to take the leaders of the Civil Community into their confidence, and establish increased points of contact, that things will go well. . . .

Sir Shenton Thomas comes back today and I have got to convince him that I am right before anything much can be done. . . ."*

In the light of this I thought perhaps that B.P. and Shenton Thomas would not have got on well together; but the evidence of Shenton's diary, and the War Council minutes, shows their agreement generally on all matters, more often than not in opposition to Duff Cooper! But virtually every writer on the campaign has strongly blamed Brooke-Popham for his lack of professional determination and energy, particularly as the war clouds gathered; this extract from a memorandum he issued to his own Staff Officers as late as September 1941, exemplifies his complacency:

Until the latter part of February [1942] the danger of a Japanese offensive against Malaya will be less than it has been during the last six months. . . .

Our preparations should include a period of leave and recreation for as many individuals as possible, so that they shall be ready on the top of their form by the early part of 1942.

We also saw in an earlier chapter how Brooke-Popham lacked the moral courage to launch Operation "Matador" and pre-empt Japanese moves into Southern Thailand. He has been blamed for that, even though the operation might have failed.

Like so many others, Brooke-Popham was caught napping; but for a military commander in war that is a crime and he paid for it. Besides, when war reached the Far East he was 63 and Major-General Woodburn Kirby, author of the *Official History*, passed this verdict on him: "Although a man of great charm, he had clearly passed his prime and was not forceful enough a personality to deal with this complicated and difficult situation." It would have been more accurate to record that he should not have been appointed – "a man of great charm" does not necessarily win battles. Brooke-Popham was another case of selecting the wrong man for the job.

Duff Cooper arrived on the Malayan scene on 9 September, 1941,

* Extract from papers in Liddell Hart Centre for Military Archives, King's College, London University.

almost three months to a day before the Japanese invasion began; but he spent all that period touring his "parish", which left insufficient time to see for himself the military situation in Singapore and mainland Malaya, before the invasion came on 8 December. Much later Shenton Thomas wrote:

> On the outbreak of war with Japan Duff Cooper found himself cooped up in Singapore; he could not criticize the armed forces, knowing nothing of the country and the problems it created. There was left only the civil side, and the chance of being bombed.

Setting aside the rights and wrongs of this very personal conflict between Duff Cooper and the Governor, it is appropriate to consider what might have happened had there been genuine co-operation between Duff Cooper, the military leaders and the Governor. Duff Cooper's arrival created a unique situation. It brought to the deliberations of the Commanders-in-Chief of the armed forces, and the civil government, the advice and influence of a Cabinet Minister who had the ear of the Prime Minister in London and was able to *communicate direct with him.* Duff Cooper had been on active service in the First World War. He could, or should, have seen the defects of relying on air power to counter a likely Japanese invasion with totally inadequate military resources; he must have known the value of fixed defences; with his previous experience of war he did not need Simson to tell him that. He could, therefore, very early on, say in October, have advised Churchill *personally* of the highly dangerous situation impending. To put it another way, Duff Cooper, with his personal contacts with the Prime Minister, must have known before he left London that it was H.M.G.'s policy to avoid war with Japan; and that defence of the Far East would have, in Churchill's view, to be based on air power until it became possible to send massive naval support to the Far East. As the P.M.'s representative, he could have strongly advised Churchill that this defence policy would lead to disaster if Japan attacked.

It is true that he did strongly urge the Chiefs of Staff in London to send much-needed reinforcements, but that was in the second half of *December*; and then early in January he muddied the waters by advising Churchill *personally* that:

(a) Brooke-Popham was on the verge of a nervous collapse
(b) Shenton Thomas could not adjust his mind to war conditions
(c) Stanley Jones, the Colonial Secretary, was universally detested
(d) Percival had been a schoolmaster and he (Duff Cooper) wished he had remained one.

What, then, will history make of Duff Cooper's contribution to the catastrophe of Singapore? The impression remains that he achieved nothing but harm; it is difficult to see any actual constructive results from his performance. Nobody invited him to assume the role of a character assassin. Yet, on the other hand, would Churchill have responded positively to the kind of unanimous plea which I have suggested he could have sent him long before Pearl Harbor?

Field-Marshal Wavell stands prominently on the stage, as it were, above all the other actors, and Ronald Lewin has ably described the part that he played after he became Supreme Commander of ABDACOM:

> From now on Singapore meant Wavell. It was he who struggled to inject marrow into the bone of the defence, and into its irresolute commander; it was he who ordered a fight to the death and a policy of "burnt earth", and it was Wavell who, when there was nothing left to do and London had lost hope, personally authorised capitulation.*

In 1970, as mentioned earlier, Brigadier Ivan Simson, the Director General for Civil Defence in Malaya (D.G.C.D.) published his book *Singapore, Too Little Too Late.* The author was highly critical of senior British civil and military leadership, both in the United Kingdom and locally in Malaya, both before and during the campaign; indeed the only senior man who escaped Simson's denunciation was Duff Cooper, who had secured the appointment of a D.G.C.D. Simson's book is important because of the scope and range of his comments and the allegations he has made. But he deserves credit for having combined his criticism with a reminder that the Japanese only captured Singapore by sheer bluff – a remark which does nothing to lessen the humiliation of the British defeat.

Simson refers to a book by John Deane Potter**, published in 1963, which told the Japanese side of the Malayan campaign, and included the personal diaries of General Yamashita. Apparently, according to the General, the Japanese 25th Army numbered only some 30,000 men, and he wrote as follows about the final battle for Singapore:

> My attack on Singapore was a bluff – a bluff that worked. I had 30,000 men and was outnumbered more than three to one. I knew that if I had to fight long for Singapore I would be beaten. That was why the surrender had to be made at once. I was very frightened all the time that the British

---

* From *The Chieftain.*
** *A Soldier must Hang*, Muller, 1963.

would discover our numerical weakness and lack of supplies, and force me into disastrous street fighting.

The *Official History* states that total battle casualties of the army in Malaya were nearly 9,000 and that the figure for prisoners of war captured by the Japanese exceeded 130,000 men of all the armed forces, but excluding all civilian internees. These details, so terrible when set against the statement of General Yamashita that his final victory was won by bluff, merely enhance the humiliation of the Singapore disaster.

Ivan Simson was a distinguished and highly professional senior officer of the Royal Engineers. He had been appointed Chief Engineer of the Army in Malaya and clearly wanted to remain as such; he did not wish to be made D.G.C.D. and objected strongly at being "pushed into" the job by Duff Cooper during the absence of Sir Shenton Thomas. The main theme of his book is his complete lack of support, either from Whitehall or from his superiors in Malaya, for the defensive measures he considered as urgent and essential; he had been briefed by the War Office to make good the military defences of Malaya. But on arrival in Singapore in August, 1941, he found that: "There were few plans or preparations at all to thwart landings or block enemy advances, or to protect the naval base from landward attack. That surely is the real tragedy of what Churchill considered to be our greatest defeat in history." In earlier chapters we saw how, throughout the long withdrawal from the frontier of Thailand, the retreating troops, when falling back to a new defence line, never once found any pre-planned and prepared defence works; there was a complete absence of anti-tank and machine gun positions sited in depth for all-round defence, including fall-back (reserve) positions and reinforcement plans.

It has to be said that Simson was right. There were no prepared defences and it was always the same until, finally, the army came to northern Johore, then the Muar River line, followed by southern Johore and, lastly, the north shore of Singapore Island.

Simson's main culprit was always General Percival, whom he blamed for consistent inertia at the highest level of military command and was therefore in his opinion very largely responsible. But Simson also strongly blamed the civil government, and particularly Sir Shenton Thomas, for the lack of those military defence works, though without giving specific reason or argument to support the accusation. Indeed, this lack of reason is understandable, for the fact is that Percival was the Governor's chief military adviser, and the man closest to the Governor from among the services. The records show clearly that before the war, and after it began, any important defence proposal falling within the purview of the civil government was always accepted by Sir Shenton Thomas. An even more telling rebuttal of Simson's accusation was made by Hugh Bryson, a senior officer of the M.C.S. in the Singapore Secretariat, who made a detailed analysis of the allegation which is filed in the Royal Commonwealth Society archives*. Bryson wrote, inter alia: "It is unworthy of Simson to record such stupid gossip that the Governor was responsible for lack of defence: he [Simson] had detailed clearly how he himself failed to persuade Percival to erect defences. How then could the Governor do it? Was the Army possibly seeking a scapegoat?"

Finally Shenton's own remark about the lack of defence works should be recorded. After he had returned from captivity he met General Bond, Percival's predecessor, and asked him why, pre-war, no defence works had been constructed on the north shore of Singapore Island, or in southern Johore. The General replied that "they had thought of it but decided against it." Bond made no mention of civilians or the civil government, or gave any reason for the military decision.

Simson also criticized the civil government for inadequate action over the scorched earth decision once complete destruction had been ordered. Again it is pertinent to read the Governor's reaction, expressed in a letter he wrote to Lord Wavell on 21 December 1947:

> Our pre-war plans, which were all discussed in our War Committee, were for denial operations which would render plant, machinery and installations useless to the enemy but would allow speedy reconditioning after the war, or rather after we were relieved; the Malaya Defence Scheme was in respect of a six-month siege. Much of it was of course scrapped after the Japs entered Indo-China in July, 1941, and I agree that a lot of what we were able to substitute was imperfect. But, due to the unexpected (retreat) nature of the campaign, and to the orders we suddenly received for scorched earth, there had to be much improvization.

Later on, in this same connection, Shenton Thomas, when commenting on the draft Official History, wrote:

> On December 23rd 1941 Duff Cooper at Singapore asked the Foreign Office whether total destruction was enjoined in view of the possibility of our *regaining* [my italics] Malaya within six months.

It sounds fantastic now, but so it was.

---

* Royal Commonwealth Society, World War II papers, File SIMSON ZA.

One particular aspect of the drama, referred to by Simson, was the odd way in which Duff Cooper had insisted on appointing him, a Sapper Brigadier, to be the "supreme overlord" for all civil defence, without reference to the Governor. This was mentioned in an earlier chapter, but it is timely to recall it here in the context of the extraordinary, some may call it sinister, manner in which Duff Cooper had also discussed personally with Simson the question of a suitable replacement for Sir Shenton Thomas.

However, for me the most important facet of Simson's story lies in his treatment after his return to England from captivity. The following extracts from *Singapore, Too Little Too Late* bear a striking resemblance to the testimony of Sir Shenton Thomas:

> During our three and a half years in prisoner of war camps I wrote two reports. The first was on the civil defence aspects, and was prepared on the order of Duff Cooper, then Resident Minister for Far Eastern Affairs, with Cabinet rank. . . . The second – and more important report – I wrote in my position of Chief Engineer, Malaya Command. . . . Like the civil defence report, the Engineer report was checked, during its writing, with senior fellow officer prisoners, British, Australian and Indian Corps.
>
> After the war I had many interviews, and exchanged correspondence with Major General Kirby, the official historian at the Cabinet Office. . . . It was only after final publication of the Official History that I discovered that the information I had supplied, and which I considered of major importance, had not been included. . . . I made two further efforts to get certain facts placed on official record, and it was only after this failure that I decided to write my book.*

We now have two proven examples of absolute refusal by a Cabinet Office department, responsible for producing the *Official History of World War II*, to publish highly significant evidence on the Malayan campaign; this refusal to publish *all the facts*, whether pleasant or unpleasant, has never been explained by H.M.G., except (and partially only) on grounds of confidentiality. While researching for this book, with special reference to Sir Shenton Thomas's plea for publication of his *Malaya's War Effort*, I noted a particular file in the Public Record Office which, from its title, appeared relevant and highly important. My efforts to see this file finally ended when I received the following letter:

---

* I have taken the liberty of altering the order of the above passages in order to reduce the length of the quotation but retain a logical sequence.

Cabinet Office
70 Whitehall, London SW1A 2AS
13 May 1982

Dear Colonel Montgomery,

As you are aware, Mr Smith of the Ministry of Defence has copied to me your letter of 8 April about early access to C.A.B. 101/148. I apologise for the delay in letting you have a formal reply. Unfortunately I can really do no more than reiterate what Mr Theobald said to you in his letter of 27 November 1981. That is that C.A.B. 101/148 contains correspondence between period 1954–55 and since it includes correspondence between General Kirby and not only Sir Shenton Thomas but also Sir James Butler, the Colonial Office and others who gave testimony about the fall of Singapore, it cannot under the rules of confidentiality in which such correspondence was conducted be opened to outside researchers until January 1986. I therefore very much regret that we are unable to grant you early access to C.A.B. 101/148.

Yours sincerely,
D. A. MORRIS
Departmental Records Officer

In the case of Simson's testimony it is noteworthy that he had also written personally to Sir Winston Churchill in 1956, hoping that the latter's intervention might result in the inclusion in the *Official History* of certain major acts of omission and commission that had a bearing on the speed of collapse in Malaya, and which Simson had submitted. But his efforts failed; as also, in the circumstances, did Simson's efforts to contact Duff Cooper again. According to Simson the Historical Section of the Cabinet Office agreed in 1954 that he should send his civil defence report to Duff Cooper (by then Viscount Norwich); but Lord Norwich died before the report could reach him. For Simson surely one of his most poignant memories of captivity must have been when General Percival, in a prison camp in Formosa, told him that a Chief Engineer's report on the Singapore disaster would not be required.

Major-General Woodburn Kirby, C.B., C.M.G., C.I.E., O.B.E., M.C., a highly distinguished army officer appointed as Official Historian of the war against Japan, published his own account of the Malayan campaign, in 1971, in a book entitled *Singapore: The Chain of Disaster*. Kirby was extremely critical of all the senior British commanders, civil and military, for their inability to stop the Japanese army's advance at any stage. In the strictures on various personalities he clearly leant heavily on Simson's book, which made Hugh Bryson remark that: "Cabinet instructions precluded Kirby from casting too many aspersions in the *Official History* on the leaders"; in his own book he has had no hesitation in doing just that.

In these circumstances it was not surprising to read Kirby's very strong, and repeated, attacks on Sir Shenton Thomas, and on Stanley Jones, the Colonial Secretary. He was highly critical of both men for their poor character and performance and, reading between the lines, it is difficult to escape the conclusion, indeed it is evident from the text, that much of Kirby's book reflects the views of Duff Cooper, particularly about Shenton Thomas's tenure as Governor. Kirby began to collect material for his official history in 1951, though this volume was not published until 1957, and it would be illogical to suppose that Kirby's staff did not have frequent contact with Duff Cooper. Also it must have been in Kirby's office that the decision was taken, or recommended, not to publish the Governor's own Review or any of his representations about the civil administration, as well as vital portions of Simson's testimony. Maybe the fact that Kirby had no personal knowledge of Malayan conditions accounts for some of his ill-informed criticism. Hugh Bryson, when reviewing Kirby's book, wrote:

> Kirby is very critical of civil defence efforts and blames Stanley Jones, Colonial Secretary, for refusing to construct air-raid shelters in Singapore City. That decision had been taken previously by a committee on which all the armed services were represented. More than half the population lived in densely congested areas only a few feet above sea level. . . . Underground shelters on a large scale were impracticable and there was no room to build above ground. A policy of dispersal was adopted and two camps were built outside the city, each capable of housing and feeding 300,000.

Looking back now I can view the senior field commanders of the Malayan campaign, naval, military and air, marching, as it were, across the pages of my script; none were successful in the sense that they fought and gained victory in battle. But they fought most gallantly, handicapped by ill-trained, inexperienced troops, inferior weapons and unsuitable transport, against an enemy superior in every respect. Some, beyond doubt, achieved considerable tactical success, but they were not given sufficient resources to exploit their local victories; their poor communications, cumbersome transport and complete lack of armour denied them much-needed mobility. They must all, at some stage, have met Sir Shenton Thomas, either at Government House, Singapore, or later on in captivity. Comparisons are invidious, but some names spring to mind: Lieutenant-General Sir Lewis Heath, the Corps Commander, one of the most experienced and highly respected officers of the Indian Army, whose sound professional advice Percival so often, unfortunately, rejected; Major-General "Billy" Key, alert and always cheerful, who commanded the brigade that faced the first massive Japanese assault on the beaches at Kota Bharu, and later was promoted to command 9th Indian Division; and Major-General Gordon Bennett, Commander of the 8th Australian Division, whose actions became so famous for very unusual reasons.

The Australian troops fought magnificently in spite of Percival's grave error in splitting the division, thereby making it impossible for Gordon Bennett to command his formation in battle. Then came the long retreat and the surrender and the attempts to escape by various parties of British troops and civilians. General Bennett was determined to escape. He had the right to communicate direct with Australian Army Headquarters in Melbourne on administrative matters, and he interpreted this as giving him the right to leave Singapore and return to Australia, come what may, in order that his experience in fighting the Japanese should be available to the Australian Army. Therefore, on the night of February 15/16 he got away in a fast motor launch with a group he had organized, without telling Percival, or any other authority, and, worst of all, *without handing over* his division to the command of another officer. It was a strange and dreadful act, for he left his men at the time of their most dire need when firm and sound leadership by their appointed commander was their prime requirement. He was a brave man and he reached Australia as he intended. But a Court of Inquiry was held to investigate his personal conduct and he was never again appointed to command troops. If he had stayed with his men, as all other commanders did, then surely no Australian troops would have taken part in those post-surrender scenes of disorder that Cicely Williams witnessed.

It will be a long time before historians cease to record their views of the events of the 70-day Malaya campaign. It was a time when rumours were rife, particularly of false optimism in many quarters in Singapore. Now, more than 40 years later, it becomes increasingly difficult to sift the truth from among the mass of contradictory records, books, type-written memoranda in public and private libraries and museums, all inevitably coloured, sometimes no doubt distorted, by the originator's personal opinions, likes and dislikes.

I therefore had no cause for surprise when I read the following reference to Duff Cooper at Singapore in December, 1941:

> Having accomplished the recall of Brooke-Popham Duff Cooper now
> increased the pressure to oust Sir Shenton Thomas. In an off-the-

record talk with Dickinson, Inspector General of the Straits Settlements Police, Duff Cooper asked for his reactions if Whitehall could be persuaded to recall the Governor. Dickinson, startled by this surprising and indiscreet question, replied that it would be a tremendous blow to morale as the Governor represented the King and had established good relations with the various native leaders.*

Duff Cooper's involvement in attempts to get rid of Shenton Thomas are not new in this story, but the significance here is the former's effort to enlist the support of the Chief of Police, who was in fact a friend and admirer of Sir Shenton.

However, I was alerted to something new when I found allegations that Sir Shenton Thomas had been deliberately kept in the dark about military developments. True, or untrue, this was surely a most serious charge, and therefore a highly relevant and important factor in assessing the performance of the man who was the Governor and High Commissioner.

While Duff Cooper was in Singapore his private office and clerical staff were provided on a temporary basis by appointments from the Colonial Service. His cypher officer was one Mrs Molly Reilly, who was normally responsible for the Governor's cypher traffic. Some 15 years ago now, Mrs Reilly had been corresponding with Dickinson about certain details of her work in Singapore and her successful escape therefrom. The following extract from a letter she wrote to him on 22 November, 1968,** is relevant to the preceding paragraph:

> I too have been wrathful of the mud thrown at Sir Shenton as I have always had the greatest admiration for him. Alas, towards the end he was kept quite ignorant of what was happening and when Duff Cooper left Singapore and I returned to Sir Shenton I was horrified to find how little he knew of conditions then prevailing. But I knew Duff Cooper had trusted me not to mention anything I had learnt whilst I was his cypher officer. . . .

Mrs Reilly's statement that the Governor was not kept properly informed of the local war situation must have derived from her reading of Duff Cooper's cypher traffic, or relevant material in his office. However, looking through the minutes of the daily meetings of the War Council, which Shenton carefully preserved, I cannot see that they in any way conceal the true, and generally deteriorating, nature of the

---

* *Out In The Midday Sun* by Kate Caffrey André Deutsch, 1975, p. 95.
** Papers on Shenton Thomas in the library of the Royal Commonwealth Society.

battle for Malaya, including the rate of Japanese advance. Finally, Percival was the Governor's military adviser, and both his official despatches, and his own book, show clearly how punctilious he was in keeping the Governor properly informed. Shenton never for one moment doubted Percival's sincerity, irrespective of his judgement.

During the seven years of Shenton Thomas's administration he had presided, by and large, over a contented population, politically and otherwise; though Malayanization of the M.C.S. was still a long way off, far-sighted administrators like Shenton knew it had to come. Meanwhile the government of the country was accepted as good and fair, in spite of the fact that right through the whole community there was no one common language and so many of the population were not British subjects; but the people prospered, the police were efficient and respected, and law and order prevailed. Justice was administered in the Supreme Courts by British judges and was never questioned.

Then, when war came in 1939, the Governor was told that the production of tin and rubber was to take precedence over all other considerations. At the same time preparations and plans for large scale, in fact national, civil defence had to be made and implemented, and this was done. Inevitably there were mistakes and faults at all levels of administration, and some friction departmentally; but a vast, new, noncombatant organization was created, and when invasion came no less an authority than the Chief of Police went on record to say: "The efficiency and fortitude of the Civil Defence Services were proven beyond doubt."

However, from the very first day of the invasion the military situation began to deteriorate and went on doing so until the conquest of the whole country was complete. During the retreat things had gone wrong with both military *and* civil action and people generally wanted to know why and how. Leaders of the armed forces and the authors of the *Official History* found it possible to argue that a large part of the responsibility must rest on the Governor; after all, he was the King's representative and the senior citizen in the land. So the Governor has been blamed for the disaster.

Was Sir Shenton Thomas a great man? Was he made of the stuff of national leaders who can impose their will on their subordinates, civil and military? Did he give this impression? I believe the answer to both these questions must be "No". He was not in the mould of supreme commanders, but he must be defined nevertheless. The best people to "define" him must be his contemporaries, men who were both his colleagues and friends and knew him intimately, men like Sir Andrew Gilchrist, Sir William Goode, and the late Sir Robert Scott. The definition I give below has been largely shaped by what they have told me.

Shenton Thomas was not a great man in the sense outlined above. But he was an admirable man, determined to do his very best for the people under his charge, completely dedicated to the public service, not a prig in any way, but a strong and upright character with a deep sense of duty. By character and upbringing he was a sincere church-man, always honest and direct, not devious in any way. Perhaps above all he came to identify himself with the people he administered, or governed, regarding himself in a sense as their trustee, their guardian; he therefore intervened as little as possible with their customs and traditions.

To put it another way, Shenton Thomas considered that his job was to run an efficient and honest administration as economically as possible. This he did and in so doing gained the respect and affection of all the people he served. One important point remains. Shenton Thomas knew very little about the regular armed forces or military matters in general. His contact with the army had been confined to his experience of the colonial forces in East and West Africa (The K.A.R. and R.W.A.F.F.) and, of course, his purely titular appointment as Commander-in-Chief. Yet, as we saw in the first chapter, he was quite prepared to speak his mind on defence problems if he felt strongly about a vital point. For him, defeat followed by retreat was alien to his personal concept of the high professional standards expected of officers and men of the armed forces of the Crown.

Having written that definition of Shenton, which I believe equally suits the thoughts and outlook of his wife, I found it easier to fit Duff Cooper, a strange, frustrated figure, completely different to Sir Shenton, into the picture of war-time Singapore that has grown in my mind. Clearly Duff Cooper could not have had, and did not have, any effect on the readiness and efficiency of the civil defence organization, which he attacked so viciously. Yet he was right when he called for a supreme theatre commander at Singapore; but Sir Shenton Thomas and Sir Archibald Clark Kerr (British Ambassador to China) had made the same plea many months earlier.

Thus Shenton Thomas has been blamed unfairly by not a few for a large share of responsibility in a great disaster. But his own case (and thereby that of those he governed) has never been officially published; yet it is there in writing, in government archives, in his review entitled *Malaya's War Effort*, in his comments on General Percival's despatches and on the draft of the *Official History*. To that extent he was a much maligned man and the case for the civil government has been deliberately left unpublished. Sir Andrew Caldecott* wrote an accurate exposé of the whole matter in a letter to Sir Shenton dated 13 September, 1948:

> Very many thanks for letting me see your *Malaya's War Effort*. It is a thousand pities that it was not published as a Command Paper last year; and one can never forgive the Colonial Office for their failure to do justice by the country and people who served us so well, by letting the public here have an authoritative account of what was done and given.

Sir Shenton should really have written his autobiography; it would certainly have caused a stir! But readers will recall that he said to me: "Many heads would roll." So, after more than 40 years, important information remains to be released in public about the Singapore disaster. Evidence, given to H.M.G. at the time, is still withheld from researchers and some of it, presumably, may never become available. In certain important respects therefore this book remains an unfinished story.

---

* Sir Andrew Caldecott, G.C.M.G, C.B.E., a former Colonial Secretary of Malaya and Governor of Ceylon.

EPILOGUE

After the surrender of Singapore there was consternation throughout the Commonwealth and a call for a public inquiry into the
circumstances of the defeat. But, as Churchill wrote later: "I judged it
impossible to hold an inquiry by Royal Commission into the circumstances of the fall of Singapore while the war was raging. . . . Years
have passed, and many of the witnesses are dead. It may well be that we
shall never have a formal pronouncement, by a competent court, upon
the worst disaster and largest capitulation in British history."* And so it
has been.

Even so there must be an explanation as to why and how it happened.
It may be forgotten by many that early in 1941 there had been secret
staff talks between Great Britain and America, at the highest political
and military level, concerning likely American action if the United
States should enter the war on the side of the British Commonwealth –
this was ten months or so *before* Pearl Harbor. It was agreed that first
priority should be given to the defeat of Germany, and that, whatever
Japan did, the latter should be contained until Germany had been
knocked out.** Then Japan attacked and Churchill was apprehensive
lest American public opinion might feel so outraged by the destruction
of their Pacific fleet as to insist on immediate revenge against Japan. It
was therefore a great relief to the British Prime Minister, when he
visited Washington in December, 1941, to be assured that there was no
intention of making any change in the agreed strategic plan.

This overall concept, to ensure first the defeat of Hitler's Empire
before any major onslaught against the Japanese Empire, was adhered
to; and surely this is a sign pointing to the underlying reason as to why
and how the Hong Kong/Singapore surrenders occurred, with the
subsequent loss of Burma, the threat to India, and the elimination of
British power in the Far East. It points to, though it certainly cannot
justify, the untimely dispatch of inadequate British troop reinforcements to Malaya and the neglect to supply the Far East garrisons with

* *The Second World War*, Vol. IV., The Hinge of Fate, Cassell & Co, 1951.
** *Memoirs of Lord Ismay*, p. 248, Heinemann, 1960.

modern naval, military, and air weaponry and war material, particularly artillery, transport and aircraft. Britain in the Far East had been left out of the Anglo-American priority list for active prosecution of the war effort. Thus, once Japan invaded Malaya in 1941, we had no real chance of avoiding defeat, for our resources in fighting men and equipment were wholly inadequate. The conclusion that follows naturally is that the Malayan campaign was lost in Washington and London, with the British share of responsibility for it pointed at the Prime Minister, who rejected the advice of his Chiefs of Staff.

Be that as it may, Professor Callahan has argued that Churchill, well knowing we could not win *alone* in the Far East, actually followed the most sensible course and ensured our eventual overall victory. Some readers may find it difficult not to agree with the logic of the Professor's argument:

> What he [Churchill] did was to see clearly that Britain could fight one war – or lose two. Britain's essential interests were more immediately threatened in Europe than in Asia. Britain could preserve her independence and position as a great European power, but not simultaneously the Asian Empire that made her a world power. From this everything else followed. . . . To the British, and their indomitable leader, survival, nothing less, was at stake. Next to this, nothing else mattered.*

If Professor Callahan's view is accepted much else flows from it. Is it surprising then that Churchill set his mind against any formal Court of Inquiry into the Singapore disaster, with accompanying assessment of blame and responsibility for the consequences? Maybe also, at a lower level, this was the reason why the Government in London decided, in 1946, not to take any disciplinary action against officers of the Malayan Civil Services who quit Malaya, without permission, before the act of surrender. Shenton Thomas, with his deep sense of loyalty and obedience, had written to the Secretary of State urging strong action against any civil officer "found guilty of deserting his post". But H.M.G. had decided that "in the circumstances it would be both fruitless and unwise to pursue such allegations." However, Shenton, understandably I feel, did not agree and, mindful always of the people he had served, wrote yet again to the Colonial Secretary saying: "I fear this decision will not be acceptable locally, though of course it will be observed."

While Shenton was doing battle with the Government in London

---

* Op. cit., p. 271.

over the question of publicizing his case for Malaya, he was much cheered to receive the following telegram from his successor as Governor of Singapore.*

The Singapore Municipal Commissioners have decided that a new highway, which joins the Harbour Board docks to Raffles Quay and will form part of a route along the sea front to Kallang Airport shall be named SHENTON WAY, to mark their gratitude for the distinguished services rendered to Singapore by Sir Shenton Thomas during his term of office as Governor of the Straits Settlements, and in particular of his decision to stay with the people of Singapore when the town fell into Japanese hands.

Shenton replied in appropriate terms stressing his pleasure "at this new link in the chain of happy memories." Shenton Way is now a broad and important thoroughfare in the heart of the financial centre of Singapore, flanked by the high-rise buildings of the chief banks and commercial businesses of the city. It is to Singapore what Wall Street is to New York City.

Shenton had long been a sufferer of asthma, intensified by his years in captivity, and the attacks on his respiratory system began to have an increasing effect at the beginning of the 1960s. But he was very happy in his old age in the comfortable surroundings of his home at Oakwood Court. There, on 15 January, 1962, in his 83rd year, he died very peacefully. Beyond doubt he was a great Pro-Consul, a most eminent and illustrious figure in the highest ranks of the British Colonial Service of the Commonwealth, whose traditions he upheld so nobly and for so long. He lived to see the emergence of the new era in Africa – the transition of one-time colonial possessions into free independent nations, within (as he had hoped) the British Commonwealth. He did not live to see the final completion of the new Malaysia, nor the new Singapore of our time; though how delighted he would have been to witness the dignity, prosperity and status of those two sovereign states of modern Asia.

A memorial service for Sir Shenton Thomas was held in St Paul's Cathedral in the Chapel of the Order of St Michael and St. George. The large congregation included numerous representatives of H.M.G., as well as High Commissioners and officials of the former Colonies and States in Africa and Asia where Shenton had served; also

---

* Sir Franklin Gimson, K.C.M.G., D.L., Governor of Singapore, 1946–1952.

representatives of the various organisations at home and overseas with which Shenton had been associated.

His wife lived on long after her husband. She must have had an astonishing constitution to have survived after all she had been through, with a physique of unusual toughness. She died on 1 September, 1978, at the ripe old age of 94.

BIBLIOGRAPHY

British Rule in Malaya, the Malayan Civil Service and its Predecessors, 1867–1942, by Professor Heussler (Clio Press 1981)

Old Friends, New Enemies by Professor Arthur Marder (Oxford University Press 1981)

Battleship, the loss of Prince of Wales and Repulse, by Martin Middlebrook and Patrick Mahoney (Allen Lane 1977)

Rulers of British Africa by L. H. Gann and Peter Duigan (Croom Helm 1978)

Happy Valley, The Story of the British in Kenya by Nicholas Best (Secker & Warburg 1979)

Nigerian Kaleidoscope by Sir Rex Niven (C. Hurst & Co. 1982)

Memories of a Malayan Civil Servant by Victor Purcell (Cassell 1965)

Seventy Days to Singapore by Stanley Falk (Robert Hale 1975)

Official History of the War Against Japan Vol. I. The loss of Singapore, The Cabinet Office, Historical Section (H.M.S.O. 1957)

Singapore, The Chain of Disaster, by Major-General S. Woodburn Kirby, CB., CMG., CIE., MC. (Cassell 1971)

The Worst Disaster, The Fall of Singapore, by Professor Raymond Callahan (University of Delaware Press 1977)

The Other Ultra by Ronald Lewin. (Hutchinson 1982)

Syonan – My Story by Mamoru Shinozaki (Asia Pacific Press, Singapore 1975)

Eastern Epic by Sir Compton Mackenzie (Chatto & Windus 1951)

Malayan Postscript by Ian Morrison (Faber & Faber 1942)

Singapore 1941–1942 by Dr. Louis Allen (Davis Poynter 1977)

The War in Malaya by Lt. Gen. A. E. Percival (Eyre & Spottiswoode 1949)

The Bitter End by Richard Holmes and Anthony Kemp (Anthony Bird 1982)

Dear Philip by Freddy Bloom (The Bodley Head 1980)

The Marquis by Professor E. J. H. Corner (Heinemann, Asia 1981)

The Emperor's Guest by Sir John Fletcher-Cooke (Leo Cooper, 1976)

The Churches of the Captivity in Malaya by The Rev. J. N. Lewis Bryan (S.P.C.K. 1946)

Singapore, Too Little Too Late by Ivan Simson (Leo Cooper 1970)

The Chieftain, Field-Marshal Lord Wavell by Ronald Lewin (Hutchinson 1980)

A Soldier Must Hang by John Deane Potter (Muller 1963)

Out in the Midday Sun by Kate Caffrey (Andre Deutsch 1975)

The Second World War, Vol. IV. by Winston Churchill (Cassell 1951)

Memoirs of Lord Ismay by H. L. Ismay (Heinemann 1960)

INDEX

Note. Figures in **bold** refer to illustration numbers.
The following abbreviations have been used: BP (Air Chief Marshal Sir Robert Brooke-Popham); DC (Duff Cooper); DT (Daisy Thomas); ST (Shenton Thomas)